TORRENT CONTROL AND STREAMBED STABILIZATION

FAO Land and Water Development Series *N° 9*

Torrent control and streambed stabilization

by

F. López Cadenas de Llano

FOOD AND AGRICULTURE ORGANIZATION OF THE UNITED NATIONS
Rome, 1993

David Lubin Memorial Library Cataloguing-in-Publication Data

López Cadenas de Llano, F.

Torrent control and streambed stabilization.
(FAO Land and Water Development Series, n. 9)
ISBN 92-5-102424-3

1. Torrents 2. Flood control 3. Dams
I. Title II. Series

FAO Code: 55 AGRIS: P10

Printed in Italy

Contents

Figures

Foreword

Damage of torrential origin is closely linked to population density, infrastructural investment and levels of agricultural and industrial development in mountain areas generally. Landslides, gully formation, torrential mudflows, river flooding and other similar periodic events would be much less destructive, if it were not for humans and their activities. Torrentiality is exacerbated by human activities, particularly those that involve developing areas downstream from unbalanced watersheds. Humans cultivate flood-prone valleys, build on alluvial fans and exploit mountain watersheds to provide water for electricity, irrigation and domestic use. The economic development of a region entails building more roads, bridges, railways and other facilities. The damage caused to these structures by exceptionally heavy rains also modifies the zone's hydrodynamic characteristics, giving rise to torrential phenomena of great destructive force.

These factors serve to explain why torrent control has come into being. Its development is based on valuable experience gained since the middle of the last century in mountainous European countries. Population density and heavy infrastructural investment over the years have made the development of protective steps necessary. In some European countries — Austria, the Czech and Slovak Federal Republic, France and Switzerland, for example — government torrent control programmes have been in operation for more than a hundred years. However, complete protection from torrential phenomena has yet to be achieved, and floods, landslides and dam bursts continue to claim victims year after year. Ever more intensive recreational use is made of mountain areas, and the risk of imbalances increases because of the ill effects of atmospheric pollution on protective forests; torrent control therefore has assumed special importance in highly developed countries.

Loss of life and property are growing problems in mountainous areas of developing countries that are characterized by rapid infrastructural and population growth. Every human settlement and each new road, bridge or railway in upland areas is potentially threatened by the effects of water erosion; in both the developing and the industrialized worlds, therefore, the scope for torrent control can only increase.

Since in most countries the forestry services are responsible for torrent control, watershed management and the management and protection of mountain areas, this document is being published as an FAO Forestry Paper. It is worth adding that, especially in developing countries, torrent control activities are normally a component of multidisciplinary mountain watershed management involving not only government agencies, but also the private sector and upland rural communities. Torrent control has a crucial place in the rehabilitation and protection of mountain areas and entails biological, structural and socio-economic measures. However, it should be pointed out that the effectiveness of the engineering works described here in controlling torrentiality and water erosion will be much reduced unless both adequate plant cover is provided to protect the soil and land is utilized in accordance with its capacity.

This publication is the fruit of FAO's decision to tap over 50 years of accumulated Spanish experience in the field of torrent control — knowledge that has been enriched by exchanges with other countries in Europe and elsewhere. The FAO Working Party on Mountain Watershed Management, which comes under the European Forestry Commission (chaired by the author of this paper), was set up in 1950 and has been responsible for other FAO publications such as the *Avalanche Control Manual* and the five-language *Torrent Control Terminology* (FAO Conservation Guides 6 and 7).

It is hoped that this manual will be of use to all those professionally involved in protecting life and property from torrential damage, both in mountain areas and downstream in the plains.

M. A. FLORES RODAS
Assistant Director-General
Forestry Department

1. Principles and scope of torrent control and streambed stabilization

1.1 General principles. Biological and hydrotechnical methods

Torrentiality is the result of erosion in the watershed. By analysing this phenomenon and studying its characteristics, the general principles underlying corrective action can be established. Torrents are characterized by sediment discharge and by sudden high flows of considerable violence. Sediment may be transported as a suspended load or as bedload.

Since suspended sediment is produced mainly by surface (sheet and gully) erosion in the watershed, the two phenomena are closely linked, as are the soil conservation and rehabilitation measures needed to prevent watershed erosion and the torrent control measures necessitated by the presence of suspended sediment.

Bedload discharge is due to tractive forces eroding the streambed: the deeper the water and the faster the flow, the greater the tractive force. Flow levels depend on the volume and velocity of precipitation-induced runoff in the watershed, itself a cause of erosion. Thus channel sediment flows and watershed degradation are parallel phenomena.

Similarly, sudden, violent floods can occur when the amount of rain exceeds the soil's capacity for retention, producing runoff. Since rain in eroded watersheds tends to compact the soil, the effects on torrent flow can be dramatic. In view of this clear connection between torrentiality and watershed erosion, torrent control activities should not be undertaken in isolation from the rest of the watershed (with the specific exception of some mountain torrents). An integrated package of biological and hydraulic engineering measures is required, split judiciously between streams and watershed.

Although this guide is concerned exclusively with hydraulic engineering works for torrent control, it should be stated that biological watershed rehabilitation also plays a crucial role.

Biological measures for watershed rehabilitation

Biological measures for the most part involve torrent control on hillsides, and techniques are similar to those used in soil conservation (plant cover and water control). They are important for keeping floodflows from eroding channel sides and for their effect on sediment transport generally.

In torrential watersheds, therefore, the conservation, improvement and establishment of forest tree cover are important for their highly beneficial effects on infiltration and water concentration time, as well as on surface runoff and floodflow control. Wherever possible, any suitable bare watershed land should be reforested in preference to any other form of land use. Fast-growing species, however, are not really advisable since they provide neither effective interception nor soil cover; they also do not tolerate the shrubs or grasses so essential to controlling soil loss and surface runoff.

The best species to use are those that show strong early growth in well-prepared soil, slowing down later to give sturdy stem and good crown development. The maintenance of natural vegetation in the shrub, thicket and field layers and of relict trees in repopulated areas should be an integral part of reforestation planning. A balance needs to be achieved between vegetation that is artificially introduced into the vacant tree layer and that already existing in other layers to maximize the effectiveness of watershed torrent control.

However, introducing trees will not by itself control torrents; the ecosystem as a whole will do that. The role of torrential watershed afforestation is to help nature by reversing degradation and speeding up the development of a complete forest ecosystem to provide maximum natural control. The aim of torrential watershed reforestation work should be a stable community of mixed, irregular stands containing both shrub and grass layers.

Another biological torrent control method, providing slopes do not exceed 30-35 percent, involves establishing permanent grass cover, which can be rationally managed and exploited as grazing land. This method, however, yields only partial control of surface runoff and floodflows.

Hillside restoration work may also involve some simple engineering such as prompt control of gullying by means of drystone walls, gabions, fascines or piling in conjunction with the planting of riparian species. Finally, modern sodding techniques, such as mulching with vegetal, mineral or industrial matter to form an artificial protective layer for grass to take root in, can be useful in rehabilitating steep, heavily eroded slopes, provided the area involved is not too large.

Hydrotechnical methods for torrent control and streambed stabilization

The principles underlying the design and use of hydrotechnical methods for torrent control and streambed stabilization are aimed at partially or totally controlling the typical effects of torrential flows on the surrounding area, namely erosion and transport/deposition of eroded materials. Control is therefore focused on streambanks and on the channel bottom with the aim of reducing sediment discharge to a minimum by taking steps to prevent such discharges from occurring or, failing that, to encourage maximum deposition.

The torrentiality of streamflows appears to be linked to the tractive force they exert on movable bed particles. This tractive force detaches and transports materials mainly as bedload and can be expressed as:

$$\tau = \gamma \cdot R \cdot I$$

where τ (t/m^2) is the tractive force exerted per unit of bed width by a flow of specific gravity: γ (t/m^3) in a section of hydraulic radius R (m) and circulating with an energy line of gradient I. Tractive force is countered by the resistance of materials to detachment and transport: weight, inertia, friction, etc. Resistance is computed by taking the tractive force of the water at the precise moment when mass movement begins, and is usually called the threshold, or critical, tractive force.

In beds formed of incohesive materials, as torrent beds generally are, the critical force can be expressed by the formula:

$$(\tau_o)_{cr} = K\,(\gamma_s - \gamma)\,d$$

where $(\tau_o)_{cr}$ (t/m^2) is the critical force for materials of characteristic diameter d (m) and specific gravity γ_s (t/m^3), given a discharge of specific gravity γ (t/m^3), with K an empirically determined dimensionless coefficient whose value varies depending on the author and the circumstances.

The torrentiality of a stream at a given moment may be ascertained by comparing the two values τ and $(\tau_o)_{cr}$ to see whether $\tau > (\tau_o)_{cr}$; if so, there will be erosion and/or sediment transport, quantifiable by the function $F[\tau - (\tau_o)_{cr}]$.

The integration of these erosion and transport processes into the overall pattern of flows and sections allows the torrentiality of a stream to be assessed and analysed. Using the relation between boundary shear stresses and the tractive force of discharges to explain torrential imbalances in a channel lies at the very heart of torrent control theory. Any form of hydrological intervention in the watershed that either lowers the parameters affecting the tractive force of discharges or increases boundary shear stresses will contribute to improving torrent control.

As mentioned above, biological methods of watershed restoration are clearly important in controlling torrentiality. By fixing the soil, they help reduce the quantity of suspended sediment contributing to the stream's turbidity and density, thereby lowering the water's specific gravity γ and weakening its tractive force. They also have a significant effect on direct runoff, helping to restrain peak flows, shorten the hydraulic radius R of wetted sections and reduce the water's tractive force.

1.2 Vertical control and establishment of equilibrium bed slope

Highly torrential streams are those in which the tractive force of discharges habitually exceeds particle resistance (as defined by the critical force at which material may be moved). This results in progressive bed degradation, mass transport of bedload materials, streambank erosion and destabilization of adjacent land. In such cases, transverse dikes across the stream (check dams) represent the simplest and most effective solution. These vertical control structures, which dam the channel from bed to spillway, have the following effects:

- They provide a fixed point on the streambed, controlling further downcutting.
- As long as the reservoir does not silt up, the stored water slows the approach speed of the sediment, encourages deposition of the coarser materials and thereby reduces the sediment load of the overflow.

- The resulting deposition causes the bed level to rise, until the equilibrium bed slope is reached (achieving a gentler gradient than that of the natural channel).
- This natural accretion results in a new bed with a wider cross-section, which allows broader-based flows, and in a hydraulic radius that is smaller by an amount roughly equivalent to the drop in water depth.

Because of these reductions in hydraulic radius R and the bed slope i (Figure 1), the tractive force of the discharge is significantly weakened.

Structures of this type have another advantage in that the accumulated sediment helps consolidate torrent bank slopes either because it acts as a fixed non-erodible support below the plane of the stabilized accretion, or because debris accumulates at the foot of the slopes until it reaches the new stabilized accretion level. As a result, there is a considerable reduction in the influence interval of the amount of debris arriving laterally in the channel bed.

Torrent control by transverse dikes relies for the most part on the sediment deposited by the stream, which produces both a milder slope than that of the natural bed as well as a wider section; the erosive effects of tractive forces are therefore offset by the resistance of the materials transported by the stream, and the resulting aggradation gives rise to what is termed an equilibrium bed slope.

A sediment-saturated stream flowing over an erodible bed provides an opportunity for the interchange of materials. This interchange involves replacement of the solid sediment in the discharge by other, equivalent materials. However, this equivalence does not refer so much to sediment volume as to transport capacity, and if the volume deposited is not equal to the volume incorporated (which occurs whenever bed materials differ in composition or particle size from those being transported), the result will be an equilibrium profile reflecting the stream's tractive characteristics. This profile will obviously vary until the necessary equivalence (between volume and transport capacity) is reached, at which point aggradation and degradation in the stream balance out and an equilibrium bed slope results.

There are a number of models for calculating the equilibrium bed slope, although strictly only some relate to the equilibrium profile aspect. The method below is based on the García Nájera theory, but has been simplified by replacing the Schocklitsch formulae by the Meyer-Peter formula, and the Bazin coefficient by the Manning one.

The variables are:

$$\tau = (\tau_o)_{cr} \quad \tau = \text{tractive force of water} = h \cdot \gamma \cdot I$$

$(\tau_o)_{cr}$ = critical tractive force = $0.047\ (\gamma_s - \gamma)\ d_{50}$ (according to Meyer-Peter)

d_{50} = characteristic diameter of the materials in metres. The coefficient 0.047, when applying the expression to alpine torrents, may be increased to 0.06

Ψ = $\frac{\tau}{\gamma}$

Q = the discharge (m^3/s)

b = average width of channel (m)

g = acceleration due to gravity (9.81 m/s^2)

γ_s = specific gravity of suspended materials (varies between 2.2 and 2.7 (t/m^3) depending on type)

γ = specific gravity of water with suspended charge (t/m^3)

X = sediment proportion (%)

a = coefficient of reduction

a = $\sqrt{\{[\gamma^3] / [(1 + X)(\gamma + X_{\gamma_s})^3]\}}$

h = depth of water (m)

v = velocity of water with suspended charge (m/sec)

C = $n \cdot R^{1/6}$ where n = the inverse of the Manning roughness coefficient (n_1)

C = $\frac{1}{n_1} R^{1/6} = n \cdot R^{1/6}$

R = hydraulic radius (m)

q = $\frac{gQ}{2b}$ (m^3/s^3)

The following equations can be derived from the García Nájera theory:

$$v^7 + qv^4 - 3\,\zeta^2 \cdot q = 0, \text{ in which } \zeta = \Psi \cdot a^2 \cdot C^2$$

and for the equilibrium bed slope:

$$I_c = \frac{g \cdot v^3}{2C^2 \cdot a^2 \cdot q}$$

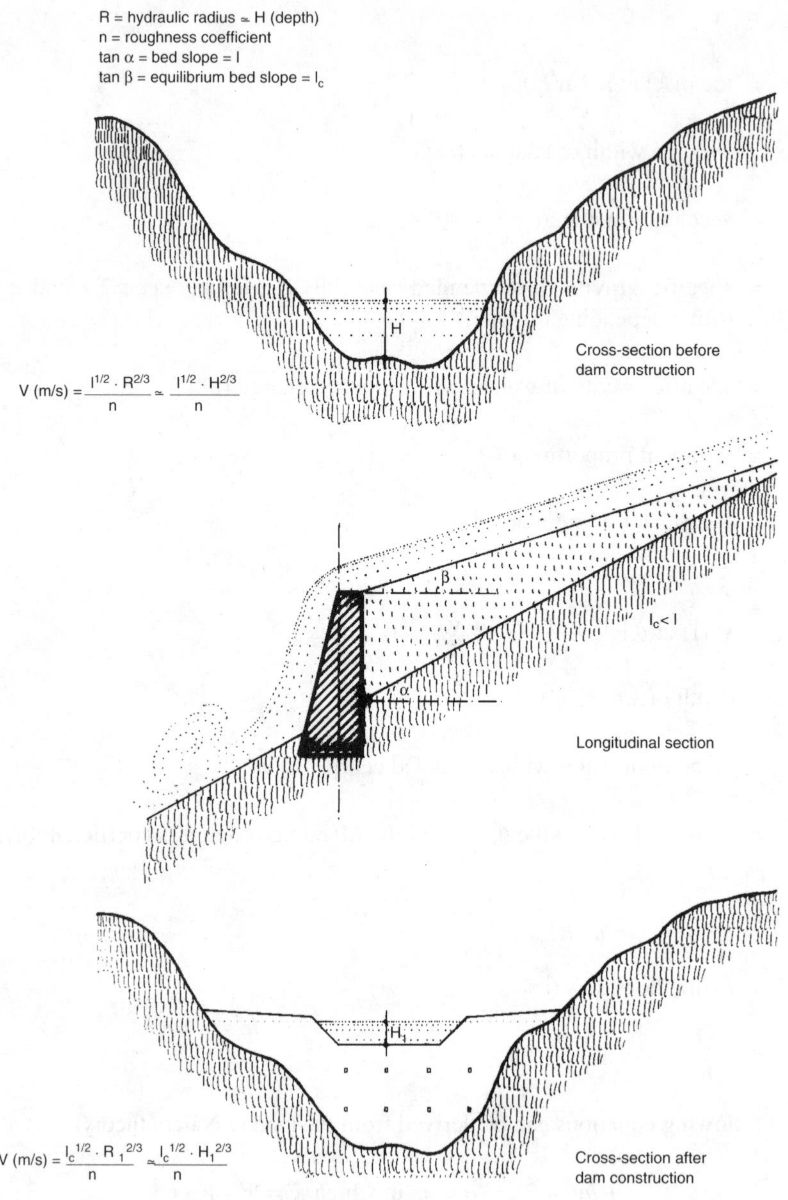

Figure 1. Cross-section of a torrent before and after construction of check dam (centre)

A few simple transformations in those formulae give us the following three basic equations:

$$v^{23/3} + qv^{14/3} - M = 0$$

$$M = \frac{3\Psi^2 \cdot a^4 \cdot n^4 \cdot 2^{2/3} \cdot q^{5/3}}{g^{2/3}}$$

$$I_c = \frac{v^{10/3} \cdot q^{4/3}}{2^{4/3} \cdot a^2 \cdot n^2 \cdot q^{4/3}}$$

The flowchart for the calculation is as follows:

$$d_{50},\ Q,\ n_1,\ \gamma_s,\ b$$

↓

$$q = \frac{gQ}{2b}$$

↓

$$\Psi = 0.047\ \frac{(\gamma_s - \gamma)\, d_{50}}{\gamma}$$

↓

$$M = \frac{3\Psi^2 \cdot a^4 \cdot n^4 \cdot 2^{2/3} \cdot q^{5/2}}{g^{2/3}}$$

↓

$$v^{23/3} + qv^{14/3} - M = 0$$

↓

$$I_c = \frac{v^{10/3}\ g}{2^{4/3} \cdot a^2 \cdot n^2 \cdot q^{4/3}}$$

↓

$$v,\ I_c$$

It can also be established that, in two sections of perimeters L and L_1 with flows of Q and Q_1, $(I_c / I_{1c}) = [(L / L_1) \cdot (Q_1 / Q)]$; this allows I_{1c} to be calculated, once the other parameters are known.

Where hydrological conditions are similar in two sections ($Q = Q_1$), the relationship between the equilibrium bed slope and the respective wetted perimeters can be shown:

$$\frac{I_c}{I_{1c}} = \frac{L}{L_1}$$

hence $I_{1c} = I_c \cdot \dfrac{L_1}{L}$

1.3 Horizontal control and channel line correction

It may be that the water's tractive force is only sufficient to overcome channel resistance in certain specific sections or at particular points — a normal occurrence in streams with a fluvial or semi-fluvial regime. In such cases, control measures will differ somewhat from those described for torrential streams, although the principles remain the same.

Erosion and sedimentation in these reaches is mainly attributable to centrifugal action in the bends that raises the free surface level at the outer banks, establishing a hydraulic gradient of transverse pressures. Consequently, flowlines are created which run downwards to the channel bed at the concave bank before rising again (Figure 2). The force exerted by flowlines at the outside bend results in bank scouring and bed erosion; solid particles are first dislodged and then deposited later when the flowlines separate and their tractive force is no longer enough to overcome particle resistance.

As Figure 2 shows, erosion of the concave bank leads to a channel bottom that is much deeper there than at the next point of inflexion.

This process of erosion and deposition tends to make the meanders unstable, to which one must add the effects of tractive forces if not offset by the resistance of boundary materials. Such stresses, however, are normally kept in balance: a fall in boundary resistance in the lower reaches, caused by an abrasion-induced reduction in the size of particles on their way downstream (Stemberg's law), is compensated for by a milder gradient and, consequently, weaker tractive force (Figure 3). Nonetheless, local imbalances of the kind mentioned above may still occur and require control.

Stabilizing a stream or reach of a stream involves applying the same control rules as for torrents; that is, a balance must be achieved between drag forces and channel resistance by reducing the former and increasing the latter. This balance is normally reached by constructing training walls, taking care to position them correctly in relation to the channel axis. They not only provide horizontal control of bank shear stresses but also allow streamline correction both by avoiding the imbalances produced by excessive meandering and by creating sections with

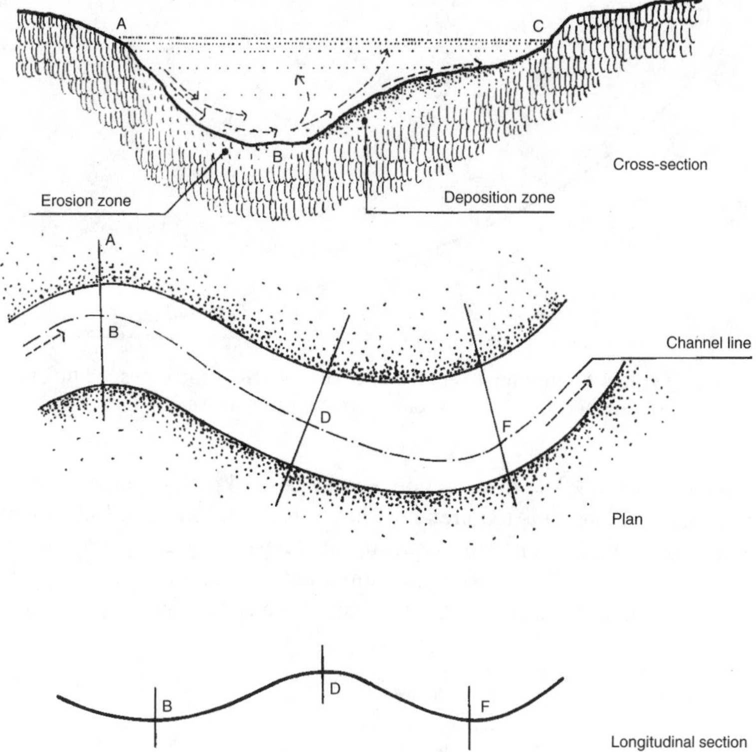

Figure 2. Typical sections of a meander

hydraulic radii that match the boundary materials' capacity to resist erosion. In streams of this type, transverse dikes are used only in special cases to fix the bed and diminish the water's tractive force by reducing the slope.

Bank shear stresses may be controlled horizontally by means of continuous walls of non-erodible materials. The walls may be rigid (concrete or masonry revetment) or flexible (gabions). Another method is to increase boundary resistance by lining the bank with loose materials of a larger diameter than those in the bed, or by planting and mulching.

Groynes are another form of horizontal control, reducing the tractive forces acting on the banks by creating low-velocity areas between the groynes in which deposition takes place (Figure 4). It should be pointed out that they reduce the flow section of the useful channel by taking away two lateral belts of dead water; this reduction increases the hydraulic radius of the flow and, consequently, its tractive force, resulting in downcutting in the centre of the bed combined with eddy effects at the groyne heads. Indeed, without preventive measures, erosion may actually destroy the structures.

Channel axis and streamflow correction works consist of training walls or firm

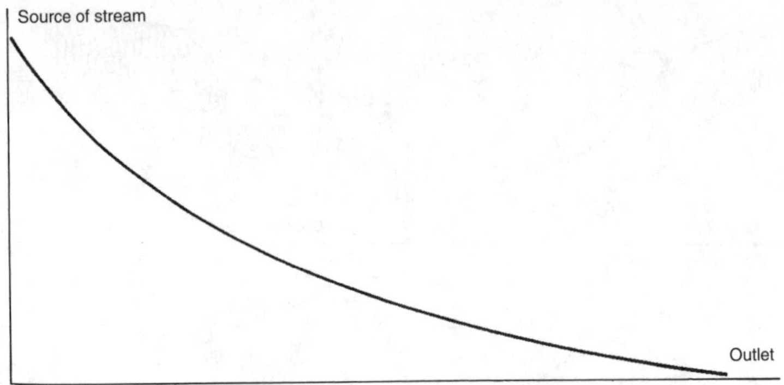

Figure 3. Typical longitudinal section of a stream (flow increases, sediment size decreases, and slope flattens out as stream nears the sea)

revetments to define the flow section and the desired path for the stream reach. A certain amount of care is required here not to force the water to follow a path different from its natural one; consequently, it is best to try and get as close as possible to what might be called the stream's natural equilibrium tendency so that lateral flow imbalances similar to those described above may be avoided.

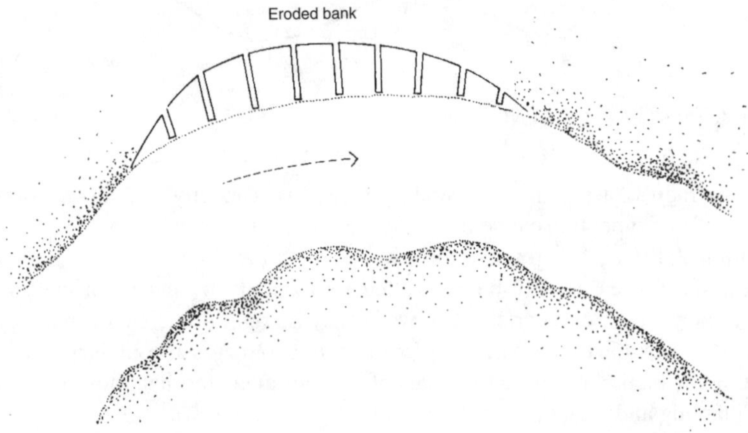

Figure 4. Plan of a stream protected by groynes

Even fixing the flow section involves a certain risk as it usually means reducing floodwater expansion areas. This reduction results in deeper floodflows with greater tractive force and erosive capacity; the reach therefore tries to stabilize itself through slope reduction, i.e. by bed erosion higher up and deposition lower down (Figure 5).

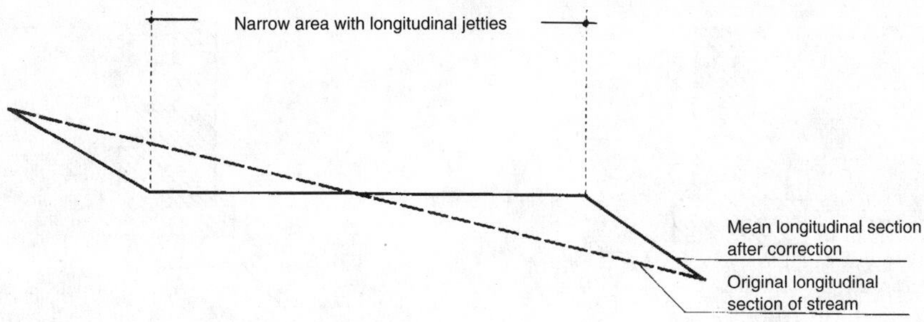

Figure 5. Effect on the slope of narrowing the reach

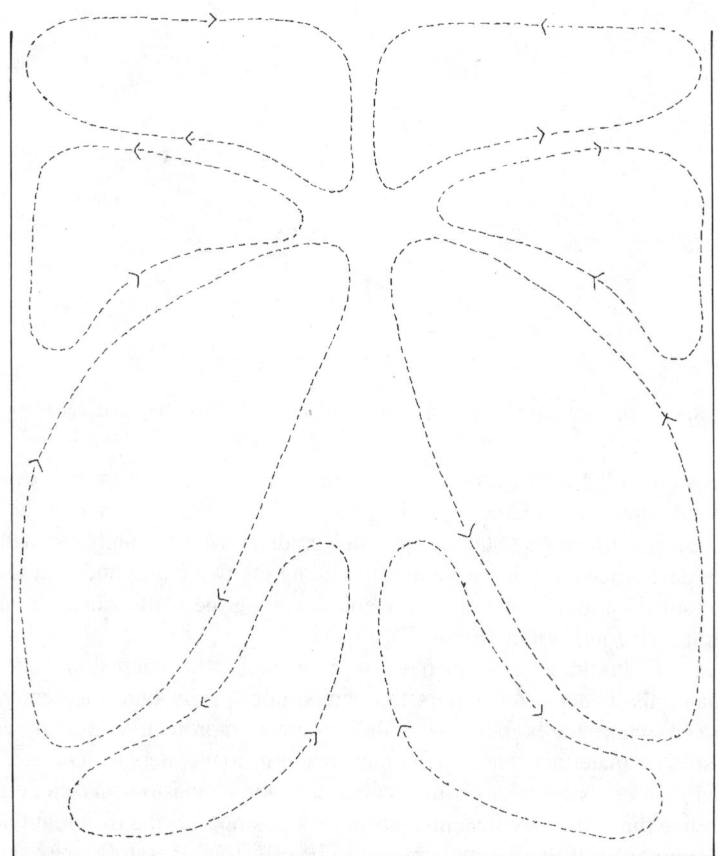

Figure 6. Transverse channel lines in a rectangular canal

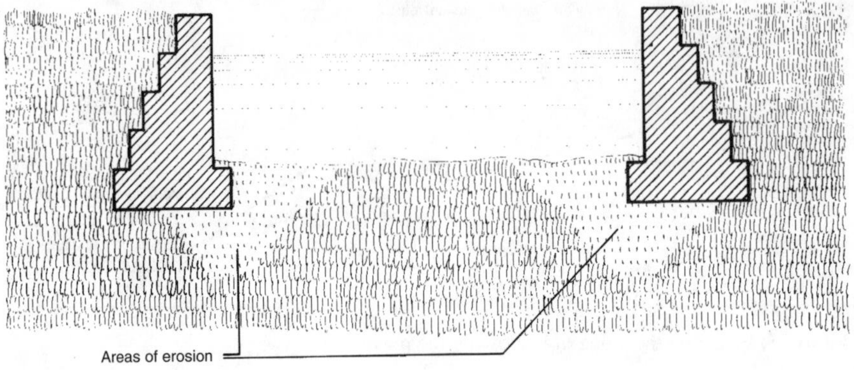

Figure 7. Danger of undercutting in a walled reach

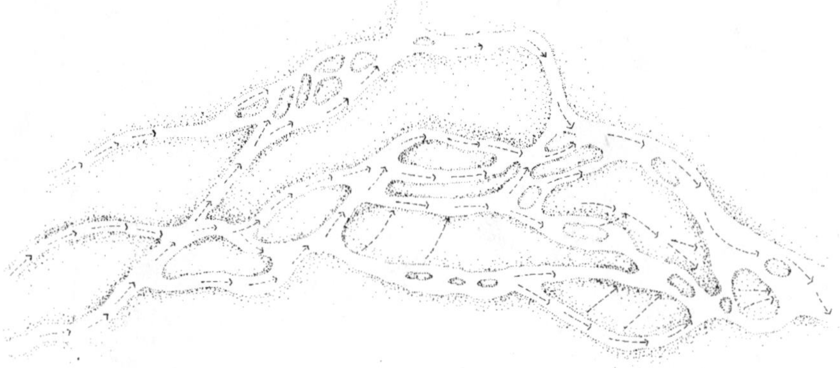

Figure 8. Plan of a stream reach with steep gradients and coarse bed materials

In designing these structures, one also has to remember that friction causes velocities in corrected streams to be lower at the banks than they are at the centre. This creates a transverse surface pressure gradient which, combined with other surface phenomena, produces streamlines along the two banks and near the channel bottom (Figure 6), causing heavy erosion along the walls which threatens to undercut their foundations (Figure 7).

Finally, it should be remembered that in channels with steep slopes and coarse bed materials, water often scours the banks more easily than the centre of the streambed, where the higher flow velocities create a protective layer by washing away smaller materials. This encourages medium flow waters to separate, branch out and then cross-connect (in the process known as anastomasis) in an attempt to stabilize the stream by matching sections and slopes to the different discharge levels (Figure 8). If these structures are to be effective, therefore, they should be used carefully, ensuring that their design takes into account all potential drawbacks.

2. Torrent bed stabilization

2.1 Types, purpose and main characteristics of torrent control structures

Transverse dikes are usually classed either as check dams or as sediment storage dams, depending on their purpose.

Check dams aim to prevent direct damage to bank slopes and streambeds rendered unstable by the effects of erosion. They are used to fix the longitudinal profile of the torrent bed and avoid downcutting by use of stepwise correction works to encourage aggradation; the torrent thus acquires a non-erodible slope with alternating dams and deposition zones. In this way, the areas most scarred by linear erosion are covered by a continuous equilibrium bed slope between the crest of one dam and the toe of its upstream neighbour, the side slopes being stabilized by accretion above the bed level.

The position and height of these dams can vary — what is important is that they ensure a continuous buildup, or stepping, of deposits, the exception being where the bed is not naturally subject to regression (e.g. rocky outcrops).

The equilibrium bed slopes in the deposition zones therefore need to be calculated on the basis of the average recurring floodflow, which is responsible for levels of aggradation and degradation as well as the general shape of the bed. This approach provides a sound economic basis for designing these structures, with plenty of scope for choosing heights and locations most suited to the area's topographic and sediment retention characteristics. Nonetheless, there are instances where the characteristics of the site impose upper and lower limits on the actual height of the dam: a maximum in cases where paths or productive bank lands might be covered over by sediment or a bridge's waterway restricted; and a minimum when a slope has to be protected against sloughing by ensuring that accretion is sufficient to contain the materials at the base.

Let us assume these primary dams are constructed along the lines shown in Figure 9, and that an equilibrium bed slope is created; now, as torrent control and watershed afforestation activities increase, particle size and sediment yield will tend to diminish, thus lowering the parameters entering into the calculation. This will produce a gentler equilibrium bed slope so that, if further bed erosion is to be avoided, a series of secondary dams will be needed to encourage the appropriate level of deposition.

Sediment storage dams are complementary structures designed exclusively to trap solid materials (and sometimes to blunt peak floodflows) when rapid action is needed to prevent damage by water and sediment discharges in torrential areas. They are positioned upstream from where damage occurs to take full advantage of places in which widening and narrowing encourages sediment deposition; they are therefore usually designed to seal the torrent gorge. Larger than check dams, their final size depends on the foreseeable sediment retention needed before other torrent and slope control structures become operational; once silted up they are of little use.

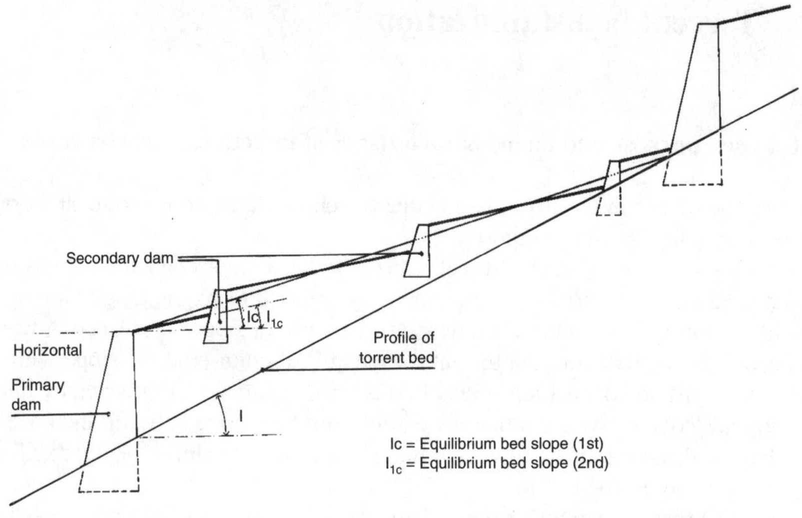

Figure 9. Determination of secondary dams in a corrected torrent

To prolong their useful life, especially in torrents of the Alpine or Pyrenean type which transport coarse materials, suitably wide openings or windows may be inserted at intervals in the dam body, in the direction of flow. These openings alleviate the impact, upstream of the dam, of discharge velocities and floodwater retention until other correction works are fully effective. Such a design allows finer materials to pass through, as well as sediment contained in flows of limited transport capacity, as these cause little or no downstream damage; thus unnecessary sedimentation is avoided and the dam's retention capacity prolonged. The dam itself will only silt up following large floods with high transport capacities. As it is these which cause the most damage, such structures help, at least temporarily, to contain them.

Any design or material appropriate to small dams may be used to construct transverse structures, whether check dams or sediment storage dams; no fixed rules can be laid down — it is up to the individual engineer to decide on the best and most economical materials in each case. It is, however, important to remember that these dams are generally small in scale (rarely exceeding 15 m in height) and constructed in steep, relatively inaccessible areas which make the use of heavy equipment impractical.

Consequently, such structures require neither expensive materials nor particularly resistant ones. They can be straight-drop gravity dams made of plain or rubble concrete, masonry or gabions, depending on the size of the structure, with a fixed, notch-shaped overfall designed for floods once every 20-100 years. The overfall should direct the free-falling water into the downstream channel, keeping it away from the sides. In dams of a certain size, the bed should be protected from the impact by an energy dissipator or simple apron. Such works can be built by relatively unskilled personnel.

To reduce uplift on the structure and prevent water from being impounded for too long (with damaging consequences for bank slope stability), small openings, or weep-holes — different from the gaps in the permeable structures described above — are usually built into the dam. Although the stability and resistance calculations for dimensioning these dams are similar to those normally employed in other hydraulic works, important differences in their functions must be taken into consideration when it comes to combining and evaluating loads.

Another typical form of torrent control occurs in debris cones and alluvial fans where the streamflow is restricted to a fixed, stable channel by means of training walls. Steps should also be taken to protect the channel bottom, since concentrating the flow upsets the natural process and makes the streambed susceptible to erosion. The same result can be achieved with small transverse grilled weirs which are stepped and help keep the flow between training walls, rather as detention dams do in corrected channels.

Except in exceptional circumstances, channelling works in debris cones should not be undertaken until the slope has been restored and the upstream bed corrected. Torrential damage may also be controlled by training walls, which run parallel to the stream. Although the channelling of debris cones might be said to fall into this category, in terms of their design and operation they have much in common with transverse dikes and are better seen as a type of hybrid.

As far as the basic aim of eliminating sediment transport and its effects is concerned, the role of training walls is in general restricted to preventing erosion and bank spilling. While training walls provide passive protection, transverse dikes act decisively upon the torrential process. In their design and operation, these structures resemble those used in streams with a fluvial regime; few modifications are required before applying them to torrents except to allow for the greater energy of flow, the marked tendency toward channel regression and the high levels of sediment discharge characteristic of torrents. For the most part, all the types, calculations, designs and specifications used in fluvial hydraulic architecture can be successfully applied to torrents, bearing in mind that the characteristics mentioned above place a premium on compactness and strength.

Streambed regression is a particularly important aspect, and special care is needed to prevent these structures from being undermined by systematic or sudden subsidence of the thalweg. With respect to torrents, therefore, it is advisable to take steps to protect training walls from undercutting.

Using longitudinal structures to prevent bed erosion instead of check dams to promote channel aggradation is not usual torrent control practice. However, there may be specific cases — short reaches that cannot for some reason be controlled in any other way, for example — where a protective apron of large rocks (with or without mortar) may be necessary to facilitate rapid flow without detachment of bed materials.

2.1.1 Classification and purpose of work

Correction in a torrential watershed

Geographical area affected	Potential problems	Preventive action	
		Classification	**Description**
Watershed	Sheet and rill erosion Gully and headwater erosion Problems with infiltration and soil moisture content Floods caused by torrential storms Deep erosion, sloughing	Biological	Reforestation Improved plant cover
		Mechanical	Terracing Drainage
		Small hydraulic works	Logs Piling Fascines
Drainage channels (torrents and torrential streams)	Unbalanced torrent profiles Unconsolidated beds (therefore unstable) Unstable slopes Substantial wash and bed-load discharges (danger of infrastructural works and hydroelectric power stations silting up) Unstable banks with channel diversion and flooding	Transverse structures	Check dams Sediment storage dams (total or selective)
		Training walls	Groynes Protective bank walls (jetties, revetments)
		Hybrid structures	Sills Stepped, non-erodible reaches
		Biological	Plant cover along channel banks

2.1.2 Siting criteria

Sediment storage dams. These are constructed upstream of the damaged area and are normally placed across the torrent gorge to take advantage of the surrounding rock and the greater width upstream, which allows large quantities of sediment to collect in the basin formed.

Check dams. When used to control bed erosion, they should be sited so as to facilitate aggradation in the erodible reach. When used to stabilize bank slopes, they should be positioned in such a way that the sediment wedge in the mean cross-section of the filtration area is high enough to ensure its stability (Figure 10). In such a case, the height of the dam will be $H = a + d_x (I - I_c)$.

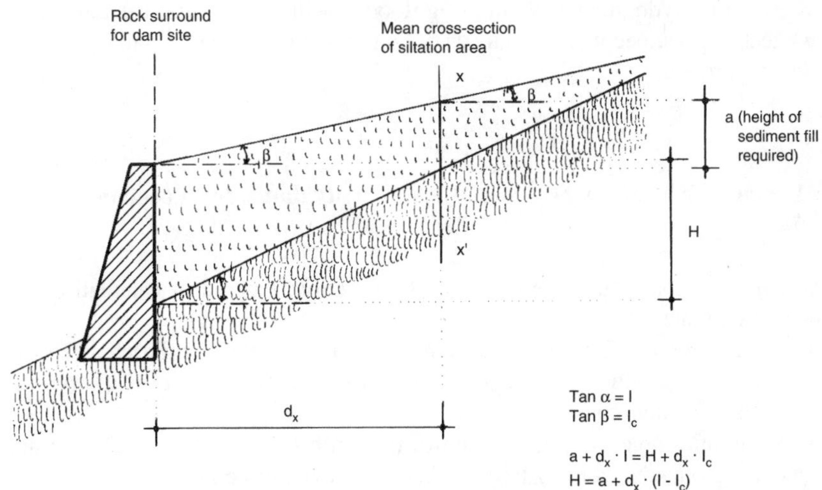

Figure 10. Check dam (xx' denotes required cross-section of sediment wedge)

Sills. These are transverse structures complementing training walls for bed erosion control in channels that do not slope steeply; they are constructed in erodible reaches where check dams cannot be used.

Jetties. These help protect banks subject to localized erosion. However, by restricting water displacement, they can have an erosive and destabilizing effect on the streambed. They are used to fill in cuts and rectify channel curvature.

Groynes. These are used to control bank erosion where the channel is wide enough to modify torrential flows; they have the advantage of being more economical than jetties.

Streambank revetments. When the channel is too narrow to divert the flow and the banks merely need protecting and strengthening, such revetments as riprapping, masonry or sodding are used.

Stepped profiles with non-erodible reaches. These are constructed in torrent debris cones and consist of training walls and grilled weirs which fix the channel and stabilize the bed.

2.2 Design and calculation of dams

Dam design involves:

- full understanding of the torrential situation requiring control;
- correct siting;
- the choice of most suitable type;
- a method of calculation appropriate to the static dimensioning of the structure;
- a cautious hydraulic design limiting floodflow damage to the structure;
- a technical and economic analysis of construction materials, availability, transport, etc.

2.2.1 Dam classification. Stress analysis. Gravity dams. Most economic profile

Dam classification. Dams are classified by function, method of calculation and construction material.

The Convention on Torrent Control Works (Vienna, 1973) proposed a classification of these structures by shape and function, with a mention of the type of material used in their construction.

The synoptic table on page 31 shows the main dam categories, classes and subclasses, grouped according to their shape, structure or composition.

Operating stages. There are three stages in dam operation: (1) filling; (2) during and immediately after aggradation; (3) once the bed has settled and become virtually impermeable.

During the first stage, hydrostatic pressure is exerted on the upstream face of the dam; the pressure may be triangular or trapezoidal, depending on whether the height of the nappe above the crest is greater than or equal to zero; the specific gravity of the water will equal or exceed 1 t/m^3 (the figure normally used is 1.2 t/m^3) as the dam begins to silt up.

In the second stage, weep-holes reduce the risk of increased sediment pressure by allowing water to filter through until the new bed is properly consolidated.

Once the third stage — bed consolidation — is complete, hydrostatic pressure is confined to the dam wings, while the rest of the structure faces the push of the saturated earth.

Analysis has shown hydrostatic pressure to be always greater than earth pressure, although the expansion and contraction of very clayey sediment as a result of changes in moisture conditions may sometimes be more damaging.

Synoptic dam classification table according to design, materials employed and purpose

Design / Type of material	Dam								
	Gravity	Gravity arch	Curved		Buttresses		Loose materials		Prefabricated components
			Fixed ring	Elastic arch	Flat deck	Curved deck	Earth	Riprapping	
Loose rocks (small structures)	S								
Gabions	S								
Masonry revetment	S and C	S and C							
Cyclopean and monolithic concrete	S and C	S and C	S and C						
Reinforced concrete	S and C	S and C	S and C	S and C	S and C	S and C			
Loose materials							S	S	
Other materials									S

S = sediment storage dam; C = check dam.

Configuration and analysis of forces exerted on dams. The first distinction to be made is between stabilizing and destabilizing forces.

Stabilizing forces are:

- the weight of the structure itself;
- the vertical component of water or sediment pressure at the upstream face (if sloping) and the above-ground part of the foundations;
- the weight of the nappe above the crest;
- the water pressure at the downstream face; and
- the passive pressure of the soil against the downstream face and foundations.

Destabilizing forces are:

- hydrostatic pressure;
- the passive pressure of the soil on the upstream face and foundations;
- uplift;
- stresses resulting from pressure drops (e.g. ice pressure and insufficient aeration below the free-falling nappe);
- dynamic forces of varying origin; and
- lateral pressure from unstable slopes.

Secondly, stresses acting on dams should be classified according to type, intensity and duration. For calculation purposes, the classification adopted here divides forces into three categories: basic, incidental and extraordinary.

In a 1-m thick calculation module, the profile will appear to have a three-part cross-section (Figures 11 and 12): a central rectangle and two laterals of previously determined shape with an area of Ω', Ω'' and Ω''' respectively. H being the height of the dam, the base of the cross-section also appears to consist of three parts, marked $k'b$, $k''b$ and $k'''b$. The height of the overflow nappe is $2/3h$, the notch itself acting as a broad-crested weir. If γ is the specific gravity of the sediment-charged water, γ_s the specific gravity of the materials used in the structure and γ_o the specific gravity of the water, the forces involved are as follows.

Basic forces

Stabilizing forces

- Weight of the structure (materials)

$$W_d = \frac{W' + W'' + W'''}{W} = \frac{(\Omega' + \Omega'' + \Omega''')}{\Omega} \cdot \gamma_s \cdot 1 \text{ [t]}$$

- Weight of earth above foundations at upstream face

$$W_{E_1 1} = Kv \cdot Kv \cdot \frac{h_{E_1 1}}{2}$$

at the downstream face

$$W_{E_1 2} = Kv \cdot \frac{h_{E_1 2}}{2}$$

Classification of torrent control dams (Synoptic table, Vienna Convention, 1972)

	Function	Morphology		Type of dam	Material employed
Torrent control dams	Check	A. Closed	A_1 Straight	$A_{1.1}$ Gravity	c, w, vm
				$A_{1.2}$ Girders and cross-braces	c, rc, s
				$A_{1.3}$ Cantilevered, self-stabilizing, on piles	rc, s
			A_2 Arched	–	c, rc, w
		B. Open or with openings	B_1 Vertical	$B_{1.1}$ With filter aperture	rc, w
				$B_{1.2}$ With comb	rc, w
			B_2 Horizontal	$B_{2.1}$ Rosic mechanism	c
				$B_{2.2}$ Modified Clauzel mechanism (Puglisi)	vm
	Sediment storage	C. Permanent (limited capacity)		Type A_1, A_2, B_1	c, s, rc, vm
		D. Temporary (release)	D_1 Without grilles	$D_{1.1}$ Mechanical storage	c, rc
				$D_{1.2}$ With energy dissipator	c, rc, vm
			D_2 With grilles	$D_{2.1}$ With fixed grilles	c, rc, vm
				$D_{2.2}$ With movable grilles	vm
			D_3 Others	–	vm
		E. Continuous (unlimited capacity)		Clauzel mechanism	vm

s = steel; c = concrete; rc = reinforced concrete; w = wood; vm = various materials.

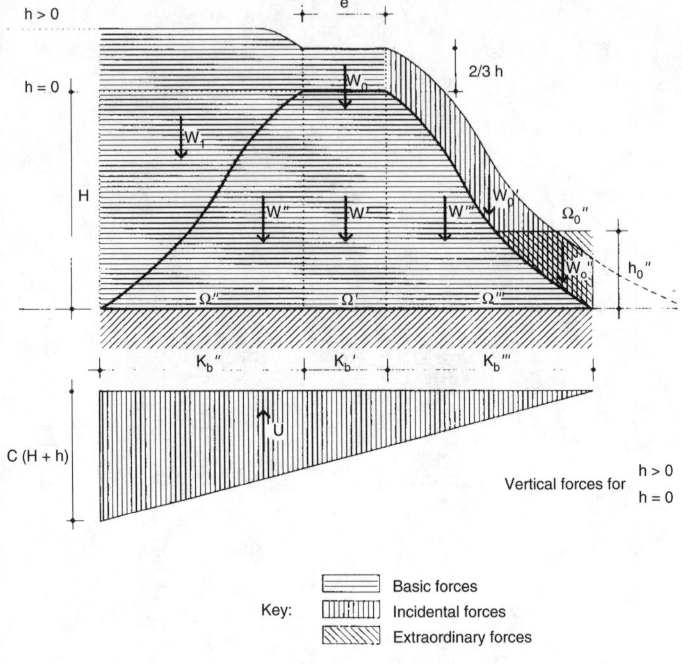

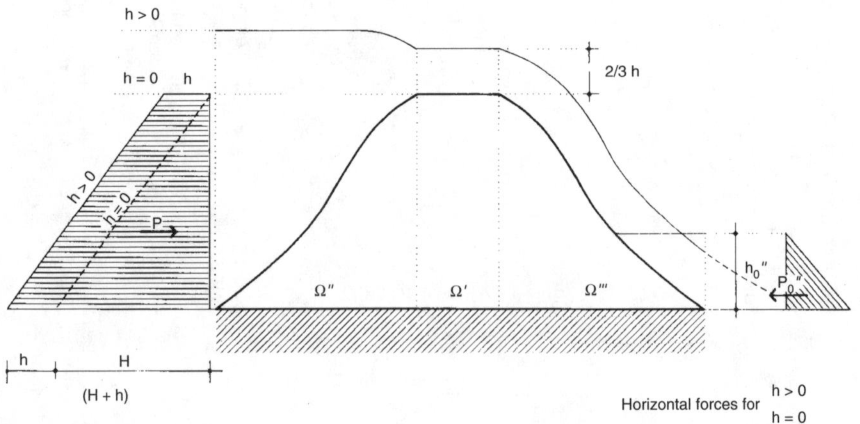

Figure 11. Forces acting on torrent control dams

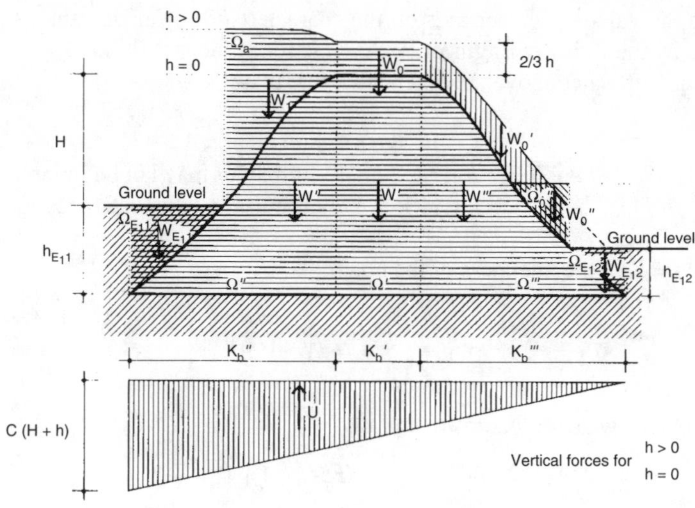

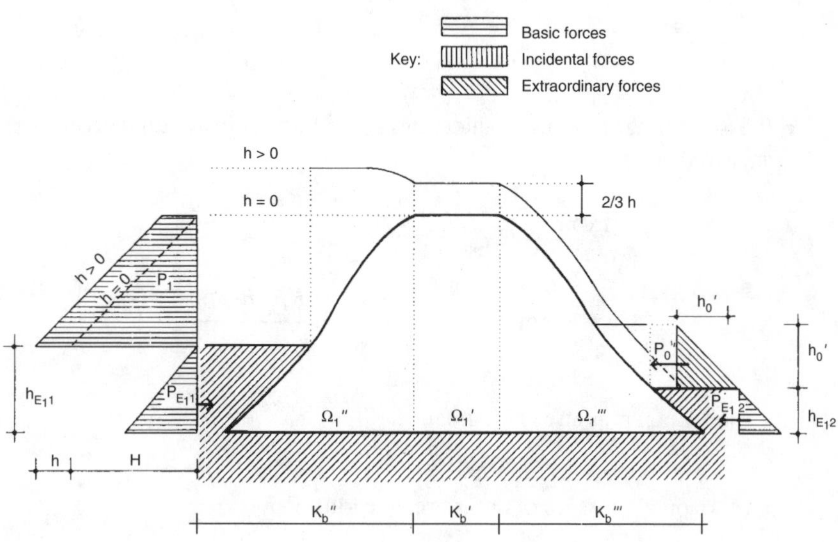

Figure 12. Forces acting on torrent control dams

where the value of *Kv* depends on the characteristics of the terrain, as per charts issued by the Railway Engineering Association, Chicago, Illinois.

- Weight of water above the notch sill. Note that if

$$t < 0.67\,h \text{ - it is ignored}$$
$$0.67 \cdot h < t < 2.5\,h \text{ - it may or may not be ignored}$$
$$2.5 \cdot h < t \text{ - it must be taken into account}$$

where t = K'b, the thickness of the notch.

$$W_0 = \frac{2}{3} h \cdot t \cdot \gamma \cdot 1 \text{ [t]}$$

- Weight of water at the upstream face

$$W_1 = \Omega_a \cdot \gamma \cdot 1 \text{ [t]}$$

Destabilizing forces

- Hydrostatic pressure at the upper face; distribution of the load may be trapezoidal or triangular, depending on whether the height of the nappe above the crest is or is not zero.

$$h = 0 \qquad P_1 = \frac{1}{2} H^2 \gamma \cdot 1 \text{ [t]}$$

$$h > 0 \qquad P_1 = \left[\frac{H}{2} + h\right] H \cdot \gamma \cdot 1 \text{ [t]}$$

- Pressure of earth on the foundations (based on Railway Engineering Association charts):

$$\text{upstream} \qquad P_{E_1} = \frac{K_H \cdot h_{2E_1 1}}{2} \text{ [t]}$$

$$\text{downstream} \qquad P_{E_2} = \frac{K_H \cdot h_{2E_1 2}}{2} \text{ [t]}$$

P_{E_1} (horizontal pressure of upstream earth) = $K_H \cdot \frac{h_{2E_1}}{2}$

P_{E_2} (horizontal pressure of downstream earth) = $K_H \cdot \frac{h_{2E_2}}{2}$

h_{E_1} = height of upstream sediment (m)

h_{E_2} = height of downstream sediment (m)

K_H = function of Rankine's formula without considering cohesion

$$= \gamma \cdot \frac{1 - \sin \sigma}{1 + \sin \sigma}$$

γ_E = weight of sediment under water

σ = angle of internal friction of earth

Incidental forces

Stabilizing forces

• Weight of water at the downstream face W_0'. This is only a factor when downstream waters are fairly deep. Friction at the lower face is not normally taken into account either.

Destabilizing forces

• Uplift. As a general rule, the destabilizing effect of the interstitial pressure of the water saturating the pores of the material does not enter into design calculations. For destabilization to occur, there would have to be continuous hydrostatic pressure on the dam face, which is prevented by weep-holes. The same applies to contact with the foundations if the dam is to be built on rock. Uplift only comes into play when foundations are laid on permeable soil. According to Levy's formula:

$$U = \frac{1}{2} (H + h) c \cdot \gamma \cdot 1 \text{ [t]}$$

where c is a reduction coefficient depending on dam foundation materials.

$c = 0$ – for rock
$c = 0.5$ – for rock fragments
$c = 1$ – for permeable materials

In evaluating this force, the trapezoidal distribution of the head of water on the downstream face is ignored as being of little significance.

Extraordinary forces

Stabilizing forces

• Weight of overfall nappe on the dam's lower face, as a result of the formation of a back current due to an energy dissipator

$$W_o'' = \Omega_o'' \cdot \gamma \cdot 1 \text{ [t]}$$

• Pressure of overfall nappe on the lower face

$$P_0'' = \frac{1}{2} h_0''^{2} \cdot \gamma \cdot 1 \text{ [t]}$$

Destabilizing forces

• Ice pressure. This arises due to the effect of temperature variations on the ice which forms on impounded water in mountain areas. It becomes relevant once the ice is more than 20 cm thick, with a value of 2.5 t/0.1 m of thickness per linear metre of crest.

• Dynamic pressure. This is produced by rapid flows, torrential washes, bedload impact or earth tremors. The forces produced by a rapidly flowing stream mainly affect the upstream dam face, because the water arrives as a jet and adds to the hydrostatic pressure. The value of these forces may be estimated by

$F = \gamma/g \cdot H \cdot v^2$ where v is the velocity of the stream and γ/g the density of the water

However, these effects are restricted to the crest area of closely spaced dams in fast-flowing mountain torrent reaches.

Torrential washes, or mudflows, consist of a mixture of semi-liquid materials whose high specific gravity (around 2.5 t/m^3), high roughness coefficient and above-average velocity (approximately 5 m/s) endow them with an immense destructive force seven to ten times that of hydrostatic pressure; consequently, they necessitate much larger structures. If the dam is to withstand the impact of the sediment load, the crest and wings need to be at least 1.3 m thick. As a general rule, the reservoir formed before the arrival of fast-flowing waters is enough to protect the structure from these dynamic forces, with the exception of torrential washes for which each case needs to be considered separately.

• Lateral pressures caused by unstable sediment loads. Unstable sediment runoff usually occurs at an angle to the channel axis and exerts considerable, but not easily quantifiable, pressure on the structure, particularly the wings. Rigid structures, therefore, should have an independent central core with flexible components.

Other destabilizing forces

Stresses arising from the depression that occurs when water flows over the notch without coming into contact with the dam face need to be considered only rarely in the case of hydrodynamic profiles. The same applies to stresses that may develop within a structure because of volume variations caused by physical, chemical and intrinsic factors.

Analysis of possible stresses on the structure shows it is necessary to distinguish between different load configurations, depending on the system adopted for the structure and the characteristics of the area where it is to be built.

First scheme. Only two forces are considered: the hydrostatic pressure resulting from a triangular pressure pattern ($h = 0$) on the dam body, and the weight of the structure itself. Application: design of step-wise correction works.

Second scheme. Two additional forces are considered: the increased hydrostatic pressure on the dam face applied by the height of the water above the notch and the weight of this water on the crest. Application: check dams not spaced in series, or built across very broad channel sections, or, more frequently, sediment storage dams on compact ground.

Third scheme. The hydrostatic force exerted by the total head of water on the whole dam face (including foundations) is taken into account as well as uplift on the foundation floor. Application: sediment storage dams constructed on permeable ground.

Fourth scheme. Sediment load and torrential wash pressures are added to the list. Structures affected by these aspects need to be designed specifically with them in mind.

Characteristic features of various dam components

Criteria	Concrete and stone/ mortar	Gabions	Earth	Riprap	Reinforced concrete	Prefabricated components
Useful life *	E G	S	S	S	E	G
Maintenance	G	S	S	S	E	S
Adaptation to site	G S	G S	E G	S	S	S
Utilization of *in situ* material +	G E	G	E	E	P	P
Transport of building materials		S	G	G	G	S S
Minimum necessary equipment	S G	G	G	G	P	G
Scope for mechanization	G S	S P	E	E	S	S
Construction time	E G	S	E G	E G	S	G
Engineering techniques	G	G	S	S	S	S
Scope for heightening	S P	S G	G	S G	P	S

E = Excellent; G = Good; S = Satisfactory; P = Poor.

* Useful life is reckoned as 50 years.
+ Only in torrents where there is appropriate construction material.

Dam utilization criteria. Economic evaluation is, of course, an integral part of any dam project, and involves not just the choice of structure, or its size, but other considerations as well: useful life of the dam; maintenance; available equipment and manpower; building supervision and so on. These considerations are summarized in the table on page 39 according to type of material employed.

Gravity dams. Gravity dams are dams whose own weight is the main influence on their stability. The following design conditions need to be met:

- At no point in the dam should tractive forces ever reach significant levels. Note that the resultant of all the outside forces acting above any particular horizontal section should remain inside the central core. (This condition gives a safety factor against overturning of more than one.)
- The dam should be stable enough to prevent sliding along the base or any horizontal joint. Consequently, the resultant of all the forces acting above a section or the base should lie at angle α to the vertical, so that tan α is less than the corresponding roughness coefficient (masonry against masonry, or masonry against foundation materials).
- Compressive forces acting on dam materials should not exceed permissible levels.

Verification of the calculation hypothesis involves (Figure 13):

- Accepting Hook's law (linear relation of stress to strain) and the conservation of plane sections, and calling the summation of all the vertical forces ΣF_v, which gives:

$$\sigma_A = \frac{2\Sigma\, Fv}{b}\left(\frac{3u}{b} - 1\right) \ [\text{kg/cm}^2]$$

$$\sigma_B = \frac{2\Sigma\, Fv}{b}\left(2 - \frac{3u}{b}\right) \ [\text{kg/cm}^2]$$

where $u = \frac{b}{3}$

$$\sigma_A = 0 \ [\text{kg/cm}^2]$$

$$\sigma_B = \frac{2\Sigma\, Fv}{b} \ [\text{kg/cm}^2]$$

- $\Sigma F_H \leq \varphi \Sigma F_v$ φ = roughness coefficient

tan $\alpha \leq \varphi$

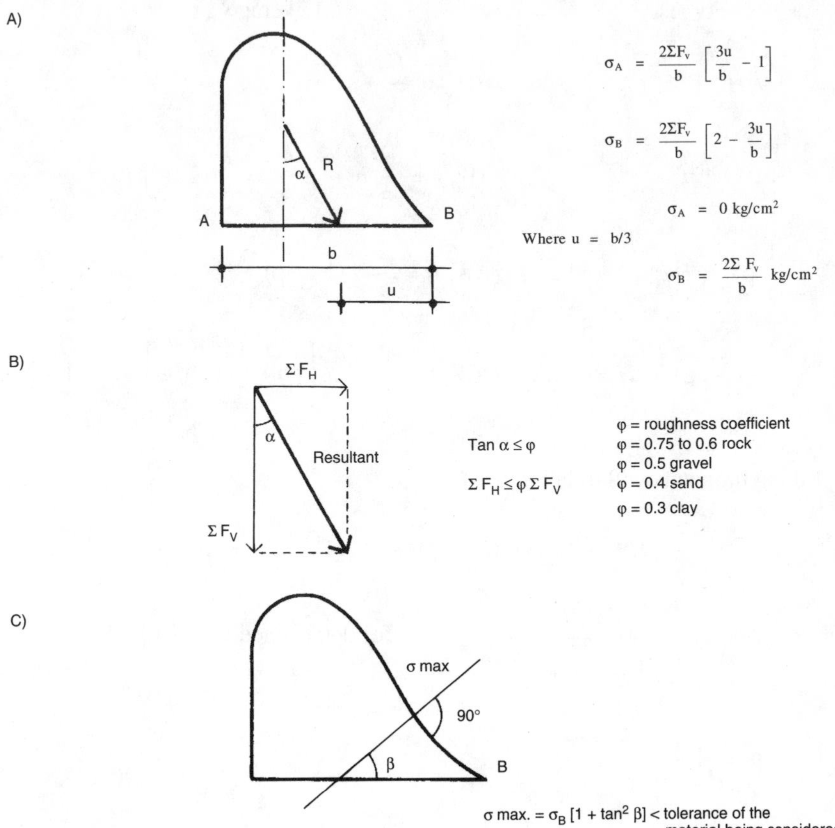

Figure 13. A. Calculation of stresses transmitted by gravity dams
B. Check for sliding
C. Verification of compressive forces within the structure

$$\varphi \begin{cases} 0.75 \text{ to } 0.6 \text{ rock} \\ 0.5 \text{ gravel} \\ 0.4 \text{ sand} \\ 0.3 \text{ clay} \end{cases}$$

- $\sigma_{max} = \sigma_B\,[1 + \tan^2 \beta] \leq$ tolerance of the material being considered.

Most economic profile (Figure 14):

γ (kg/m³) water with sediment
γ_s (kg/m³) masonry

Forces	Leverage
$P = \frac{1}{2} \gamma H^2$	.... $\chi(P) = \frac{H}{3}$
$W_o = \frac{1}{2} \rho \cdot b \cdot H$	.... $\chi(W_o) = \frac{2}{3} b - \rho \frac{b}{3} = \frac{b}{3}(2 - \rho)$
$W_1 = \frac{1}{2} \rho \cdot b \cdot H \cdot \gamma_s$	.... $\chi(W_1) = \frac{2}{3} b (1 - \rho)$
$W_2 = \frac{1}{2}(1 - \rho) b \cdot H \cdot \gamma_s$	.... $\chi(W_2) = \frac{2}{3} b - \left[\rho b + \frac{1}{3}(1-\rho) b\right] = \frac{b}{3}(1 - 2\rho)$

Taking moments with relation to *M*:

$$- \gamma H^2 + b^2 [\gamma \rho (2 - \rho) + \gamma_s (1 - \rho)] = 0$$

hence $b = \dfrac{H}{\sqrt{\frac{\gamma_s}{\gamma}(1 - \rho) + \rho(2 - \rho)}}$ for determined values of $H \dfrac{db}{d\rho} = 0$

so that: $\rho = 1 - \dfrac{\gamma_s}{2\gamma}$

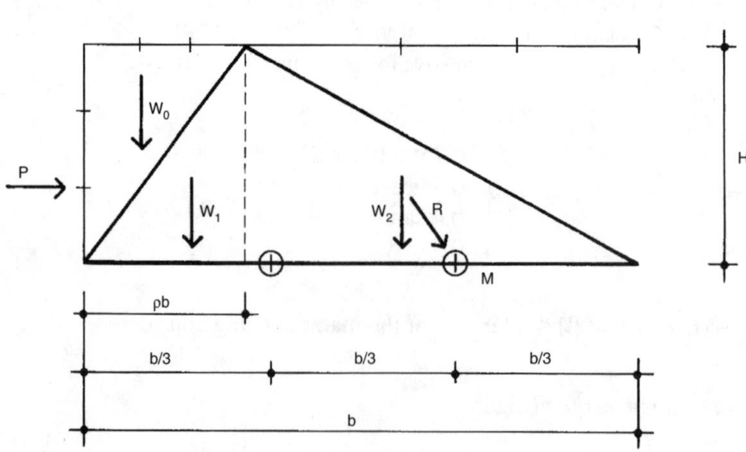

Figure 14. Most economic dam profile

Approximate values are: $\gamma_s = 2\ 400$ kg/m^3 and $\gamma = 1\ 200$ kg/m^3, $\rho \approx 0$. The most economic theoretical profile is, therefore, a triangular one with a vertical upstream face.

2.2.2 Overflow design and calculation

Types of overflow

Dams are usually designed with a notch or overflow to let water through. Generally, the overflow can take two forms: free fall, where the nappe separates from the downstream face, or a hydrodynamic (S-shaped) profile that allows water to run down the face.

The free-fall type of overflow is the easiest to build and the most common, since it reduces face erosion by sediment. Overflows with hydrodynamic profiles should only be used where the height of the nappe above the notch sill is significant in relation to the height of the dam.

Stages of hydrodynamic operation

The stages depend on the amount of siltation. The two boundary cases are: when no silting has occurred; and when the storage pool has completely silted up, and the accumulated sediment has attained the equilibrium bed slope. Overflows are usually designed on the latter basis.

Design of free overflows

Free overflows normally have flat sills, no rounding of the edges or walls, a trapezoidal section to facilitate aeration below the nappe and the passage of lesser flows and slopes of between 1/1 and 2/1. They are generally centred over the downstream channel to prevent bank erosion (Figure 15).

Narrow downstream channels call for a composite notch (Figure 15) consisting of a lower section centred over the channel for normal floodflows and a shallower ($h_1 < 1$ m) upper section for larger but less frequent discharges. As the overflow may cause bank erosion, complementary protection works will be needed.

Design of overflows with hydrodynamic profiles

The notch is rectangular in section, with vertical sides, and is centred over the downstream channel. The design of the overflow crest and the downstream face follows the curvature of the hydrodynamic profile adopted. The shape of the profile depends on the head, the inclination of the upstream face of the overflow section and the water's velocity of approach. The profile is defined as it relates to axes at the apex of the crest (Figure 16) and follows a parabola whose equation is: $\gamma/h = K(x/h)^n$ where K and n are constants depending on the slope of the upstream face and the velocity of approach.

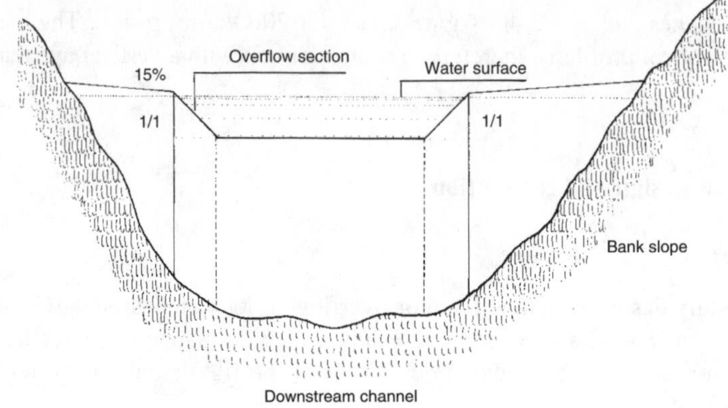

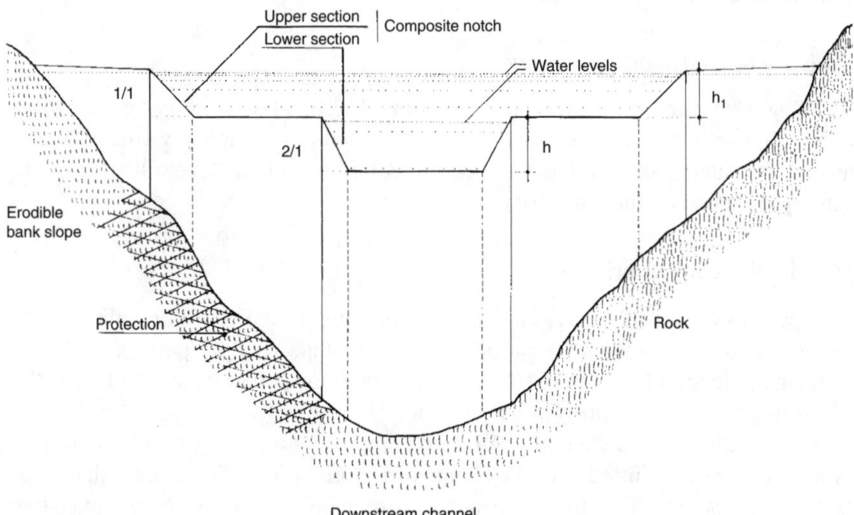

Figure 15. Design of free overflows

Although the Creager profile is the one normally used: $\gamma/h = 0.47\ (x/h)^{1.8}$, the Bureau of Reclamations profile is better suited to sediment-filled dams: $\gamma/h = 0.5\ (x/h)^{1.87}$.

The approximate profile shape for a crest with a vertical upstream face and a negligible velocity of approach is constructed in the form of a compound circular

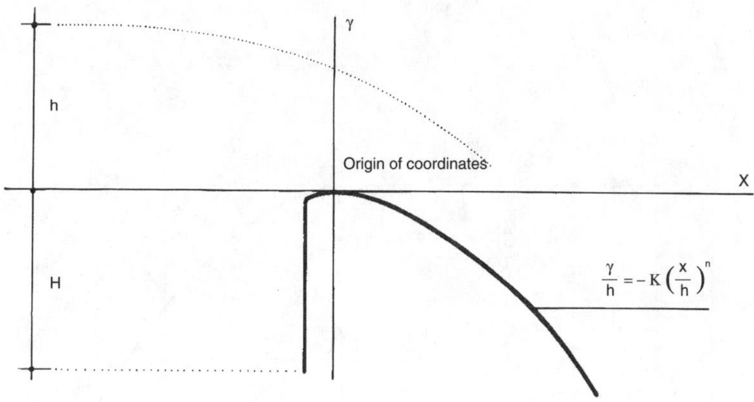

Figure 16. Design of an overflow with a hydrodynamic profile

curve with radii expressed in terms of h (Figure 17). In normal conditions, with small spillways where the height (H) of the dam is greater than or equal to $h/2$, this profile is sufficiently accurate. However, where H is less than $h/2$, the parabolic profile should be used.

Length of notch

As mentioned above, the notch length is determined by the width of the downstream channel. Furthermore, if the length (L) entails a significant contraction of the flow upstream of the overflow, this needs to be taken account of in the calculations by adopting a useful length $L_o = \varepsilon L$, in which $\varepsilon = L - 2Kh) / L$ where $K = 0.2$ (for sides with faces normal to the flow and right-angled edges); $K = 0.1$ (the same, but with rounded edges); $K = 0$ (for splayed sides at 45° to the flow, with rounded edges).

Height of notch

The height depends on whether the dam is filled or not and on the discharge Q (m^3/s).

Unfilled dams with free overflows usually have thick-walled notches, i.e. $t > 2.5h$, in which case the formula $h = (Q / 1.705\ L)^{2/3}$ can be used.

The notch height of unfilled dams with a hydrodynamic profile can be calculated on the basis of $h = [Q / (0.3\ L \sqrt{hg})]^{2/3}$.

In filled dams with a free overflow, the critical depth is reached. In these circumstances, the formula $h = \sqrt[3]{Q^2 / (gL^2)}$ should be used for rectangular notches. It can also be applied to trapezoidal notches providing they are not too high, L then being the average length of the notch.

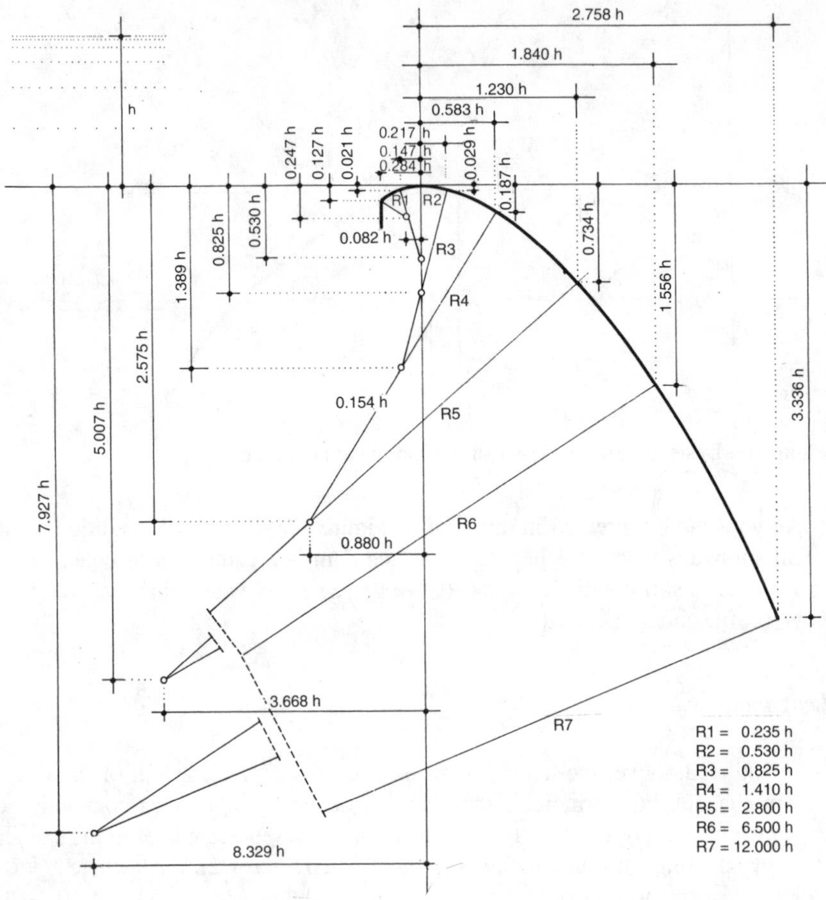

Figure 17. Design of an overflow with a hydrodynamic profile: compound circular curve with radii (R) expresssed in terms of the head (h)

For higher trapezoidal sections, use $h = (Q^2\ L_o\ /\ g)^{1/3}\ (L_o - mh)$ where m = slope of notch walls.

Finally, filled dams with hydrodynamic profiles should use either $\gamma\ /\ h = 0.5\ (x/h)^{1.87}$, or the compound circular curve profile. In both these cases, h = is obtained from:

$$Q = 1.705\ L\ \{h + [Q\ /\ (hL)]^2\ /\ 2g\}^{3/2}$$

2.2.3 Design components

Although design components have to be defined on a case-by-case basis according to stress patterns, calculation methods and so on, definitions of the following are always required:

- dam height
- thickness of crest
- thickness at base and face slopes
- foundations
- weep-holes
- energy dissipators (baffles, launching ramps, etc.)
- contraction joints

Height of dam

Height will depend on the purpose of the structure and on economic considerations. For sediment storage dams, the site with the largest sediment-holding capacity will need to be carefully determined and the height which gives the largest rates of stored volume to dam volume calculated. If, however, consolidation is the immediate objective, then the height will be such that the tail of the sediment fill is situated a distance *d* from the original site (Figure 18).

However, even where there is a rock surround to ensure the dam's stability, a check still needs to be made that the height of the accumulated sediment does not cause any difficulties further upstream, such as the silting up of a bridge or the flooding of crops due to too steep a rise in the streambed level. Sometimes, it will also be necessary to check whether aggradation in the average cross-section is having the expected stabilizing effect on banks (Figure 18).

Thickness of crest

Although triangular dam profiles are the most economic, the upper part of the structure needs to be thick enough to absorb pressure from the silt-laden water behind (Figure 19).

Taking AA' as the horizontal plane, the upper part needs to be able to resist horizontal slide pressures. If φ is the coefficient of roughness (material against material), then for a 1-m wide section φ must be W/P, where

$$W = (t\,x + 1/2x^2 \tan\alpha)\,\gamma_s \ [\text{t}]$$

$$P = x\left(\frac{x}{2} + h\right)\gamma \ [\text{t}]$$

hence $$\varphi\,(t + x/2 \tan\alpha)\,\gamma_s = (x/2 + h)\,\gamma$$

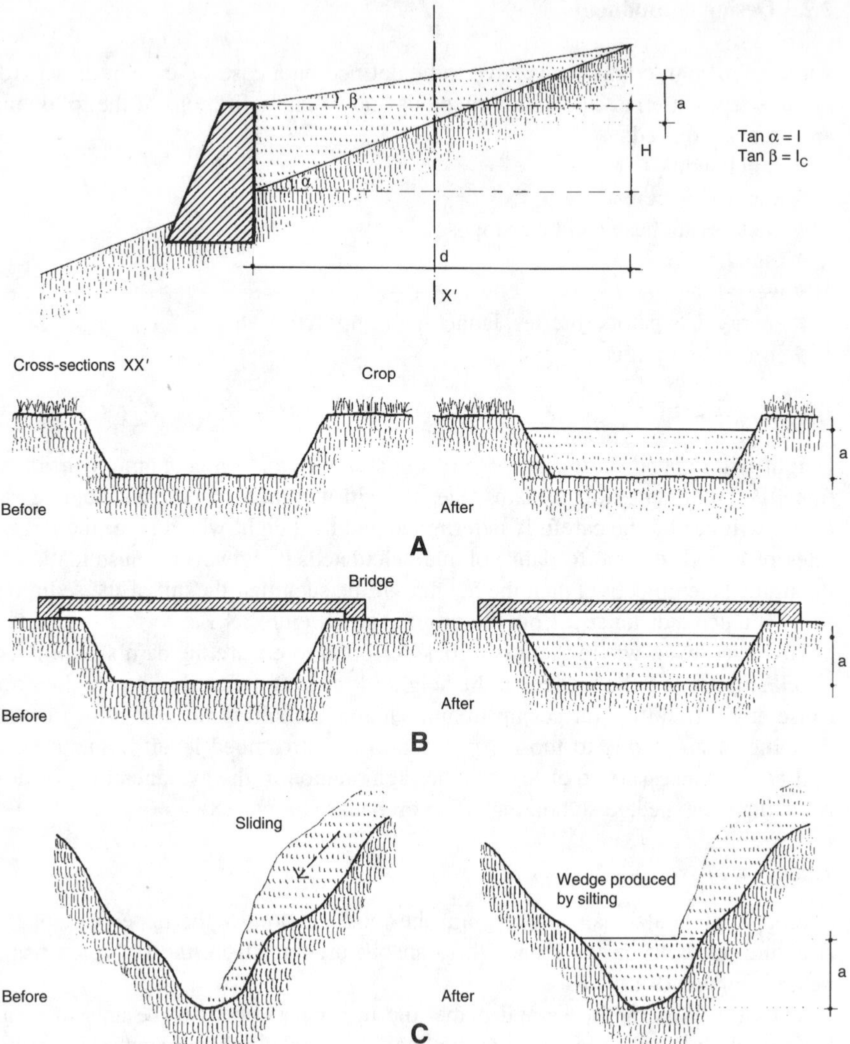

Figure 18. A. Sediment storage dam: its height threatens crops on the bank
B. Sediment storage dam: its height reduces the bridge's flow section
C. Detention dam: its height helps stabilize the bank

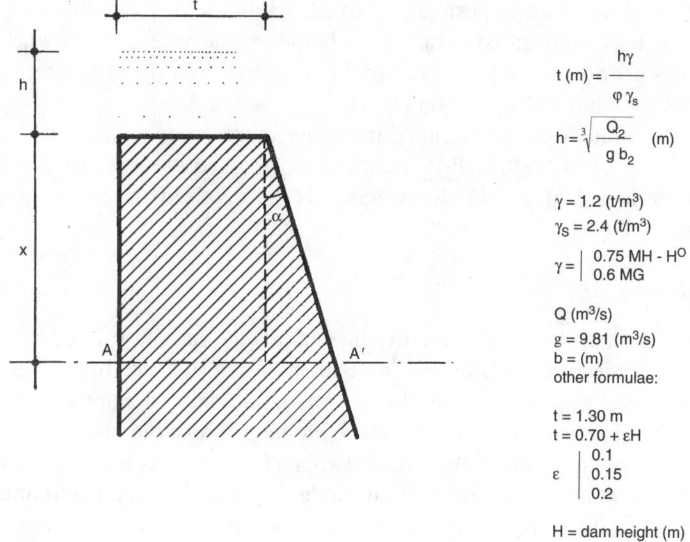

Figure 19. Thickness of crest in a gravity dam

And, where x is small enough, $t \cdot \varphi \cdot \gamma_s = h \cdot \gamma$

hence $t = \dfrac{h \cdot \gamma}{\varphi \cdot \gamma_s}$

When all the values of γ, φ and γ_s are known, an approximate value for h may be obtained from the formula for critical depth in a rectangular channel given a design flow Q : $h = \sqrt[3]{Q^2 / b^2 g}$ (m), in which b is the overflow width (m), Q the design flow (m^3/s) and $g = 9.81$ (m/s^2).

Among the other experimental formulae used by various authors, one gives the thickness directly as a function of dam height and a coefficient ε (a function of particle size) which varies between 0.1 and 0.2:

$$t = 0.7 + \varepsilon \cdot H \text{ [m]}$$

If there is a risk of mudflows, the thickness should not be less than 1.3 m.

Thickness at base and face slopes

Thickness is defined on the basis of the stability conditions given by the chosen method of calculation and, on occasion, by the slopes of the upstream and downstream faces.

The upstream face is normally vertical, while the downstream face slope depends on how slim the structure is to be. Over the years, the downstream face slope has been increased from 0.2 to 0.6, resulting in a slimmer structure and reductions in volume of up to 30 percent.

On the minus side, streamlined dams are more prone to damage from the increased impact of the overflow on the dam face. To prevent this damage, tan α should be less than $\sqrt{(2h / H)}$, where h is the depth of the overflow and H the height of the dam.

Foundations

Foundations are designed primarily in such a way that the soil's carrying capacity is not exceeded, and there is no danger of subsidence. In certain instances, therefore, and especially in the loose soils commonly encountered in riverbeds, some kind of substructure will be needed to help spread the load.

Dam foundations are usually shallow, since the load is transmitted directly to soil level without any lateral friction. In these conditions, the maximum and minimum load values, assuming linear distribution of structure-transmitted stresses, are:

$$\sigma_{max} = \frac{2\Sigma\ Fv}{b}\left(2 - \frac{3u}{b}\right) \text{ [kg/cm}^2\text{]}$$

$$\sigma_{min} = \frac{2\Sigma\ Fv}{b}\left(\frac{3u}{b} - 1\right) \text{ [kg/cm}^2\text{]}$$

Base the average load transmitted to foundation level that is permissible for the type of ground on: $\bar{\sigma} = 1/4\ (3\sigma_{max} + \sigma_{min}) < \sigma$.

Type of ground	**σ permissible (kg/cm²)**
Gravel	5 - 10
Coarse sand	3 - 5
Medium sand	1.5 - 2.5
Fine sand	0.9 - 1.5
Clay	very variable (requires special studies and analyses)

The hydrodynamic impact on soils is another important factor, since it may cause siphoning (which can destroy the structure) as well as directly affecting uplift. Each case needs to be looked at individually to see whether indented foundations would help counteract the effect.

Weep-holes

Weep-holes are normally built into dams to reduce the height of the nappe above the crest and to provide drainage once the structure has completely silted up, avoiding prolonged hydrostatic pressure at the upstream face. Weep-holes can be built in several different ways and may take various forms, from simple plastic tubes traversing the structure to proper openings (usually 20 $\times$ 30 cm). In any event, there should always be a downward gradient of 3 percent between the upstream and downstream faces. Normal practice is to have one weep-hole for every 6 m^2 of face.

Energy dissipators

The velocity of the overflow may result in toe scouring, undermining the structure's stability. A study of the hydraulic characteristics of the overflow will reveal what work is required at the downstream base of the structure to preserve it. In some cases, all that has to be done is to protect the torrent bed with erosion-resistant materials. In others, a stilling basin (usually enclosed at the downstream end by a subsidiary weir) may be required. Alternatively, launching ramps can be built to direct water away from critical points (Figure 20).

Contraction joints

When a structure measures several tens of metres across, contraction joints should be used to prevent cracking. Although not absolutely essential, these joints do help absorb variations in volume caused by changes in temperature or retraction of the concrete as it hardens (differential settlement may occur when a structure rests on different kinds of material). There are various ways of making these joints, but the cheapest methods are the commonest: waterproofed plane joints coated with asphalt or a similar bituminous substance.

2.2.4 Masonry and concrete dams

For calculation purposes, these consist of straight plan gravity dams which are less than 15 m high and made of masonry or monolithic or cyclopean concrete. The calculation methods given here will ensure structures are satisfactory from the economic point of view. As the weight of the material is the main favourable force, it should naturally be as great as possible. The following weights are guides:

		(kg/m^3)
Masonry:	Granite, gneiss or limestone	2 400
	Sandstone	2 100
Concrete:	Granite aggregate	2 360
	Limestone aggregate	2 280

The weight of masonry or concrete usually varies between 2 300 and 2 400 kg/m^3. The concrete or masonry dam typically used in hydroforestry work consists of a main body and two wings as illustrated in Figure 21.

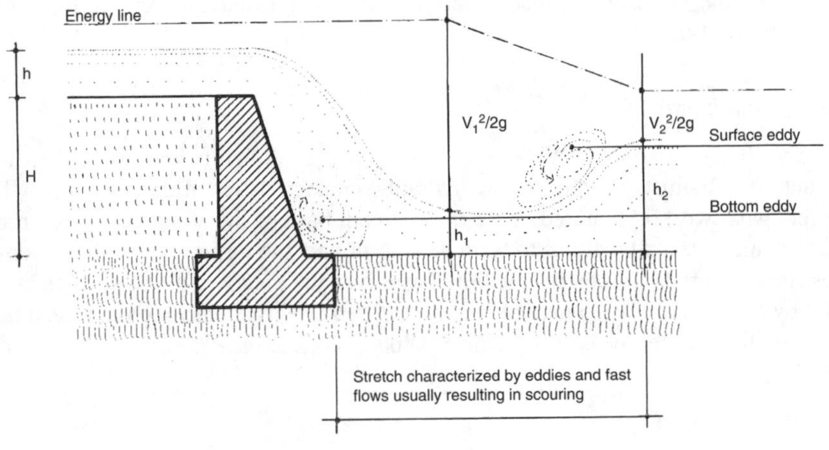

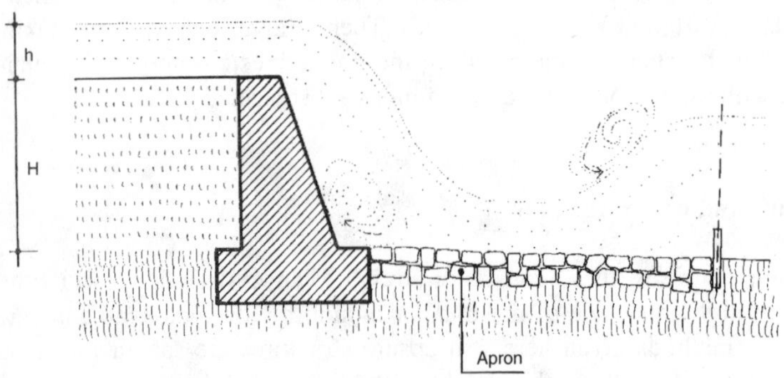

Figure 20. Energy dissipators

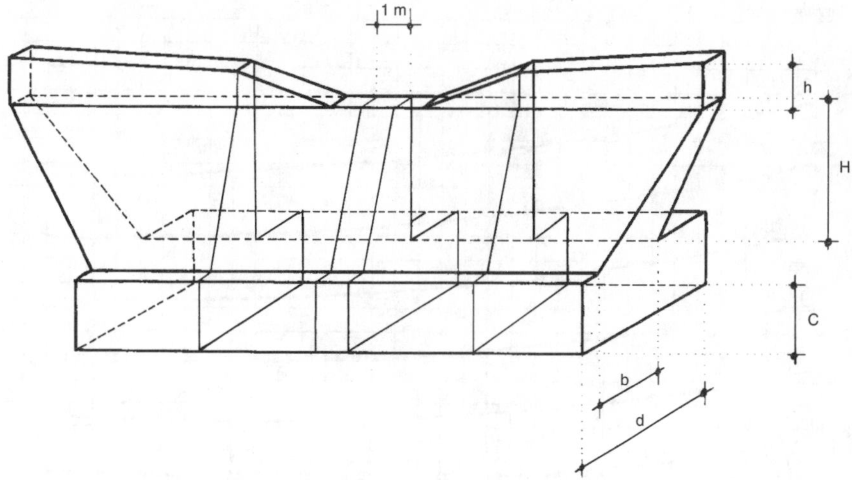

Figure 21. Perspective of a gravity dam

The main body is a trapezium with a vertical upstream face and a sloping downstream one. At the wings, a rectangle is superimposed on to the trapezium, which rests on the crest of the main body and whose height corresponds to that of the notch or overflow. After calculating the useful height H (m), the height h of the nappe above the crest (m), and the thickness of the crest t (m) or the slope n of the downstream face, the schemes described below may be used for calculating the main body.

First calculation scheme

Only two forces are considered: the weight of the material W (favourable) and the hydrostatic pressure P (unfavourable), assuming $h = 0$. In order to keep the volume of the structure down, the resultant of W and P is made to pass through the downstream end of the central core. For a length of 1 m, the thickness of the base can therefore be obtained from the following formula:

$$b\ (\mathrm{m}) = \sqrt{[(5t^2/4) + H^2\ (\gamma/\gamma_s)]} - t/2$$

In channels with a slope exceeding 15 percent, it may be more economical to have a trapezoidal profile with a vertical downstream face. Working on the same basis as before, this gives:

$$b\ (\mathrm{m}) = \sqrt{H^2 - [(\gamma_s - \gamma)\ /\ \gamma]\ t^2}$$

The diagrams for calculating b (m) and the area A (m^2) of the section corresponding to this first scheme are given in Figures 22 and 23.

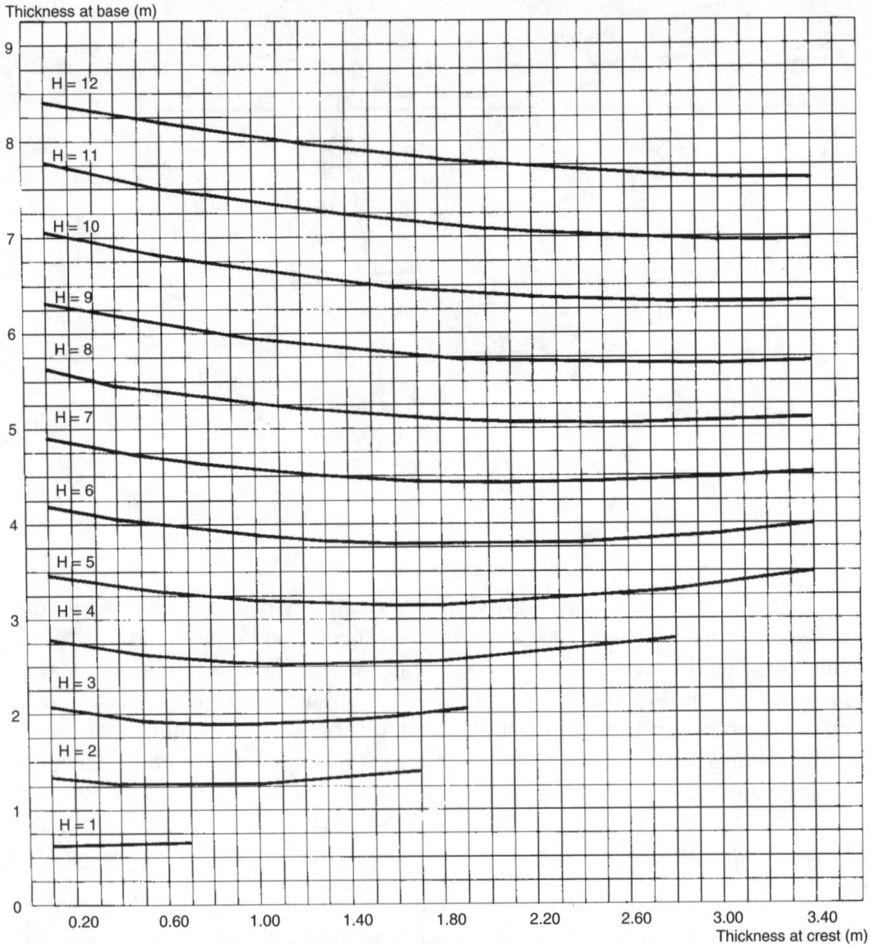

Figure 22. Graph for calculating the dimensions of a gravity dam (crest and base thickness) according to its height

Second calculation scheme

Figure 24 shows the dam in section and the forces that have to be taken into account when calculating the main body. The dam *ABCD* not only has to be stable along its base *CD* but also across any intermediate section *A'B'*. The stability of the portion *ABA'B'*, in which *A'B'* is any horizontal section between *AB* and *CD*, must therefore be studied.

Since all the calculation expressions obtained are homogeneous, it is easiest to take the total height of the dam *AC* as unity and relate all the other measurements to it. To obtain the actual dimensions, just multiply the results by *H* (the height of the dam).

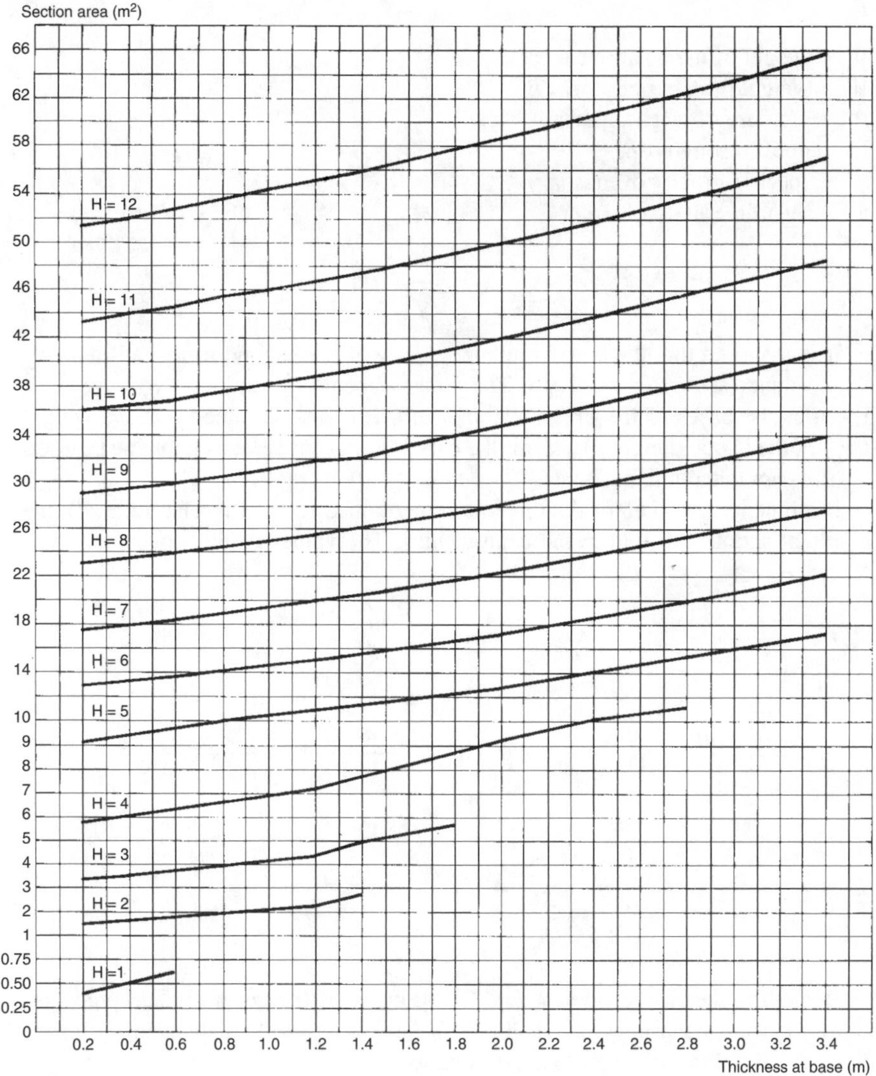

Figure 23. Graph for calculating the dimensions of a gravity dam (section area and base thickness) according to its height

Lengths

AC = overall height of dam = 1 m
$m = AB$ = thickness of crest
$m + n = CD$ = thickness of base
$q = AA'$ = height of section $A'B'$
p = height of nappe

Forces

W_0 = weight of nappe above crest
W = weight of dam body $ABA'B'$
P = pressure of water against AA'
U = uplift through $A'B'$
γ_s = specific gravity of masonry
γ = specific gravity of water

$$\Delta = \frac{\gamma_s}{\gamma}$$

It is assumed that the water pressure at A' will correspond to a head of water $(q + p)$ and, at A, to a head (p). The measurements (p) and $(p + q)$ have been taken as the bases of the pressure trapezium. It is also assumed that the weight (W_0) of the nappe (height p) acts on the crest AB. For the reasons explained earlier, uplift is not taken into account.

If moments are taken of the three aforementioned forces (in relation to A'), the resultant should fall within the central third. The values of the forces and their leverage are

$$W_o = p \cdot m \cdot \gamma \qquad X(W_o) = \frac{m}{2}$$

$$W = \frac{2m + nq}{2} \cdot q \cdot \gamma_s \qquad X(W) = \frac{-m^2 + (m + nq)^2 + m(m + nq)}{3(2m + nq)}$$

$$P = \frac{2p + q}{2} \cdot q \cdot \gamma \qquad X(P) = \frac{q(q + 3p)}{3(q + 2p)}$$

Regarding the relation $\Delta = \gamma_s / \gamma$, 2 400 kg/m^3 is the generally accepted specific gravity for masonry and 1 200 kg/m^3 for water with suspended sediment; therefore $\Delta = 2$ is a reasonable approximation.

The requirement that the resultant should pass through the downstream end of the central core leads to the expression

$$n = m(p + 1.5) + \sqrt{m^2(p^2 + 2.5p) + 1.25 + 1.5p + 1}$$

The central core condition in the wing section gives rise to the following conditions:

$$n \geq \frac{p(p + 3) - m^2}{4m}, \text{ and } m \geq p$$

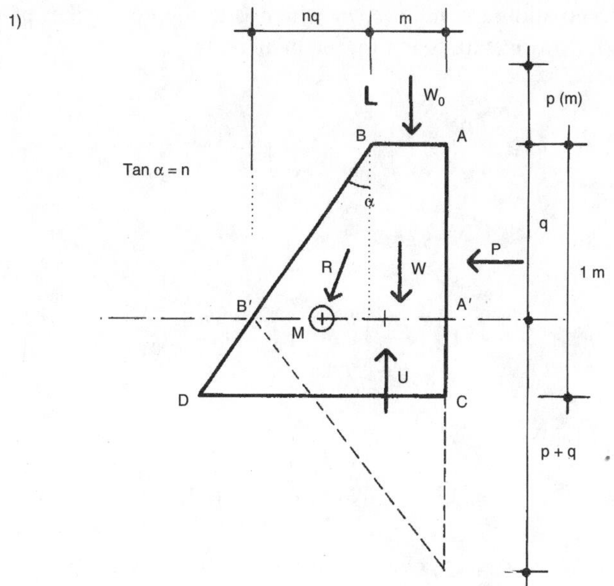

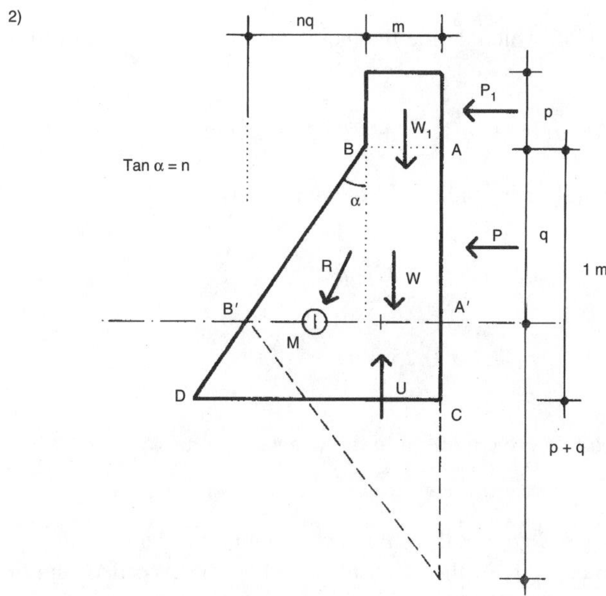

Figure 24. Forces acting on a gravity dam

In addition, the no-sliding condition, in which φ is the coefficient of static friction, gives the following expression for the main body:

$$n \geq \left(\frac{p}{q} + 2\right)\left(\frac{1}{\varphi} - \frac{m}{q}\right) - \frac{3}{2\varphi}$$

and in the wing section:

$$n \geq \left(\frac{p}{q} + 1\right)\left[\frac{1}{2\varphi}\left(\frac{p}{q} + 1\right) - \frac{2m}{q}\right]$$

which, with $\varphi = 0.75$, gives

$$q^2 (3n - 2) + 2q (3m - 2p) + 3pm \geq 0 \text{ for the main body}$$

$$q^2 (3n - 2) + 2q (3m - 2p) + 2p (3m - p) \geq 0$$

which, given the values adopted for the thickness of the crest ($m \geq 2p/3$), ensures that the wing section is at least as stable as the main body.

Summary

The values of m and n, which define the dam's dimensions, should fulfil the following conditions:

$$n \geq -(1.5 + p)\, m + \sqrt{1.25 + (2.5\, p + p^2)\, m^2 + 1.5\, p + 1} \qquad \text{(I)}$$

imposed by the central core condition in the main body of the dam.

$$m \geq p \qquad \text{(II)}$$

$$n \geq -\, 0.25\, m + \frac{p\,(p + 3)}{4m} \qquad \text{(III)}$$

imposed by the central core condition in the wings.

Observations

The conditions imposed are not the only ones essential for dam stability. For example, the bearing capacity of the material should not be exceeded, and the dam should be just as stable when the basin is full as when it is empty. However, since these conditions are not especially relevant to the size of structure dealt with here, we will not elaborate on them.

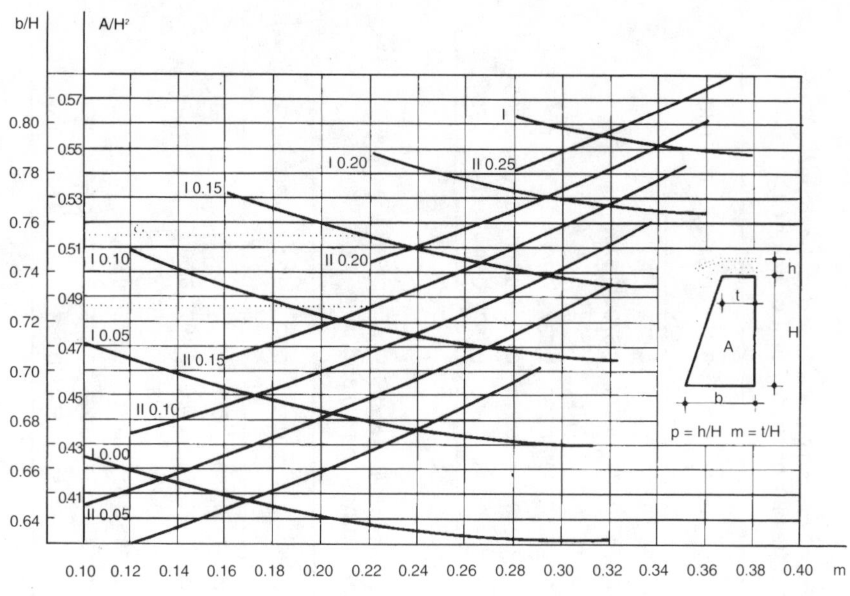

I – $(b/H)_p$

II – $(A/H^2)_p$

Example: m = t/H = 0.22 cuts the curve I (b/H) p = 0.15 with *m* b/H = 0.754 b = 0.754 H

p = h/H = 0.15 cuts the curve II (A/H^2) p = 0.15 with *m* A/H^2 = 0.487 A = 0.487 H^2

Figure 25. Graph for calculating the dimensions of a gravity dam according to the record calculation scheme

Since the objective is to present results in the form of tables and graphs (Figure 25), a number of these are provided in the following pages. However, the assumptions adopted in the calculations are by no means exhaustive; the reason for choosing them in particular is that they are the ones usually encountered in this type of structure. Some of the factors undermining dam stability have not been considered here — for example, the dynamic force of the water, uplift and the friction between the nappe and the crest. At the same time, one favourable condition that has not been taken into account either is the fact that the dam is anchored to its foundations and its wings to the ground. This is the reason for not suggesting here that some kind of safety coefficient be applied to the dimensions resulting from the above calculations, as this precaution is best left to the individual to decide in the light of his or her own experience.

The table on page 60 gives the values for $m + nq$, in line with the conditions set out above, for a series of values of m and p within the normal range for this type of structure. From now on, b will be used to represent $(m + qn)\, H$.

Main base $\left(\frac{b}{H}\right)$

Calculation of main dam base per unit of height b/H, as a function of $m = t/H$, the lesser dam base per unit of height, and $p = h/H$, the depth of the water at the crest (lesser base) per unit of height

p \ m	0.10	0.12	0.14	0.16	0.18	0.20	0.22	0.24	0.26	0.28	0.30	0.32	0.34	0.36	0.38	0.40
0.00	0.666	0.660	0.655	0.650	0.646	0.642	0.639	0.637	0.635	0.633	0.632	0.632				
0.05	0.712	0.705	0.699	0.694	0.688	0.684	0.680	0.677	0.674	0.672	0.671	0.670	0.670			
0.10		0.748	0.740	0.734	0.728	0.723	0.718	0.714	0.711	0.709	0.707					
0.15				0.772	0.765	0.759	0.754	0.750	0.746	0.742	0.739	0.737	0.736			
0.20							0.788	0.783	0.778	0.774	0.771	0.768	0.766	0.764	0.763	0.762
0.25										0.803	0.800	0.797	0.794	0.791	0.789	0.784

Area $\left(\frac{A}{H^2}\right)$

Calculation of the area of the central section (notch section) of the dam per H^2 (square height of dam) as a function of n and p

p \ m	0.10	0.12	0.14	0.16	0.18	0.20	0.22	0.24	0.26	0.28	0.30	0.32	0.34	0.36	0.38	0.40
0.00	0.383	0.390	0.397	0.405	0.413	0.421	0.429	0.438	0.447	0.456						
0.05	0.406	0.412	0.419	0.427	0.434	0.442	0.450	0.458	0.467	0.476	0.485	0.495	0.505			
0.10		0.434	0.440	0.447	0.454	0.461	0.469	0.477	0.485	0.494	0.503					
0.15				0.466	0.472	0.479	0.487	0.495	0.503	0.511	0.519	0.528	0.538			
0.20							0.504	0.512	0.519	0.527	0.535	0.544	0.553	0.562	0.571	
0.25										0.541	0.550	0.558	0.567	0.576	0.584	0.592

The values for area/H^2 are also given in tabular and graph form. The following notations have been employed in the graphs and tables: H = height of dam; h = height of nappe; t = lesser dam base.

These data allow us to calculate $p = h/H$, giving the curve of the graph, and $m = t/H$, giving the abscissa. For example, if $p = h/H = 0.15$ and $m = t/H = 0.22$, this gives a figure of 0.754 for b/H and 0.487 for A/H^2.

Thus for the main dam base and its area

$$b = 0.754 \cdot H$$
$$A = 0.487 \cdot H^2 \text{ (notch section)}$$
$$A' = (0.487 + 0.22 \cdot 0.15)\, H^2 \text{ (wing section).}$$

It will be seen that the only values for p used are 0.05, 0.1, 0.15, 0.2 and 0.25. Other values may be interpolated, or the next highest one chosen instead.

Other graphs can be drawn using this calculation scheme to obtain the thickness of the base b (m), in relation to the height H (m) and the height of the nappe above the notch sill h (m) together with the maximum acceptable stress K (kg/cm^2) and the coefficient of safety G (Figures 26-29).

The following table gives values for dimensioning the dam body (σ_m = 0.5 kg/cm^2; γ_s = 2.4 t/m^3; γ = 1.2 t/m^3 and θ_v = 0.10).

H (m)	***e* = 0.80** **b** (m)	**A** (m^2)	**σ_m** (kg/cm^2)	**G**
2.00	1.00	1.80	1.21	1.34
2.50	1.32	2.64	1.53	1.48
3.00	1.71	3.76	1.69	1.62
3.50	2.10	5.08	1.85	1.73
4.00	2.51	6.62	2.02	1.83
4.50	2.92	8.38	2.18	1.93
5.00	3.34	10.35	2.35	2.01
5.50	3.76	12.55	2.52	2.08
6.00	4.19	14.97	2.69	2.15
6.50	4.62	17.61	2.87	2.21
7.00	5.05	20.47	3.04	2.26
7.50	5.48	23.56	3.21	2.31
8.00	5.92	26.87	3.38	2.36
8.50	6.35	30.41	3.55	2.40
9.00	6.79	34.17	3.72	2.44
9.50	7.23	38.15	3.90	2.47
10.00	7.67	42.37	4.07	2.51

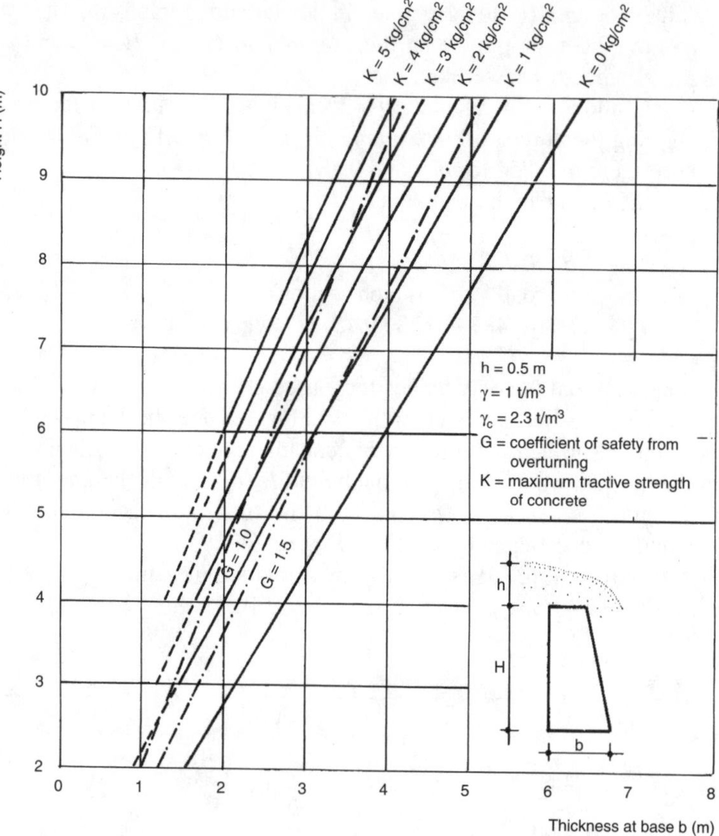

Figure 26. Graphs for dimensioning the dam body for various values of *h*, in accordance with the second calculation method

Although the use of graphs and tables helps in predimensioning the dam, a number of other checks will still need to be made to ensure that:

- There is no risk of sliding over the foundations (safety coefficient ≥ 1.3). N. B. These safety coefficients are merely illustrative.
- There is no risk of overturning with respect to the downstream end of the foundations (safety coefficient ≥ 1.5).
- The bearing capacity of the ground supporting the foundations is not exceeded (safety coefficient ≥ 2).
- The maximum allowable stresses on the various materials are not exceeded at any point in the structure.

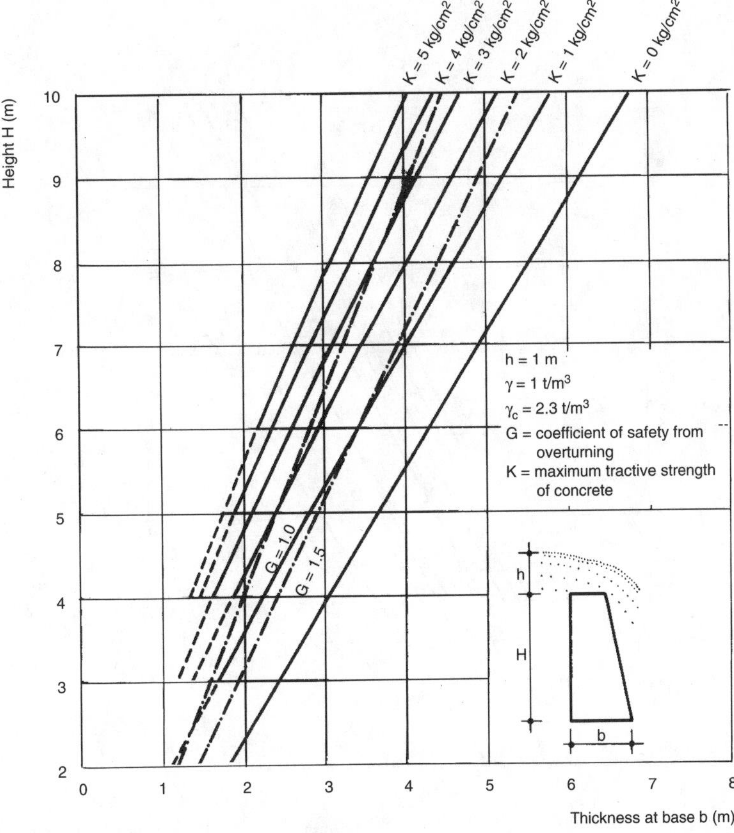

Figure 27. Graphs for dimensioning the dam body for various values of h, in accordance with the second calculation method

As regards the maximum tensile stress of concrete or masonry, most countries' regulations do not allow any traction and fix a limit of 35 kg/cm^2 for compression (higher than the materials in gravity dams normally bear). Experience shows, however, that monolithic structures can withstand a small amount of traction.

Third calculation scheme

This scheme is similar to the previous one, but also takes account of uplift U. For reasons of economy, the resultant should pass through the bottom of the central core M (Figure 24).

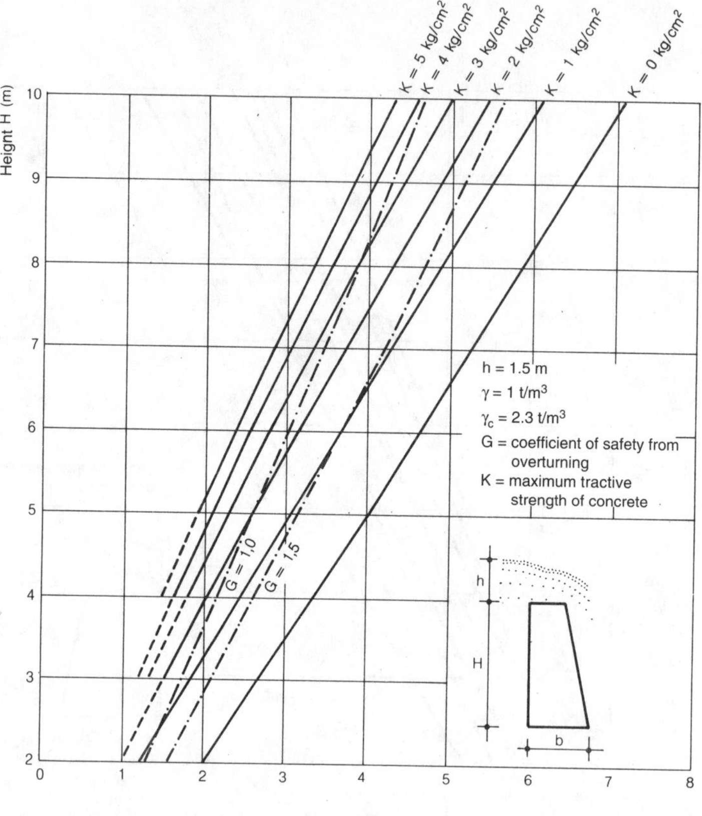

Figure 28. Graphs for dimensioning the dam body for various values of *h*, in accordance with the second calculation method

The calculation is as follows:

- Coordinates of *c* (centre of gravity of the trapezoidal section), with respect to *M*:

$$x = \frac{(nq + m)^2 + m(m + nq) - m^2}{3(nq + 2m)}$$

$$y = \frac{q(nq + 3m)}{3(nq + 2m)}$$

Forces	*Leverage with respect to* M
$W_0 = m \cdot p \cdot \gamma \; (\gamma = 1\,200 \text{ kg/m}^3)$	$x(W_0) = \frac{1}{6}(4nq + m)$

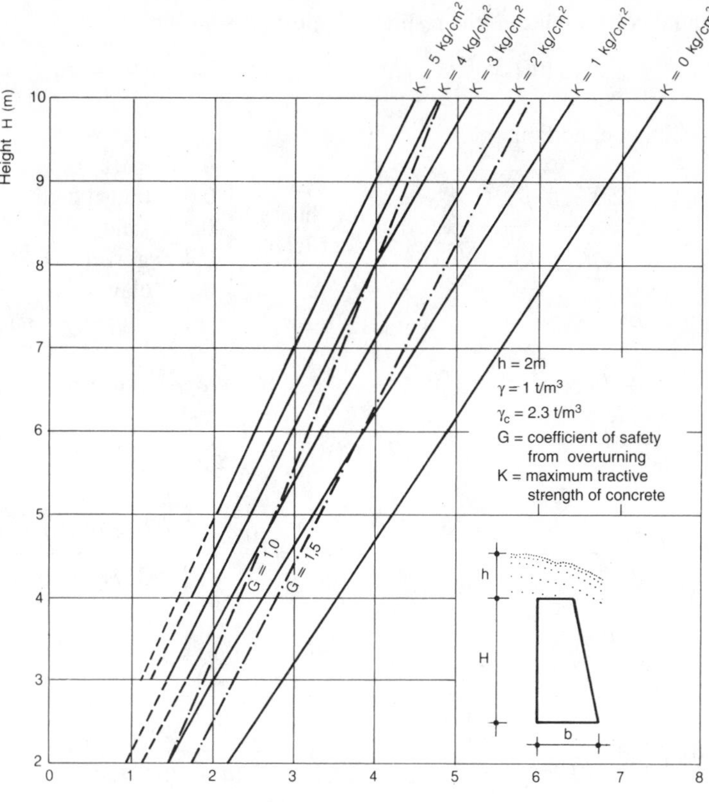

Figure 29. Graphs for dimensioning the dam body for various values of *h*, in accordance with the second calculation method

$$W = \frac{nq + 2m}{2} \cdot q \cdot \gamma_s \; (\gamma_s = 2\,400 \text{ kg/m}^3) \qquad x\,(W) = \frac{(nq+m)^2 + m(nq+m) - m^2}{3\,(nq+2m)}$$

$$U = \frac{1}{2}\,(nq + m)\,(q + p)\,\gamma_0 \cdot c \qquad x\,(U) = \frac{1}{3}\,(ng + m)$$

$$(\gamma_0 = 1\,000 \text{ kg/m}^3) \qquad c = \begin{cases} 0 & \text{rock} \\ 0.5 & \text{loose rock} \\ 1 & \text{soil} \end{cases}$$

$$P = q\left(\frac{q}{2} + p\right) \cdot \gamma \qquad x\,(P) = \frac{q\,(q + 3p)}{3\,(q + 2p)}$$

- Central core condition (the resultant *R* must pass through *M*):

$$W_0 \cdot x(W_0) + W \cdot x(W) - U \cdot x(U) - P \cdot x(P) = 0$$

- No-sliding condition:

$$\frac{P}{W + W_0 - U} \qquad \text{roughness coefficient} \begin{cases} 0.75 & \text{rock} \\ 0.6 & \text{transit earth} \\ 0.5 & \text{sand} \\ 0.4 & \text{gravel} \\ 0.3 & \text{clay} \end{cases}$$

Forces	*Leverage with respect to* M
$W_1 = m \cdot p \cdot \gamma_s$	$x(W_1) = \frac{1}{6}(4\,nq + m)$
$W = \frac{nq + 2m}{2} \cdot q \cdot \gamma_s$	$x(W) = \frac{(nq + m^2) + m\,(nq + m) - m^2}{3\,(nq + 2m)}$
$U = \frac{nq + m}{2}(q + p)\,\gamma_0 \cdot c$	$x(U) = \frac{1}{3}(nq + m)$
$P = q\left(\frac{q}{2} + p\right)\gamma$	$x(P) = \frac{q\,(q + 3p)}{3\,(q + 2p)}$
$P_1 = \frac{1}{2}p^2 \cdot \gamma$	$x(P_1) = \left(q + \frac{p}{3}\right)$

- Central core condition:

$$W_1 \cdot x(W_1) + W \cdot x(W) - P \cdot x(P) - P_1 \cdot x(P_1) - U \cdot x(U) = 0$$

- No-sliding condition:

$$\frac{P + P_1}{W + W_1 - U} \leq \text{roughness coefficient}$$

Permissible ground load:

$$\frac{3}{2}\,\frac{W_1 + W - U}{nq + m} \leq \begin{array}{l} 3\ \text{kg/cm}^2\ \text{(gravel)} \\ 2\ \text{kg/cm}^2\ \text{(coarse sand)} \end{array}$$

2.2.5 Gabion check dams

The characteristics of gabions are described in Chapter 4. Calculations for these structures, however, should give particular importance to determining their apparent specific gravity γ_g, which is a function of the stone's specific gravity γ_s, size and porosity. The values of γ_s for the various types of rock are:

Rock	Specific weight γ_s (kg/m^3)
Basalt	2 900
Granite	2 600
Hard limestone	2 600
Trachyte	2 500
Sandstone	2 300
Porous limestone	2 200
Tufa	1 700

The diagram in Figure 30 enables γ_g to be obtained in function of γ_s and n where $\gamma_g = \gamma_s(1 - n)$. Experience shows that γ_g varies between 1 200 kg/m^3 and 1 900 kg/m^3 for values of γ_s between 2 000 and 2 700 kg/m^3 and values of n between 0.25 and 0.40.

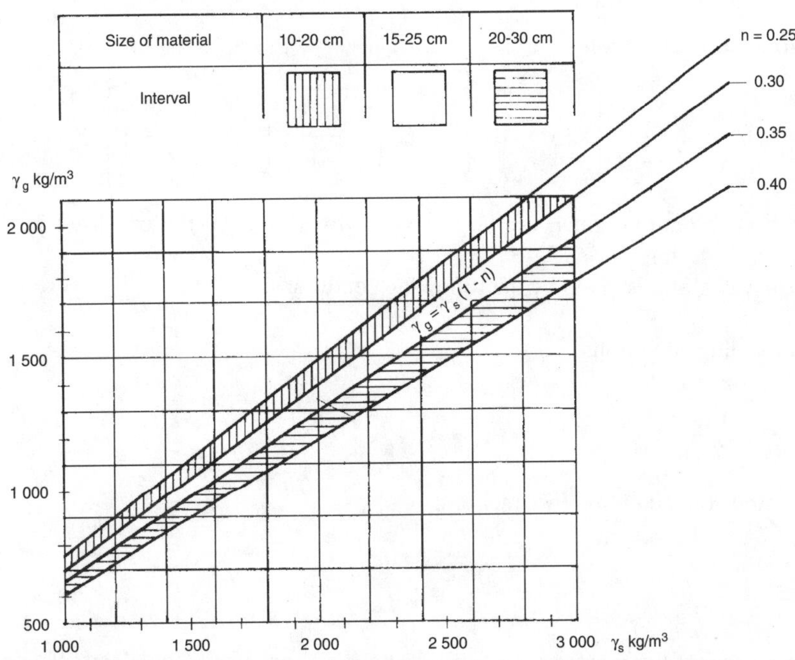

Figure 30. Diagram showing the determination of the apparent specific gravity of the gabion γ_g, given to γ_s of the fill material and the porosity of the gabion n

Calculation of gabion check dams

This calculation basically involves applying two conditions to each horizontal joint: no sliding and no tractive stresses in the body of the structure.

In masonry dams, for which the calculation conditions are very similar, the least-volume profile was shown to be a triangular one with a vertical upstream face. It is even more appropriate for gabion structures, because the gaps lessen the vertical pressure of the water on dams with sloping upstream faces.

In calculating each of the three profiles referred to, it is assumed that pressure is exerted on the upstream face when water containing suspended sediment of specific gravity γ (t/m^3) reaches the notch sill. Such a simplified load hypothesis is acceptable for small dams of this type that are built in highly torrential channels and silt up very quickly; in other words, the height of the water flowing over the notch during the siltation period is only of relative importance and can be left out of the calculation, particularly in view of the fact that the sizes of gabions available commercially will result in a structure that is bigger than necessary anyway.

Application to regular stepped profiles (type II)

- No-sliding condition:

$$d \geq \frac{2}{i - 1}\left(\frac{i\gamma}{2\varphi \cdot \gamma_g} - a\right)$$

- No-traction condition:

$$d \geq \frac{1}{2i - 3}\left[-3a + \sqrt{q\,a^2 - 2\left(\frac{2i - 3}{i - 1}\right)\left(a^2 - i^2\,\frac{\gamma}{\gamma_g}\right)}\,\right]$$

For each dam height i, the largest value for d will be the one used in the structure's design.

The value of a is given by the following conditions:

- No-sliding condition:

$$a \geq \frac{\gamma}{2 \cdot \gamma_g \cdot \varphi}$$

- Central core condition (no traction):

$$a \geq \sqrt{\frac{\gamma}{\gamma_g}}$$

These conditions are amply fulfilled by the usual values of γ and γ_g, with $a = 1$ m (the width of the standard commercial gabion).

	Profile	No-sliding condition	Central core condition
I	d_1, a_1, d_2, a_2, d_i, a_i, i (m)	$\varphi \cdot \gamma_g (a_1 + a_2 + \ldots + a_i) \geq \frac{1}{2} \gamma i^2$ hence: $a_i \geq \frac{\gamma i^2}{\varphi \gamma_g} - (a_1 + a_2 + \ldots + a_{i-1})$	$\gamma_g \left[a_1 \left(\frac{2}{3} a_i - \frac{a_1}{2} \right) + \ldots a_i \left(\frac{2}{3} a_i - \frac{a_1}{2} \right) \right] = \frac{1}{6} i^3 \gamma$ hence: $a_i \geq -2(a_1 + \ldots + a_{i-1}) +$ $+ \sqrt{4(a_1 + \ldots + a_{i-1})^2 + 3(a_1^2 + \ldots + a_{i-1}^2) + \frac{\gamma}{\gamma_g} i^3}$
II	d, a, a + d, d, a + (i – 1) d, i (m)	$\varphi \cdot \gamma_g [a + (a+d) + \ldots (i-1)d)] \geq \frac{\gamma i^2}{2}$ hence: $d \geq \frac{2}{i-1} \left(\frac{i\gamma}{2\varphi \gamma_g} - a \right)$	$\gamma_g \left\{ a \left[\frac{2}{3} a + (i-1)d - \frac{a}{2} \right] + \ldots \left[a + (i-1)d \right] \right.$ $\left. \left[\frac{2}{3} (a + (i-1)d) - \frac{a + (i-1)d}{2} \right] \right\} = \frac{\gamma i^3}{6}$ hence: $d \geq \frac{1}{2i-3} \left[-3a + \sqrt{9a^2 - 2\left(\frac{2i-3}{i-1} \right) \left(a^2 - i^2 \frac{\gamma}{\gamma_g} \right) \left(a^2 - i^2 \frac{\gamma}{\gamma_g} \right)} \right]$
III	d, a_1, d, a_2, d, a_i, i (m)	$\varphi \cdot \gamma_g (a_1 + a_2 + \ldots + a_i) \geq \frac{1}{2} \gamma i^2$ hence: $a_i \geq \frac{i^2 \gamma}{2\varphi \gamma_g} - (a_1 + a_2 + \ldots + a_{i-1})$	$\gamma_g a_1 \left[(i-1)\, d + \frac{a_i}{2} - \frac{a_i}{3} \right] + \ldots + \gamma_g a_i \left[\frac{a_i}{2} - \frac{a_i}{3} \right] = \frac{\gamma i^3}{6}$ hence: $\sum_{j=1}^{j=i} \left[d(i-j) + \frac{1}{2} a_j - \frac{1}{3} a_i \right] a_j \geq \frac{1}{6} i^3 \frac{\gamma}{\gamma_g}$

For $\gamma = 1.2$ t/m^3, $\gamma_g = 1.55$ t/m^3, $\varphi = 0.6$ and $a = 1$ m, the following table gives values for the width of step d (m) and volume V (m^3) per metre of length, for dam heights H (m) of 2-8 m.

(I)

H	2	3	4	5	6	7	8
d	0.63	0.94	1.05	1.11	1.15	1.17	1.19
V	2.63	5.82	10.30	16.10	23.25	31.57	41.32

Step design and volumes for commercial gabions, at intervals of 0.5 m:

(II)

H	2	3	4	5	6	7	8
d	1.00	1.00	1.50	1.50	1.50	1.50	1.50
V	3.00	6.00	13.00	20.00	28.50	38.50	50.00

This design involves a volume increase of between 3 and 26 percent depending on how closely the size of the commercial gabion corresponds to the theoretical dimensions.

With the above type of dam, which has a fixed-width crest (1 m), step widths can range in practice from 1-1.5 m. Damage, however, can be caused when large volumes of water loaded with coarse sediment fall on to the lower steps of the downstream face — even if the top of the step is coated with cement mortar. To prevent this damage (always assuming it can be predicted from the torrent's characteristics), another design should be used with a fixed step width of 0.5 m (the smallest commercial gabion size), and a crest width a (m),which depends on dam height and stability requirements. On this hypothesis, a should fulfil the following conditions:

- No-sliding condition:

$$a \geq \frac{\gamma i}{2\varphi \cdot \gamma_s} - \frac{i - 1}{4}$$

- No-traction condition:

$$a \geq \frac{-3(i-1) + \sqrt{i^2\left(5 + 16 \cdot \frac{\gamma}{\gamma_s}\right) - 8i + 3}}{4}$$

Without changing the values of the parameters considered earlier, the table below gives the crest width *a* (m) for dam heights *H* (m) of 2-8 m, together with the volume *V* (m^3) per metre of length.

(III)

H	2	3	4	5	6	7	8
a	1.13	1.44	1.83	2.23	2.62	3.02	3.41
V	2.76	5.82	10.32	16.15	23.22	31.64	41.28

This design gives similar volumes to those above but with the additional advantage of reducing water impact on the downstream face; it should therefore be used in preference to the others.

Adapting these results to commercial gabion dimensions gives the following values in practice:

(IV)

H	2	3	4	5	6	7	8
a	1.50	1.50	2.00	2.50	3.00	3.00	3.50
V	3.75	6.00	11.00	17.50	25.50	31.50	42.00

These volumes are much the same as, or lower than, those for the other model, except in the relatively infrequent case of dams 2 m high.

For the wings on either side of the overflow notch, the following measurements apply, depending on the height *h* (the values of γ, γ_s and φ remaining the same as before):

(V)

h	1	1.50	2.0
Upper row width	1.0	1.0	1.0
Lower row width	–	1.0	1.5

The following remarks are in order:

- A height of 1.5 m can be achieved by using commercially available 0.5 m gabions in the upper row.

- However, the figures are not applicable to the type of dam considered in (I), where $h = 2$ m, and no other size is stable without altering the thickness of the crest ($a = 1$ m).
- The 1.5 m width given for the lower row when $h = 2$ m is slightly less than the theoretical value (1.63 m) for a nappe height of 2 m; it is, however, perfectly adequate in most cases as it fulfils the stability conditions for heights of up to 1.9 m.

2.2.6 Earthfill dams

Loose materials are used because of their advantages for construction, their structural simplicity (for heights up to 10 m) and the limited demands they make on foundations or bank connections (they are flexible and able to adapt to differential consolidation in compressible ground).

Despite these advantages, earthfill dams present considerable difficulties when used as check or sediment storage dams, because water cannot be allowed to flow directly over the downstream face. A different type of overflow design is therefore called for, unless special precautions are taken to waterproof the face to protect it from erosion: waterproof sheeting must be covered with a layer of fine granular material on top of which is placed riprapping strong and large enough to resist the tractive force of overflow waters along the downstream face. This operation is really only feasible for small overflows (maximum height 0.5 m).

It is quite common to divert the overflow laterally into a fast-flowing channel along one or both of the sides where the dam is anchored; the water then returns to the main channel further downstream from the dam. Although this is a frequently employed device in loose material structures functioning as storage works, diversion weirs or small reservoirs, it is not well suited to check and sediment storage dams because it drives the water against the bank fills, threatening their stability. In addition, the sediment load, and bedload in particular, carried by the water, is forced into a sharp bend over the lower part of the siltation zone, resulting in a steep increase in deposition, the possible destruction of the overflow section and consequent overtopping of the crest.

This type of torrent control structure is best suited to wide gullies. There should be a central overflow built of masonry, gabions or concrete, with two long wings composed of loose materials. Precautions must be taken to moderate the velocity of seepage water in the sections adjoining both structures.

The development of soil science, together with the possibility of using modern earth-moving and compaction equipment requiring 15-20 times less manpower per cubic metre than concrete, are justification enough for taking earthfill dams into consideration. They are built of gravel, sand, silt and clay placed in successive compacted layers. Wagner's (simplified) unified soil classification system as well as the corresponding table of usages on page 74 are particularly helpful in designing these structures.

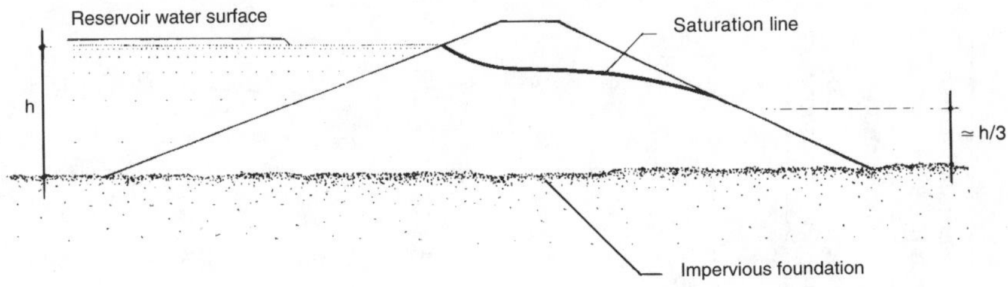

Figure 31. Homogeneous earth dam

Earthfill dams are of three types: the diaphragm type, the homogeneous type and the heterogeneous type.

The first type is not to be recommended, since the construction both of internal earth diaphragms with their accompanying filters and of rigid internal diaphragms must be of particularly high quality and call for a greater degree of control than is possible in correction works. They also involve considerable extra expense.

Homogeneous dams are built of only one material, excluding the facing surfaces. The material should be sufficiently impermeable to ensure adequate watertightness, and the slopes, for reasons of stability, need to be relatively flat (Figure 31). These dams are the most common type used in torrent control.

The heterogeneous, or zoned embankment, type has a central impervious core flanked by zones of much more pervious materials, which cover, support and protect the core. Because this type is economical to build, it tends to be used wherever different kinds of soil are available. For a classification of the materials used to construct earthfill dams, see the table on page 75.

The general conditions these dams need to meet are:

- The overflow capacity should be sufficient to ensure that the water never overtops the dam. The design requires a safety gap between the maximum foreseeable water level and the dam crest.
- The slopes of the dam walls should be adequate to ensure the stability of the materials used.
- The saturation line, or the line dividing the dry from the wet part of the dam body, should be angled as low down the downstream face as possible, to intersect with the base of the dam. In earthfill torrent control dams, the line can be determined by Casagrande's semi-empirical method. It may sometimes be advisable to install drainage at the toe of the downstream face so as to prevent the saturation line from penetrating deeper into the body of the structure.
- Water passing through and below the dam should do so slowly so as to not detach any material.

Soil use characteristics (according to Wagner)

Group [1]	Permeability (compacted ground)	Resistance to shearing (compacted and saturated ground)	Compressibility (compacted and saturated ground)	Ease of use in construction	Classification according to use (from 1 = high to 14 = low)		
					Homogeneous fill	Foundation	
						High filtration	Low filtration
GW	Permeable	Excellent	Negligible	Excellent	–	–	1
GP	Very permeable	Good	Negligible	Good	–	–	3
GM	Semi-permeable to impermeable	Good	Negligible	Good	2	1	4
GC	Impermeable	Good to fair	Very low	Good	1	2	6
SW	Permeable	Excellent	Negligible	Excellent	–	–	2
SP	Permeable	Good	Very low	Fair	–	–	5
SM	Semi-permeable to impermeable	Good	Low	Fair	4	3	7
SC	Impermeable	Good to fair	Low	Good	3	4	8
ML	Semi-permeable to impermeable	Fair	Average	Fair	6	6	9
CL	Impermeable	Fair	Average	Good to fair	5	5	10
OL	Semi-permeable to impermeable	Poor	Average	Fair	8	7	11
MH	Semi-permeable to impermeable	Fair to poor	High	Poor	9	8	12
CH	Impermeable	Poor	High	Poor	7	9	13
OH	Impermeable	Poor	High	Poor	10	10	14
P_t	–	–	–	–	–	–	–

[1] As per the Unified Soil Classification System

Design

Earthfill dams have a trapezoidal profile with sloping faces that ensure that the dam is stable whatever the water level in the basin and that the foundations are not overloaded. Filtration through the foundations and wings should be controlled to prevent erosion within the structure.

The thickness of the crest is determined by the type of material, the minimum filtration distance through the fill when the water level in the basin is at its maximum and the height and volume of the structure. In any event, the crest should be thick enough to take compaction equipment. For large structures, the formula used to calculate the thickness of the crest is:

$$t\ (\mathrm{m}) = 3.624\ (H - 1.5)^{1/3}$$

in which H is the effective height in metres.

Classification of materials for construction of earthfill dams

Description	Characteristics		Group[1]
Coarse-grained materials (more than 50% retained on a No. 200 BS sieve)	Gravel (more than 50% of the coarse fraction consists of gravel-sized particles)	Well-graded gravel, sandy gravel, with little or no fine material	GW
		Poorly graded gravel, sandy gravel, with little or no fine material	GP
		Silty gravel, sandy silty gravel	GM
		Clayey gravel, sandy clayey gravel	GC
	Sand (more than 50% of the coarse fraction consists of sand-sized particles)	Well-graded sand, sand and gravel, with little or no fine material	SW
		Poorly graded sand, sand and gravel with little or no fine material	SP
		Silty sand	SM
		Clayey sand	SC
Fine-grained materials (less than 50% retained on a No. 200 BS sieve)	Silt, clay (liquid limit 50%)	Inorganic silts, fine clayey or silty sand of low plasticity	ML
		Inorganic clay, silty clay, sandy clay of low plasticity	CL
		Organic silts and silty clays of low plasticity	OL
	Silt and clay (liquid limit 50%)	Inorganic silts of high plasticity	MH
		Inorganic clay of high plasticity	CH
		Organic clay of high plasticity	OH
Highly organic soils		Peat and other highly organic soils	P_t

[1] As per the Unified Soil Classification System.

In torrent control dams, the minimum thickness is 3 m, using the formula:

$$t \text{ (m)} = \frac{H + h + h_1}{5} + 1.5$$

in which:

H (m) = effective height of dam

h (m) = height of nappe above the crest

h_1 (m) = freeboard remaining above maximum water level at dam face ($h_1 = 0.76 + 0.34\ L^{1/2} - 0.26\ L^{1/4}$, in which L = maximum length of impounded water in km).

As for the slope of each of the dam faces, it should be remembered that while the upstream face is initially in direct contact with the stored water, this situation gradually changes as the basin silts up; in the long term, the stability requirements for the upstream face need not be so stringent as for the downstream one, which is permanently exposed.

The slope is determined by filtration network characteristics within the structure. In the case of homogeneous materials (according to Casagrande), the network follows a modified parabola: the saturation line is normal to the upstream face slope and at a tangent to the slope of the downstream face.

The stability of the downstream slope is related to the height at which it intersects the upper line of the filtration network at the face — a height that should not exceed a third of the dam's useful height (Figure 32a).

Flow conditions can be improved by having a triangular wedge-shaped toe of pervious material at the base of the downstream face, one third the height of the dam's useful height (Figure 32b), or a filter of pervious granular material at the downstream toe. The filter's dimensions are defined by the formula $t \text{ (m)} = \sqrt{(2LQ/K)}$, in which t (m) is the thickness of the filter, L (m) the length of the filter, Q (m^3/s) the filtration rate and K (m/s) the coefficient of permeability for the material used (Figure 32c). In these conditions, the faces of homogeneous earthfill dams on stable ground may be given the following slopes, depending on the type of soil used.

Soil used[1]	Upstream slope	Downstream slope
GC, GM, SC, SM	2.5:1	2 :1
CL, ML	3 :1	2.5:1
CH, MH	3.5:1	2.5:1

[1]As per the Unified Soil Classification System.

Note: Soil Types OL and OH should not be used on account of their high organic matter content. Types GW, GP, SW and SP are permeable and therefore unsuitable as well.

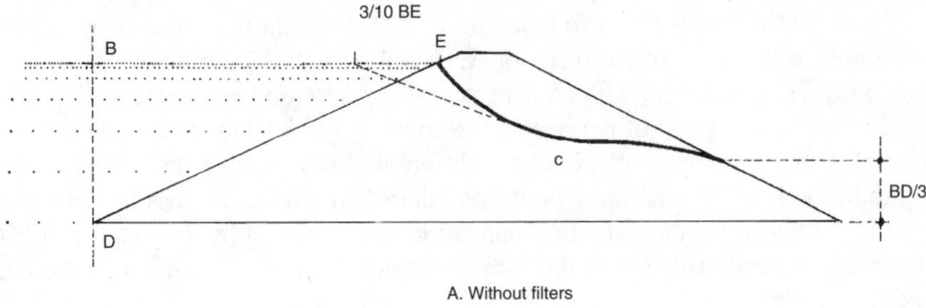

A. Without filters

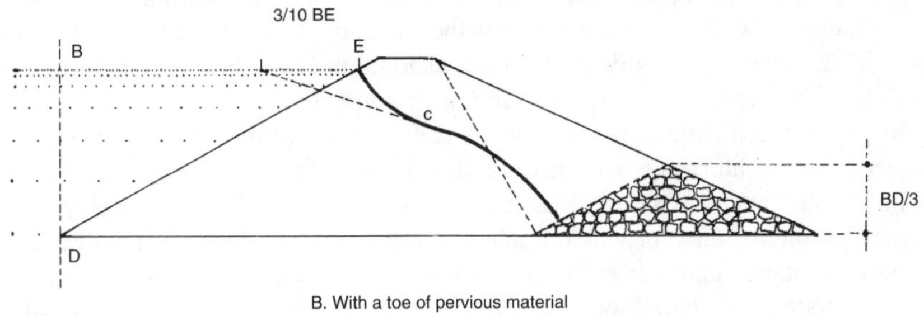

B. With a toe of pervious material

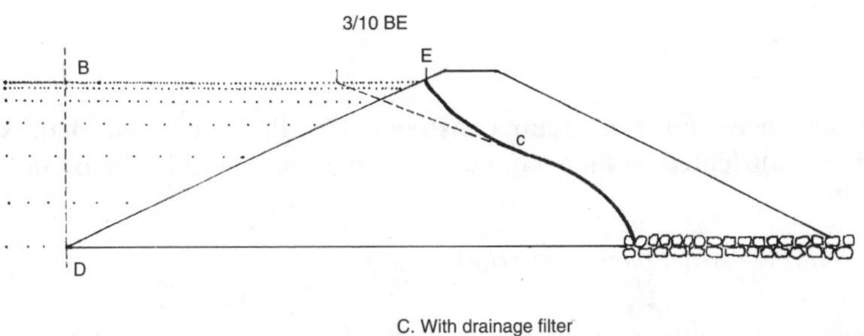

C. With drainage filter

Figure 32. Upper filtration limit in homogeneous dams

Foundations

The essential requirement for an earthfill dam is that the foundations and the torrent bed and banks should be capable of withstanding the vertical pressures exerted by the structure. Three types of foundation material are considered here: rock, coarse-grained particles and fine-grained particles.

Intact bedrock is the best foundation. It is so resistant that there is no need to set limits to the slope of the fill. Slopes, therefore, will depend solely on the type of construction material, with no danger of water filtration below the dam.

Torrent beds formed of permeable materials — gravel and sand — do not pose any particular problems of stability or differential settlement either. Nonetheless, filtration below the structure should be controlled whenever possible and good contact between the dam and the foundation floor ensured by digging a cutoff (a trapezoidal trench filled with the same compacted material from which the dam itself is made).

The cutoff is placed near the middle of the structure, or slightly upstream, and parallel to the central line of the dam. The sides normally have a slope of 45°, and the formula giving the relation between the width of the bottom of the cutoff W to its depth d is $W = h - d$, where h is the hydraulic head above the ground surface. In any event, the width at the bottom should not be less than 6 m to accommodate excavation, filling and compaction equipment.

Impermeable membranes may also be used. Placed in the upstream face, they reduce filtration and the risk of erosion, thereby improving dam stability.

Last, foundations consisting of fine materials, especially silt and clay, pose several problems, most of which relate to possible sliding of the structure caused by low resistance and settlement of the materials during consolidation. In these circumstances, the dam should be built in successive layers, at intervals of at least two years, to speed up consolidation of the loose materials. Vegetation should always be cleared from the foundation floor and from horizons containing organic matter. The surface should then be compacted prior to applying the first layers of earth.

2.2.7 Heterogeneous dams. Cellular construction with interlinked girders. Made with prefabricated metal components. Grille, comb and lattice dams

Dams of cellular construction with interlinked girders

These dams may be either straight or curved in plan, with a large radius, and stepped upstream and vertical downstream faces. The type of bank is not important because of the monolithic nature of the structure. The dam is built using reinforced concrete or iron girders arranged parallel and perpendicular to the channel axis and embedded in masonry or concrete supports to form cells. These supports have a stepped upstream profile, the girders being fixed on top of the steps. The cells are then filled in with gravel or stone.

A certain amount of care is needed to prevent the erosion of the structure internally or at the downstream toe through siphoning. Damage can be prevented by using cutoffs and aprons of the kind referred to earlier. To ensure stability, the structure needs to be well keyed in to the banks and the remainder covered over with impervious material.

Design

Thickness at base. This is usually expressed as a function of dam height H (m). If b (m) is the thickness at the base:

Gravel and mortar	$b = 0.67\ H$
Dry stone	$b = 0.80\ H$
Wood and stone	$b = H$

where $b = 0.8\ H$ is the value normally used to prevent siphoning and to exploit the characteristics of cellular construction to the full.

Notch thickness. In small dams this can be as little as 1.05 m, corresponding to the thickness of half a cell. However, for dams more than 3 m high, the notch is usually 2 m thick, especially if there is a likelihood of floodflows or strong dynamic flow pressures. In the latter case, it may be safer to cover the upstream face with riprapping, either triangular in section or trapezoidal if the dam is a high one.

Stepping of upstream face. Figure 33 illustrates the design of the structure. Above 3 m, the initial thickness is reduced by 2 m and ribbing inserted at intervals of no more than 3 m.

- The notch can be either trapezoidal or rectangular; the same criteria apply as those laid down in this chapter on overflows.
- In small torrents with low discharges, notch revetment is unnecessary. Braces are used to secure the girders at the upstream notch face to those at the downstream face.
- For large flows carrying coarse sediment, the notch should be covered with mortar or concrete. Special attention must be paid to the construction of the downstream outside edge of the notch, facing it with stonework if necessary.

Stability checks

The characteristics of cellular construction, with its typically horizontal stratification, act to prevent sliding.

With regard to overturning, the following factors come into consideration:

Specific gravity of the cellular structure	1 800 kg/m^3
Specific gravity of water	1 100 kg/m^3
Specific gravity of sediment acting on dam	1 800 kg/m^3

The hydrostatic pressure of water must also be taken into account (with riprapping, it will normally be exerted on a 1/1 slope so that $\cos\varphi = \sin\varphi = 0.71$).

The dimensioning of dams 3 m, 5 m and 7 m high, the calculation of the coefficient of safety against overturning, the point of application and eccentricity of the resultant, as well as the maximum and minimum forces transmitted to the foundation plane, are shown schematically in Figure 34. In practice, modifications will be needed to take account of actual load conditions and the channel slope (here assumed to be horizontal).

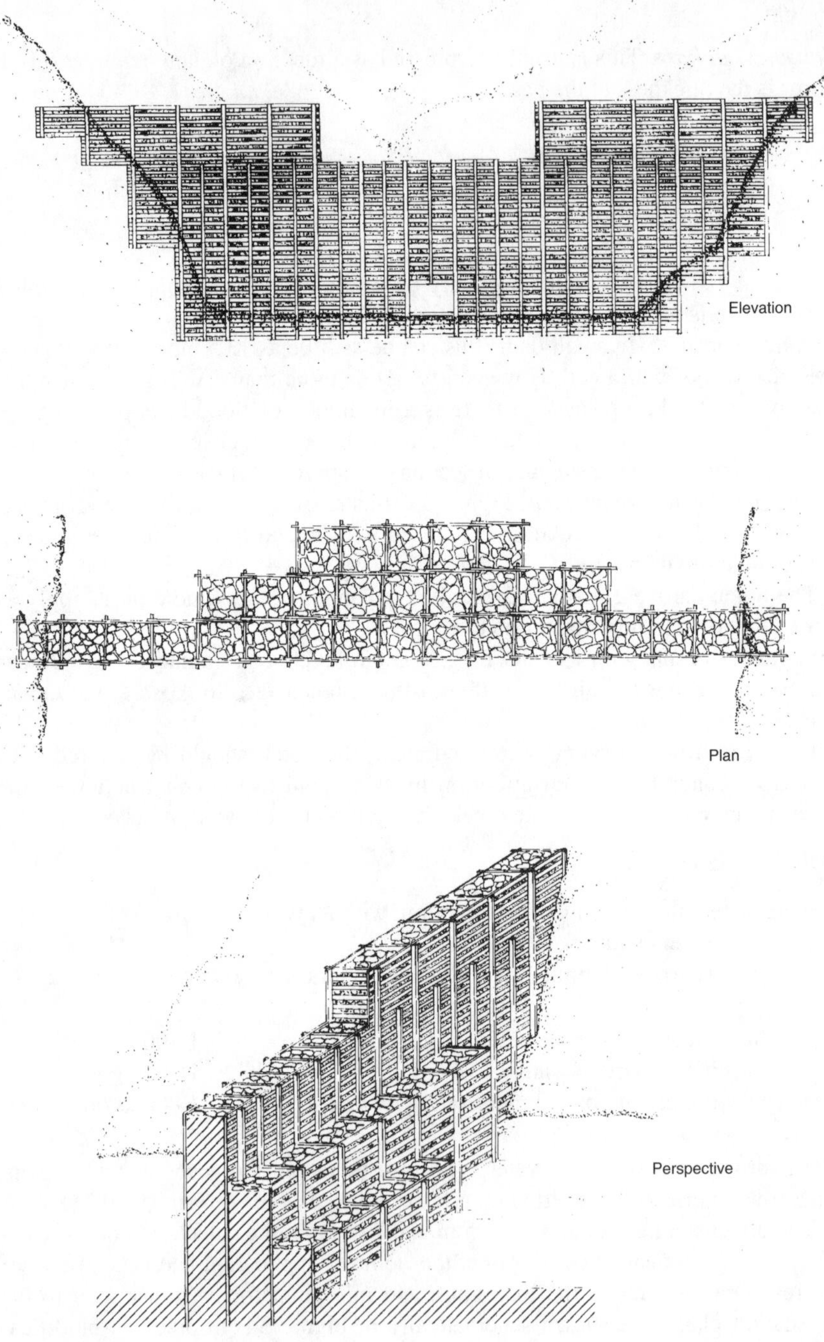

Figure 33. Dam of cellular construction with interlinked girders

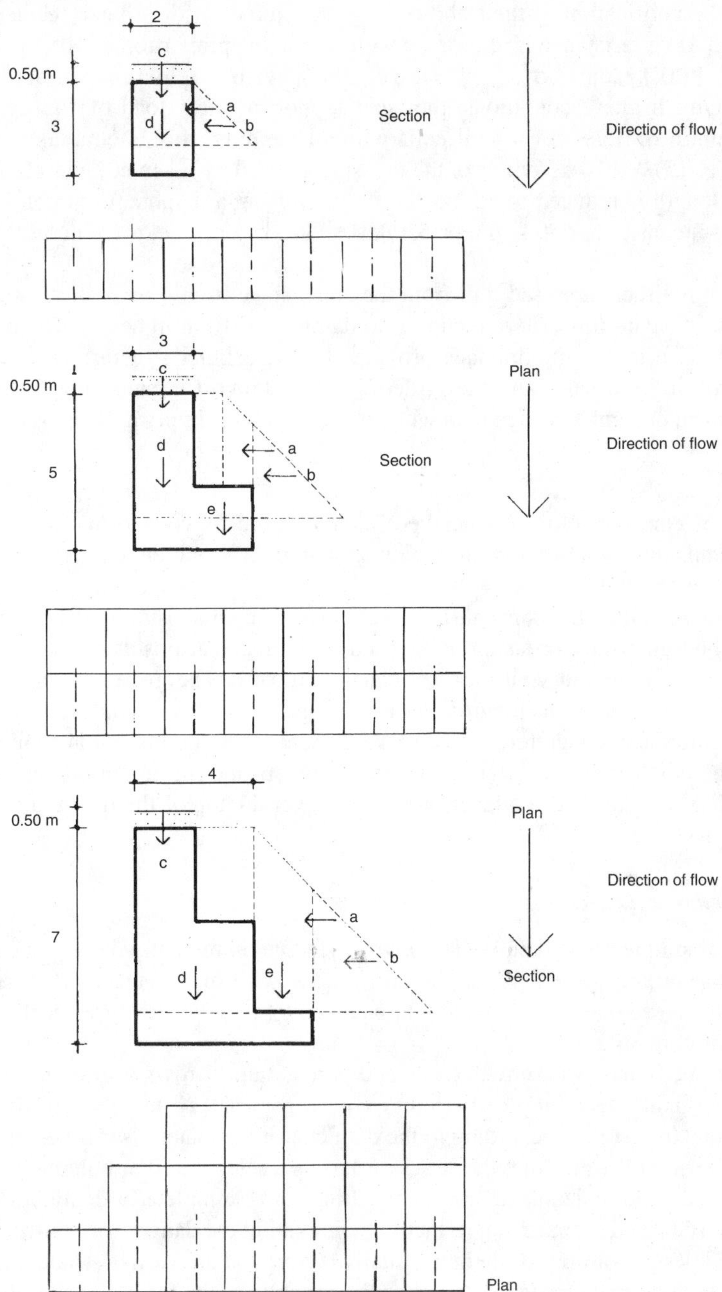

Figure 34. Stability calculation for a dam of cellular construction with interlinked girders

As for the verification of the stability of girders joined with ordinary cement, they have 500 kg resistance if reinforced with iron in the proportion of 105 kg/m^3 (σ_{iron} = 1 800 kg/cm^2, $\sigma_{concrete}$ = 60 kg/m^2), with a resistance moment M = 55 kg/m. In these conditions, they can support a safety load of 145 kg/m along a length of 1.79 m (normal cell) without bending; this is equivalent to 1.45/(100 × 15) = 0.10 kg/cm^2, i.e. the pressure exerted by a l-m column of water. If the length is reduced to 85 cm (half a cell) using a diaphragm girder, the safety load increases to 650 kg/m, or 650/l50 = 0.43 kg/cm^2, i.e. a 4.3-m head of water.

Diaphragm girders are used 3 m from the crest, since from 4 m earth pressure is virtually constant; this criterion applies to dams up to 10 m in height. The reasoning behind it is that the drainage provided by the cellular structure helps reduce hydrostatic pressure, and the girders have to support greater stress when they are keyed or semi-keyed in than when they are acting simply as supports.

Application

This type of dam is useful in watersheds characterized by clay formations and frequent landslides, with bottom and thalweg materials strong enough to be employed in fills (Figure 35).

In these conditions, the dam must be accompanied by a subsidiary dam, wing walls and bottom grilles, or an apron between the dam and a subsidiary dam. The dam, subsidiary dam and wings are cellular in structure. The grilles and aprons are built on a grid pattern using girders; each gap is at least 0.3 m^3 and filled with stones and mortar or concrete-covered rocks. A revetment of cut stone is applied, if not to the whole overflow section, at least to its outside rim in both dams. As for the rest of the dam crest, a layer of concrete over the top of the fill should be sufficient.

Precast concrete filter dam

This type of simple rustic dam is particularly effective in reducing the volume of bedload discharge. Since it is employed in areas with highly unstable slopes composed of loose materials, care should be taken to give the structure sufficient elasticity (Figure 36).

The dam body has two vertical faces and is made up of rows of precast concrete blocks, laid one on top of the other with a gap of 0.20 m between them. This gap may in fact vary according to the diameter of the materials it is designed to retain. During its useful life, the structure acts as a selective filter holding back sediment of a certain size upstream; once silting up is complete, it continues to drain off surface and seepage water, thereby eliminating the dangers of uplift.

The modules are of uniform height (usually 0.5 m) and are vertically and horizontally linked by metal rods inserted into the concrete in the form of a star, thus giving a degree of flexibility. The lower foundation blocks are longer, so that the number of gaps is reduced. A continuous coating of concrete is applied to both the overflow and the crest.

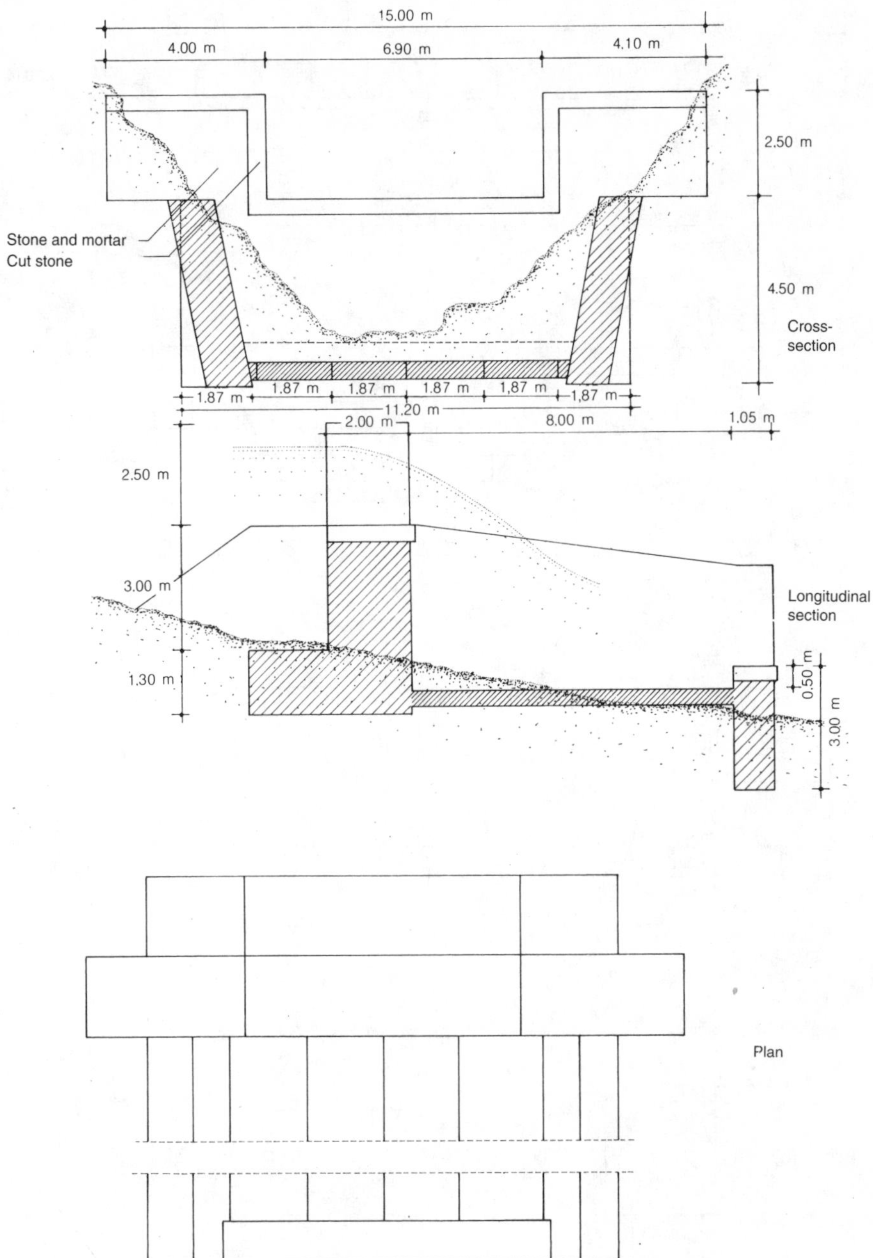

Figure 35. Practical application of a dam of cellular construction with interlinked girders

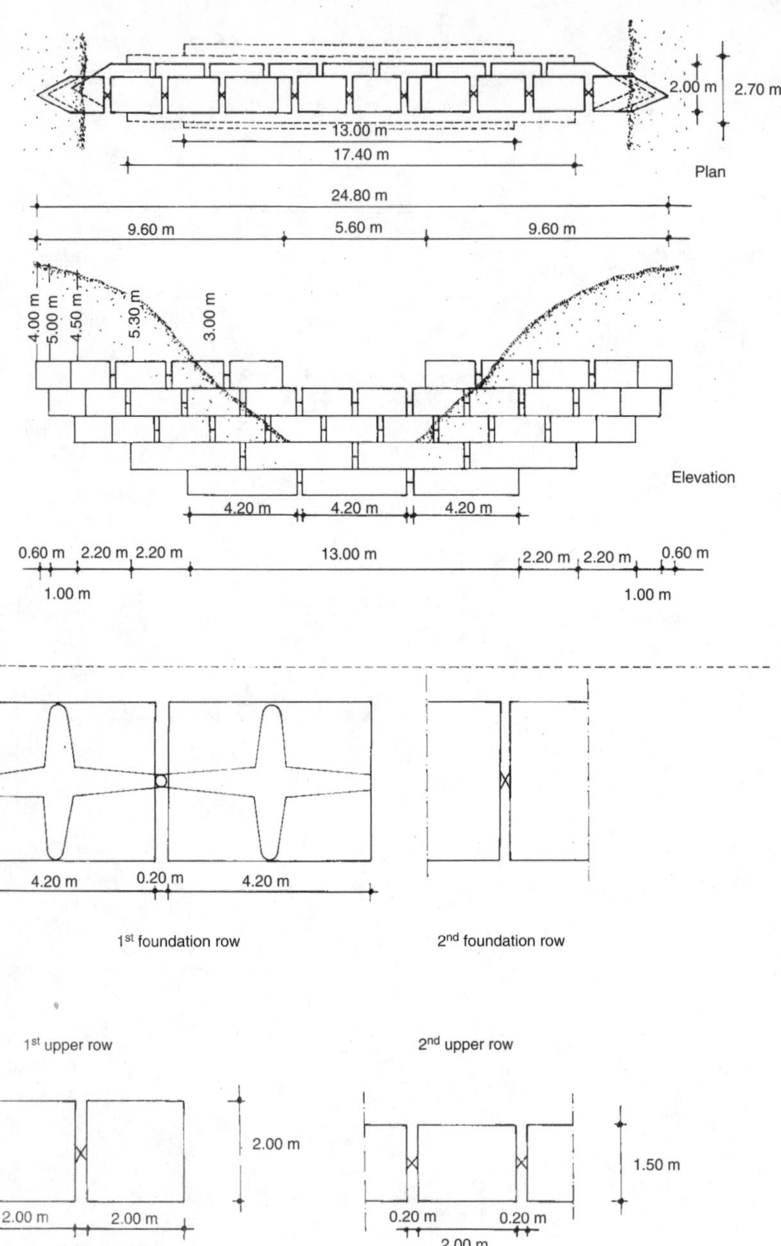

Figure 36. Precast concrete filter dam

The end blocks of the rows keyed into the banks are wedge-shaped to improve the structure's resistance to the lateral pressure exerted by bank slopes; by cutting into the active mass, the wedges reduce the forces borne by the structure as a whole.

Dams built of prefabricated metal components

Prefabrication is certainly cost-effective if carried out on an industrial scale with standardized components and modular design for structures that facilitate mass production. Given the characteristics of control structures, the easiest thing to do is to look at the various prefabricated materials on the market that are designed for other uses and see how they might be employed in dam construction (after modification, if necessary); for example, there are commercially available metal components for building bin walls used in earth retention.

Description

The metal components are put in place and bolted together to form bins or cells, which are then filled with loose materials. The result is a structure consisting of bins approximately 3 m long (the same as the front and back ledgers) and varying depth according to the height of the structure and the load to which it is subjected.

The use of diaphragms of variable length and thickness allows compartments of different depths to be obtained. The bigger the structure, the thicker the ledger. All the components are of corrugated iron, making them light, easy to handle and, since they take up very little space, easy to transport and store as well. This aspect is a big advantage in torrent control works, which are often located in rugged, out-of-the-way areas. Moreover, assembly is quick and does not call for skilled labour.

The bins or cells making up the dam are positioned directly on top of the previously levelled and compacted soil. Material that has been removed can be used to fill the bins. In some cases, a 40-cm bed of aggregate may be laid first.

Once this operation is completed, a row of 7-mm thick bedplates (599 × 406 mm) is placed at the upstream face of the dam and another at the downstream face. A U-shaped pillar is then bolted to each plate; the ledgers and diaphragms are then fastened to it.

The ledgers are reinforced with struts and an *ad hoc* plate placed at the end of each column. The side walls of each compartment are formed of the superposed diaphragms, which are the structural elements connecting the two dam faces. For static reasons, these transverse walls are full. The upstream face, on the other hand, forms a kind of lattice with spaces between the ledgers.

One example of a dam prototype made of prefabricated metal components consists of open steel Itacor 1 bins, each one measuring 1.5 × 1.0 m, joined by HR bolts and with a rectangular notch and a silt ejector at the bottom. The standard diaphragm is embedded in the wing walls and the concrete floor. It is 10.5 m long and 2.5 m high from the notch to the surface. The notch is 1 m high with an area of 4.5 m^2; the silt ejector is 0.5 m high and 1.5 m^2 in area.

Calculation of coefficient of safety from overturning, depending on dam height

H(m)	Forces		Leverage		Moments +	Moments −	Calculation
3	*a)* $0.5 \cdot 2 \cdot 1\,100 \cdot 0.71$	780	–	2	–	1 560	$c = \frac{11\,900}{4\,160} = 2.85$
	b) $2 \cdot \frac{2}{2} \cdot 1\,100 \cdot 0.71$	1 560	$1 + \frac{1}{3} \cdot 2$	1.66	–	2 600	$x = \frac{7\,740}{11\,900} = 0.65$
	c) $0.5 \cdot 2 \cdot 1\,100$	1 100	–	1	1 100	–	$u = \frac{1 \cdot 2}{2} = 0.65$
	d) $2 \cdot 3 \cdot 1\,800$	10 800	–	1	10 800	–	$\upsilon = 0.35$
	Σv	11 900			11 900 − 4 160	4 160	$\delta = \frac{11\,900}{2} 1 \pm$
							$\pm \left(\frac{6 \cdot 0.35}{2}\right) =$
				$\Sigma M =$	7 740		$= \begin{cases} 1.2\ \text{kg/cm}^2 \\ 0.03\ \text{kg/cm}^2 \end{cases}$
5	*a)* $0.5 \cdot 4 \cdot 1\,100 \cdot 0.71$	1 560	–	3	–	4 680	$c = \frac{72\,430}{18\,880} = 3.85$
	b) $4 \cdot \frac{4}{2} \cdot 1\,100 \cdot 0.71$	6 200	$1 + \frac{1}{3} \cdot 4$	2.33	–	14 200	$x = \frac{53\,550}{37\,420} = 1.43$
	c) $0.5 \cdot 3 \cdot 1\,100$	1 640	–	1.50	1 640	–	$u = 2 - 1.43 = 0.57$
	d) $2 \cdot 5 \cdot 1\,800$	18 000	–	1	18 000	–	$\delta = \frac{3\,742}{4} 1 \pm$
	e) $2 \cdot 4.75 \cdot 1\,800$	17 000	–	2.95	50 000	–	$\pm \left(\frac{6 \cdot 0.57}{4}\right) =$
	a) $0.5 \cdot 1 \cdot 1\,100 \cdot 0.71$	390	$3 + 0.50$	3.50	1 360	–	$= \begin{cases} 1.7\ \text{kg/cm}^2 \\ 0.14\ \text{kg/cm}^2 \end{cases}$
	b) $1 \cdot \frac{1}{2} \cdot 110 \cdot 0.71$	390	$3 + \frac{2}{3} \cdot 1$	3.66	1 430	–	
	Σv	37 420			72 430 − 18 880	18 880	
				$\Sigma M =$	53 550		
7	*a)* $0.5 \cdot 6 \cdot 1\,100 \cdot 0.71$	2 350	$1 + \frac{6}{2}$	4	–	9 400	$c = \frac{223\,400}{51\,700} = 4.30$
	b) $6 \cdot \frac{6}{2} \cdot 1\,100 \cdot 0.71$	14 100	$1 + \frac{1}{3} \cdot 6$	3	–	42 300	$x = \frac{171\,700}{76\,440} = 2.23$
	c) $0.5 \cdot 4 \cdot 1\,100$	2 200	–	2	4 400	–	$u = 3 - 2.23 = 0.77$
	d) $4 \cdot 7 \cdot 1\,800$	50 400	–	2	100 800	–	$\delta = \frac{76\,440}{6} 1 \pm$
	e) $2 \cdot \frac{7 + 5}{2} \cdot 1\,800$	21 500	$4 + 0.95$	4.95	106 000	–	$\pm \left(\frac{6 \cdot 0.77}{6}\right) =$
	a) $0.5 \cdot 2 \cdot 1\,100 \cdot 0.71$	780	$4 + \frac{2}{2}$	5	3 900	–	$= \begin{cases} 2.25\ \text{kg/cm}^2 \\ 0.29\ \text{kg/cm}^2 \end{cases}$
	b) $2 \cdot \frac{2}{2} \cdot 1\,100 \cdot 0.71$	1 560	$4 + \frac{2}{3} \cdot 2$	5.33	8 300	–	
		76 400			223 400 − 51 700	51 700	
				$\Sigma M =$	171 700		

In addition to consolidating the torrent bed, the dam should also help reduce floodflows. Under reduced flow conditions, the silt ejector has no limiting effects and stops the dam from silting up; at higher flows, it acts as an escape and provides temporary storage. A series of dams can be used to create a flood wave difference, thus expanding over time the watershed's storage capacity. The modular components are obtained from 5-mm thick sheets, which are cold-corrugated and prepared in series. Prior to use they are bolted together with high-resistance 10 K screws (UNI standard 3740-65). The advantages are that modular components are very light (about 120 kg each); they are quick to assemble because of their interchangeability and because of the use of friction joints; furthermore, the compnonents can be used to build dams that can be adapted to environmental conditions by altering the dimensions of the silt ejector and the notch according to flow conditions.

Grille, comb and lattice dams

In some types of control work, grille dams (Figure 37) are often used. The central part consists of a wide-meshed grid of iron profiles anchored to a firm floor and masonry wings. Simplified versions exist using only horizontal or vertical bars made of steel or reinforced concrete. Alternatively, a comb structure, composed exclusively of vertical members with their base embedded in concrete (Figure 38), may be employed. Another possibility is a lattice framework of modular elements — usually steel, but sometimes reinforced concrete — supported directly by the torrent bed and slopes (Figure 39). Mesh dams, consisting only of steel netting anchored to the banks, fall into the same category.

Despite their similarities, these structures all have distinct functions. Grille and comb dams, for instance, act as check dams; the base helps fix the bed, while the grille or comb retains the coarse sediment and any floating material (logs, branches, roots, etc.). Lattice dams, on the other hand, have no other purpose than to keep back floating material.

Grille and comb dams generally function as gravity dams. In the hypothetical event of sediment filling the dam up to the overflow sill, the overturning moment is produced by hydrostatic pressure and the stabilizing moments by the respective weights of the foundation floor and the water above the sill.

Calculating the reticular structure of lattice dams is fairly simple as each element in the mesh behaves like a beam embedded in the subfoundation and is subject to hydrostatic pressure (which is exerted along a line equal in length to the distance separating the midpoints of adjoining spaces). However, detailed analysis of all the elements in the lattice is much more complicated if the structure is treated as hyperstatic. In practice, the main elements which behave isostatically are identified, and the hydrostatic pressure spread between them. The remaining elements are no more than links, although they do take some of the pressure off the main elements. The connecting parts are just there as support (embedded or semi-embedded).

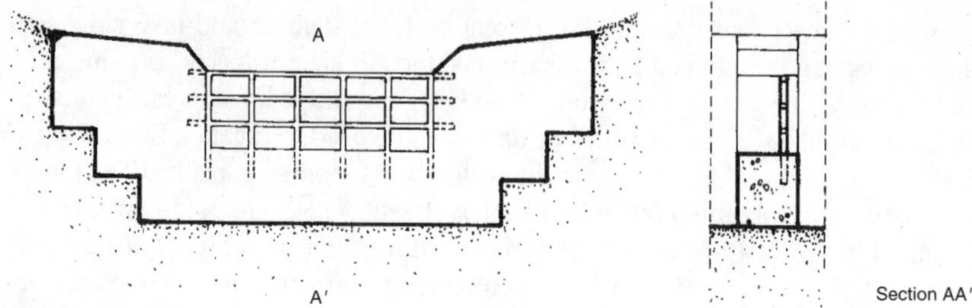

Figure 37. Grille dam

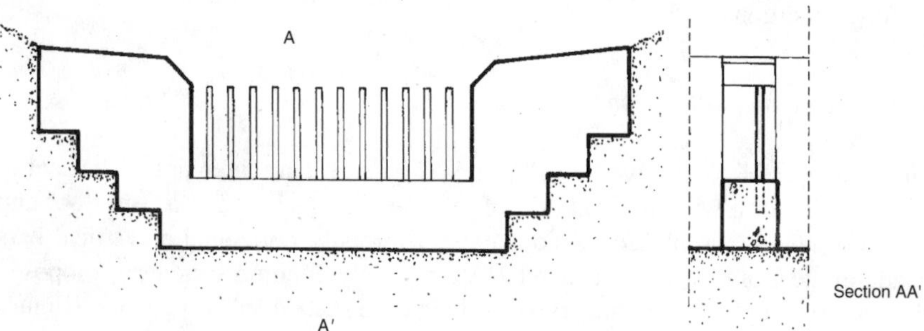

Figure 38. Comb or vertical grille dam

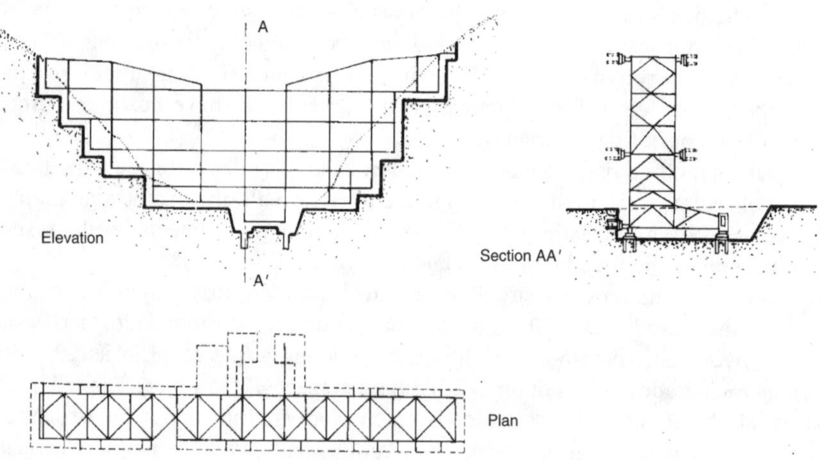

Figure 39. Lattice dam

2.3 Foundations, building materials and methods

Foundations

This aspect should be studied closely to ensure it is safe to build a structure at a particular site. Sometimes, simple inspection of the site may be enough to determine what type of structure is most appropriate.

Rock foundations. Because of its load-bearing capacity and resistance to erosion and seepage, rock poses very few constraints on the type of dam (gravity, earthfill, etc.) that can be built on it.

Gravel foundations. Well-compacted gravel is a suitable foundation for earthfill, rockfill and gravity dams. However, adequate control measures are needed against seepage.

Sand and silt foundations. These are suitable for gravity and earthfill dams, but not for rockfill dams. Possible problems include subsidence, heavy seepage losses and toe erosion.

Clay foundations. These can support earthfill dams, providing they are properly consolidated and do not have too high a moisture content. They are unsuited to rockfill or gravity dams unless special care is taken in their design. Tests should always be carried out on their consolidation characteristics and load-bearing capacity.

Non-uniform foundations. With this type of foundation (e.g. rock and earth), each case has to be looked at separately. Masonry dams, which are at most risk from break-up caused by differential settlement of the foundation, can be divided up into separate blocks linked by plane joints to allow independent settlement.

In short, all the characteristics of the site and its materials have to be considered. If necessary, soundings and inspection samples should be taken as well.

The design parameters for dams with earth foundations can be derived from the Unified Soil Classification System. The system distinguishes between coarse and fine particles, those with a diameter exceeding 7.62 cm being excluded altogether. Coarse grains have a diameter larger than 0.074 mm (200 sieve) and are subdivided as follows:

Gravel: particles retained by a No. 4 sieve (4.75 mm)
- coarse gravel: between 1.90 cm and 7.62 cm;
- fine gravel: < 1.90 cm.

Sand: particles passing through a No. 4 sieve (4.75 mm)
- coarse sand: passing through a No. 4, but not a No. 10 sieve;
- medium sand: passing through a No. 10, but not a No. 40 sieve;
- fine sand: passing through a No. 40, but not a No. 200 sieve.

Fine grains passing through a No. 200 sieve are of two types — silt and clay — and are less than 0.002 mm in diameter.

It would be wrong, however, to suppose that particle size is the only relevant factor in determining the technical characteristics of these materials. The table on page 91 assigns values to the parameters defining USCS soil types.

Materials

Building materials available at or near the dam site are: (a) rock for riprapping, revetment and masonry; (b) aggregate for concrete (sand, gravel and crushed stone); (c) earth for embankments.

(a) Riprapping consists of rock fragments and forms part of earth and rockfill dam structures. Revetments are made of large, non-erodible blocks of stone to hold slopes or infrastructure in place and prevent scouring.

The search for a suitable quarry extends radially outwards from the dam site until a rock deposit whose quality and volume are sufficient to meet requirements is located. Full use should be made of any available data such as geological and topographical maps, aerial photographs and so on. Local people are a useful source of information too. The most obvious place to begin exploration of the rock source is where durable rock crops out. Vertical faces cut back to unweathered material should be thoroughly examined for fracture patterns, bedding and cleavage planes and zones of unsuitable material. The joints and the cleavage and bedding plane systems are especially important as they indicate the sizes likely to be produced.

The suitability and quality of a rock is assessed on the basis of physical tests, petrographic analysis and previous experience of its use. Since the rock has to produce fragments of the right size, qualitative trials should be complemented by data derived from direct examination and by the results of borings carried out in the quarry itself. One may come across piedmonts containing undisintegrated rocks of sufficient size and quantity for quarrying to be unnecessary.

The most important rock properties from an engineering standpoint are:

Type of rock	Specific gravity (t/m^3)	Porosity (% space)	Compressive strength (kg/cm^2)	Hardness[1] (Sievers penetration value)	Durability[2] (Sievers abrasion coefficient)
Basalt and igneous	>2.9	0.02-1	1 800-2 600	8.5	8
Granite	2.6-2.8	0.05-2.8	750-2 500	3.5	8
Quartzite	2.6-2.8	0-8	1 000-3 600	–	–
Schist	2.0-2.6	0.4-20	200-1 200	180-250	50
Limestone	2.2-2.7	0.8-25	170-1 600	35-125	25
Sandstone	2.2-2.7	2.2-35	500-1 800	6-440	12
Marl	2.3	16-52	35-180	–	–

Source: J. Talobre, *La mecanica de las rocas.*
[1] Value declines with increasing hardness.
[2] Value declines with increasing abrasive strength.

Mechanical properties of soils[1]

Group	Geotechnical description	Average particle size				Plastic properties			Standard properties			Compaction (Proctor)		Permeability 10^{-6}/cm^{2}*	Compressibility		Resistance to 2% constant stress		
		Clay %	Silt %	Sand %	Gravel %	W_L %	W_p %	I_p %	γ t/m^3	W %	n %	γ_d t/m^3	W_{opt} %		Load 1.4 kg/cm^2 %	Load 3.5 kg/cm^2 %	C_o kg/cm^2	C_{sat} kg/cm^2	tg Ø
GW	Well-graded gravels	0	2	26	72	*	*	*	2.00 ± 0.25	5 ± 3	30 ± 6	1.91	13.3	27 000 ± 13 000	< 1.4	*	*	*	0.84 ±0.05
GP	Poorly graded gravels	0	2	26	72	*	*	*	1.90 ± 0.30	3 ± 2	32 ± 8	1.76	12.4	64 000 ± 34 000	< 0.8	*	*	*	0.78 ± 0.05
GM	Silty gravels	2	8	30	60	17	13	4	2.10 ± 0.25	8 ± 5	28 ± 8	1.83	14.5	> 0.3	< 1.2	< 3.0	*	*	0.78 ± 0.04
GC	Clayey gravels	3	9	23	65	25	15	10	2.05 ± 0.20	11 ± 6	32 ± 8	1.84	14.7	> 0.3	< 1.2	< 2.4	*	*	0.73 ± 0.06
SW	Well-graded sands	0	2	76	22	*	*	*	1.95 ± 0.20	13 ± 10	36 ± 10	1.91 ± 0.08	13.3 ± 2.5	> 15.0	1.4 ± x	*	0.40 ± 0.04	*	0.79 ± 0.02
SP	Poorly graded sands	0	2	76	22	*	*	*	1.85 ± 0.25	11 ± 9	38 ± 10	1.76 ± 0.08	12.4 ± 1.0	> 15.0	0.8 ± 0.3	*	0.23 ± 0.06	*	0.74 ± 0.02
SM	Silty sands	2	9	75	14	26	22	4	2.00 ± 0.25	17 ± 7	37 ± 10	1.83 ± 0.02	14.5 ± 0.4	7.5 ± 4.8	1.2 ± 0.1	3.0 ± 0.4	0.52 ± 0.06	0.20 ± 0.07	0.67 ± 0.02
SM SC	Silty clayey sands	9	32	45	14	19	13	6	2.10 ± 0.20	15 ± 8	32 ± 10	1.91 ± 0.02	12.8 ± 0.5	0.8 ± 0.6	1.4 ± 0.3	2.9 ± 1.0	0.51 ± 0.22	0.15 ± 0.06	0.66 ± 0.07
SC	Clayey sands	5	7	76	12	25	15	10	1.95 ± 0.20	20 ± 10	40 ± 10	1.84 ± 0.02	14.7 ± 0.4	0.3 ± 0.2	1.2 ± 0.2	2.4 ± 0.5	0.77 ± 0.15	0.11 ± 0.06	0.60 ± 0.07
ML	Inorganic silts	6	64	29	1	30	26	4	1.90 ± 0.25	32 ± 21	47 ± 15	1.65 ± 0.02	19.2 ± 0.7	0.13 ± 0.07	1.5 ± 0.2	2.6 ± 0.3	0.68 ± 0.11	0.09 ± x	0.62 ± 0.06
ML CL	Silts and clayey silts	12	58	26	4	20	14	6	2.10 ± 0.15	19 ± 7	35 ± 8	1.75 ± 0.03	16.8 ± 0.7	0.59 ± 0.23	1.0 ± 0.2	2.2 ± 0.0	0.65 ± 0.17	0.22 ± x	0.62 ± 0.06
CL	Inorganic clays (average plasticity)	20	61	16	3	33	17	16	2.00 ± 0.15	25 ± 10	41 ± 8	1.73 ± 0.02	17.3 ± 0.3	0.08 ± 0.03	1.4 ± 0.2	2.6 ± 0.4	0.89 ± 0.11	0.13 ± 0.02	0.54 ± 0.04
OL	Organic silts	8	70	21	1	42	29	13	1.70 ± 0.15	48 ± 13	57 ± 8	**	**	0.16 ± 0.10	**	**	**	**	0.44 ± 0.10
MH	Special inorganic silts	10	65	25	0	68	38	30	1.55 ± 0.15	73 ± 20	67 ± 7	1.31 ± 0.06	36.3 ± 3.2	0.16 ± 0.10	2.0 ± 1.2	3.8 ± 0.8	0.74 ± 0.30	0.20 ± 0.09	0.47 ± 0.05
CH	Inorganic clays (high plasticity)	22	59	18	1	64	25	39	1.75 ± 0.15	47 ± 24	56 ± 9	1.51 ± 0.03	25.5 ± 1.2	0.05 ± 0.05	2.6 ± 1.3	3.9 ± 1.5	1.05 ± 0.34	0.11 ± 0.06	0.35 ± 0.09
OH	Organic clays	12	70	17	1	71	40	31	1.55 ± 0.15	68 ±22	56 ± 8	**	**	0.05 ± 0.05	**	**	**	**	0.40 ± 0.08

[1] According to Unified Soil Classification System.
(*) Permeable soils unsuited to dams.
(**) Soils unsuited for use in dams because of their high organic matter content.

(b) Aggregate should be of the right quality to produce strong and durable cement. Sand and gravel from natural deposits or crushed rocks may be used. For classification purposes, particles that pass through a 5-mm sieve are called sands, and those retained by it are called gravel. The proportion of fine materials by weight should not exceed the following levels:

	Sand	*Gravel*
Lumps of clay	1.00	0.25
Fine materials that pass through a 0.08–mm sieve	5.00	5.00

Maximum gravel size is 8–mm.

Good aggregate is strong and capable of withstanding the elements without disintegrating. Soft or highly porous rocks are not suitable (e.g. clay schists, crumbly sandstones, some micaceous rocks, clays and very coarse crystals). The rock's specific weight is a quick and effective indication of the aggregate's quality: a low figure implies a soft and porous material.

The gravel/sand ratio for concrete is 2. The amount needed to obtain 1 m^3 of concrete varies according to the characteristic strength of the structure, the type of aggregate (rounded or crushed) and its maximum size. The values in the table below are for the types of concrete normally employed in torrent control works. The table also gives the quantities of water and cement to use in the mixture.

Specifications of concretes using rounded aggregate

Characteristic strength (kg/cm^2)	Maximum size of 40-mm aggregate				Maximum size of 20-mm aggregate			
	Cement	Water	Sand	Gravel	Cement	Water	Sand	Gravel
	................................(kg)................................							
60	175	160	715	1 430	200	180	690	1 380
90	220	160	700	1 400	240	180	680	1 360
120	250	160	690	1 380	290	180	670	1 340
150	290	160	680	1 360	330	180	655	1 310

Specifications of concretes using crushed aggregate

Charac-teristic strength (kg/cm²)	Maximum size of 40-mm aggregate				Maximum size of 20-mm aggregate			
	Cement	Water	Sand	Gravel	Cement	Water	Sand	Gravel
	............................(kg)............................							
60	160	180	700	1 400	175	200	680	1 360
90	190	180	695	1 390	210	200	670	1 340
120	220	180	685	1 370	240	200	660	1 320
150	245	180	675	1 350	270	200	650	1 300

(c) Soil for embankments, as for earth dams, is always taken from borrow pits, although soil excavated from the foundations can also be used. To allow for possible design changes, calculation errors and the like, large safety coefficients should be built into estimates of the volumes available in borrow areas. If these areas are well known, the specifications usually only insist on one-and-a-half times the necessary quantity; larger coefficients are employed when the available information suggests that deposits are not uniform; if less than 10 000 m^3 of a material are required, coefficients as high as 10 may be applied.

Building methods. Design calculations are based on a series of hypotheses as to the quality that will be achieved during construction. Although the requirements for the various sections and structural components have been covered earlier, they are listed schematically on page 94.

2.4 Weirs

A weir is a structure built across the streambed to check the water and raise its level for diversion purposes; it is designed to allow overtopping. The main aim is to raise the water-level, but it can also play a storage role.

Weirs may be straight, curved or broken in plan. The alignment of straight weirs may be normal or oblique to the flow. The former is the norm providing the overflow is sufficiently long to discharge floodwaters (without unduly raising the backwater level), and streambed sediment deposition is not so heavy that siltation prevents water from entering the lateral inlet.

The problem can be avoided by designing a weir oblique to the flow, thus facilitating water entry into the inlet channel. The disadvantage of this placement is that the overflow nappe is normal to the axis of the weir but oblique to the channel axis, necessitating bank protection measures. Curved weirs are larger structures, but they channel flow towards the inlet without directing overflow waters

General characteristics of operations used to construct different types of torrent control structures

Land preparation	Excavation		Foundations		Visible structure			Other operations
	Rock	Other materials	Rock	Other materials	Earthfill dams, embankments	Other types of dam		
						Materials	Concrete	
Channels with temporary flows (streams): summertime operations, land clearance and brush removal Channels with permanent flows (torrents and rivers): River diversion Following may be used: ● Wood piling: made of 7.5x30 cm planks and 10x10 cm ledgers ● Metal piling ● Concrete piling: minimum thickness 30 cm ● Earth coffer dams	Massive materials (rocks) movable only by blasting, drilling or wedging, all rock fragments > 0.75 m^3	All materials not defined as rock: earth, gravel, cemented gravel, and soft or disintegrated rocks that can be extracted without explosives, and rock fragments < 0.75 m^3	Igneous rocks (granite, gneiss), well-cemented limestone, compacted silicas Cribbing Caissons: protection of completed excavation Final preparation of foundations (depending on type of dam), including concreting, if appropriate	Earth, decomposed rock, heavily weathered rock, (transit earth)	Selection of materials Moisture content (Proctor test) Shaping Compaction equipment: ● Sheep's-foot roller; minimum weight fully loaded: 6 000 kg/ linear m ● Compaction: at least 12 passes of the roller; compaction tests ● Filters, selection and proportioning of materials	Cement, water, aggregate (sand, gravel), stones, gabions	Composition: Concrete should not contain less than 160 kg of cement/m^3 if the maximum (crushed) aggregate size is 40 mm and 175-200 kg for rounded aggregate Batching and mixing: The sand and coarse aggregate are weighed in proportions corresponding to a whole number of bags of cement (minimum mixing time: 90 seconds in a concrete mixer) Formwork and priming Compaction, protection and curing with water Placing in foundations Concrete joints: Concrete surfaces that have set and on which fresh concrete is to be placed Wash down with jets of water before coating with new concrete Contraction joints: The concrete of one end is allowed to set before concreting the other end; the first concrete surface is then coated with a sealant before concreting the other face	Weep-holes to reduce uplift effect Drainage in foundations to reduce uplift and avoid siphoning problems

against the banks. In addition, the arch effect helps close any cracks, thus averting leaks. Broken weirs share some of these advantages and can be useful in exploiting the streambed's foundation possibilities to the full — for example, where a bank of rock lying oblique to the channel only outcrops in part of the bed.

Since weirs are low structures normally located in channels in which the flow is strong and steady enough to justify diversion, the ratio between the height of the flow nappe and that of the actual structure is usually a high one. It is therefore better for the dam body section to have a hydrodynamic profile, which holds the overflow against the structure, rather than a trapezoidal or triangular section, which results in a free-falling nappe (inadequate aeration in the lower part of the nappe may destabilize the structure).

With sediment-bearing waters, deposition takes place in the manner already described, and the weir functions as a storage dam. If the waters are sediment-free and there is a gentle flow regime, a backwater curve will form upstream; this curve will define the longitudinal profile of the water level until the backwater effect is no longer noticeable. Moreover, in the area affected by the backwater, the relationship between the adjacent land and the water-level will change, because land will be flooded that was not flooded before. A rise in the water table will occur as well.

The height of the weir

The Poire and Funk parabola, $x^2 = 4a/l^2$ (Figure 40), is used to obtain the height H of the weir providing the following parameters are known: the depth, the discharge, the channel slope and the length of the backwater (defined by measuring the distance between the upstream boundary of the concession and the site of the weir).

Calculation of the structure

As far as calculation hypothesis, most economic profile, and calculation schemes are concerned, the technique is the same as that already described for concrete gravity, masonry and gabion dams, the only exceptions being the use of $\gamma = 1$ (t/m^3), the omission of weep-holes and, for the first two dam types, the inclusion of uplift. A practical method of calculation (Figure 41) is to take moments of the stresses P, W and U to obtain

$$b = \frac{H\sqrt{\gamma}}{\sqrt{\gamma_s - \gamma}}$$

Suppose the height of the nappe to be h. Let M be the point at which the vertical face intersects the water surface, and draw a line MK so that $TK = b$. If the weight of MNQ allows it to withstand pressure MNS ($P_1 = 1/2 \cdot \gamma \cdot h^2$), and that of

MTK to withstand pressure *MRT* ($P_2 = 1/2 \cdot \gamma \cdot H^2$), then clearly *NQTK*, the difference between the two, will be able to withstand pressure *SNTR* [$P = \gamma/2\ (H^2 - h^2)$]. Thus the weir's cross-section would be *NQTK*.

Weirs on permeable ground

Because of the role of weirs in water exploitation, controlling seepage beneath those constructed on permeable soil is particularly important. The same precautions should be taken as for dams to prevent seepage velocity through foundation materials from exceeding the scouring velocity of solid soil particles, thereby causing piping. Furthermore, weirs should also be strengthened with piling that extends from the upstream face as far as the end of the apron or stilling basin; this precaution will reduce seepage-induced water losses, which can have a considerable effect on the volume of water diverted, especially at low water.

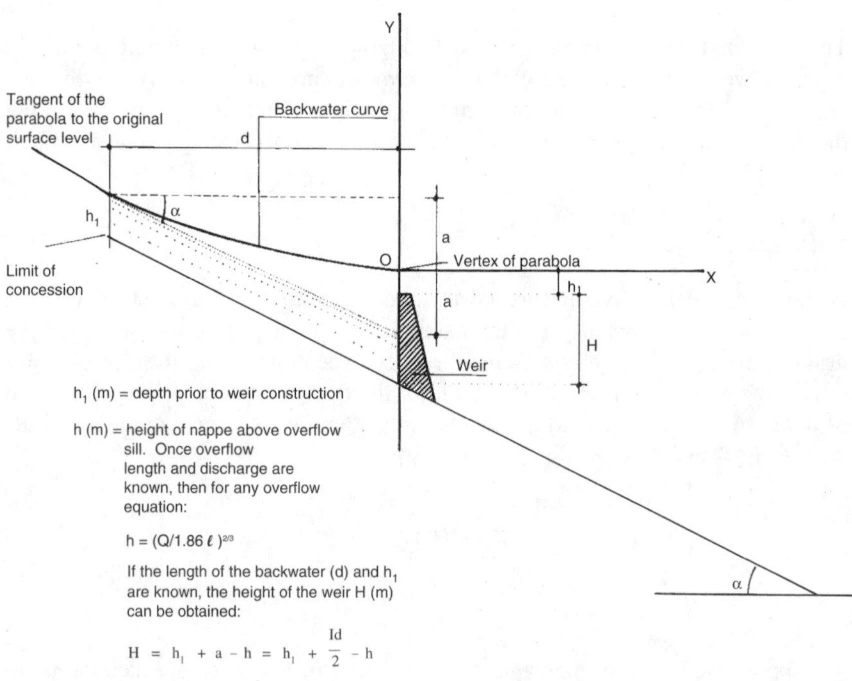

Figure 40. Longitudinal channel profile (Poire and Funk parabola)

2.5 Settling basins

Both biological and stabilization works help control sediment in erosion-prone torrents. In mixed torrents with shell-shaped erosion scarps and in glacial torrents, however, sediment discharge into the main reach continues after the dams have silted up. This discharge may need to be countered by the use of settling basins, constructed in accordance with the area's topography.

Figure 42 gives a schematic representation of a typical settling basin. A masonry-lined channel is built just downstream of a check dam to guide water and sediment to a hexagonal basin with earth or stone boundary walls. As far as possible, the main diagonal of the hexagon should follow the channel axis. About a third of the way along this diagonal a rockfill or masonry revetment dam is constructed perpendicular to the axis to force the water to spread out and discourage fan-shaped sediment deposition; a second, identical structure is built the same distance further along. Both dams should be lower than the boundary walls. Finally, before reaching the masonry-lined outlet channel, the water has to pass through three comb grilles made of strong posts driven into the ground to retain undeposited materials. Once filled, settling basins can be reforested or put to some other use.

It should be remembered that although sediment is never completely absent from glacial torrents or torrents with shell-shaped erosion scarps, it is nevertheless very much reduced; because of the milder bed slope, damage to the bed will be partially or totally averted. Consequently, settling basins are only a solution in specific cases, e.g. when a torrent runs into a waterfall.

2.6 Training walls and lined channels

In the overall context of torrent control, where the aim is to eliminate sediment discharge and its consequences, these structures play a passive, defensive role (for example, by preventing local sediment detachment, reinforcing unstable banks or slope bottoms and centring the flow).

They are usually employed as local solutions to specific problems of torrential origin and are not suitable for use as the main form of control in a torrential channel. As regards their design and functions, they closely resemble the structures used in rivers. Their use in torrential channels does not substantially affect their characteristics, except where flows are particularly strong, downcutting has occurred or there is heavy sediment discharge.

In view of the seriousness of erosion and downcutting, special care needs to be taken in designing these structures and their foundations and in assessing the effectiveness of protective works. Various methods are available:

- Small transverse structures (such as grilled weirs or bottom sills) placed at bed level or slightly above it to stabilize the channel bed in a particular reach.

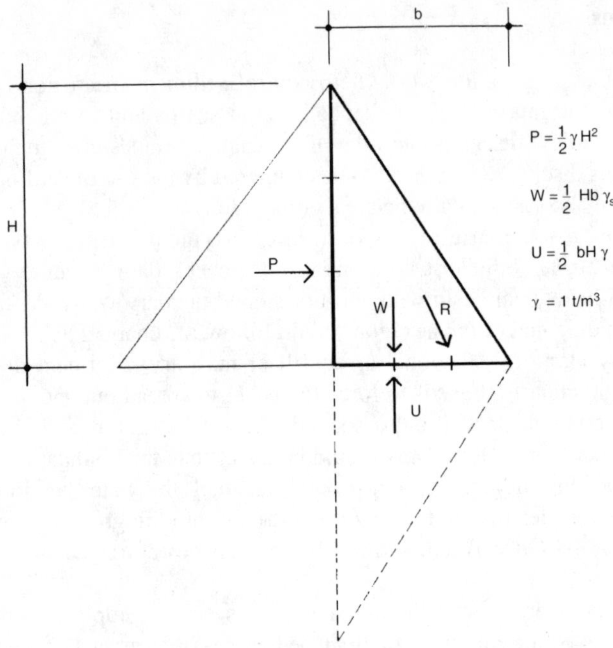

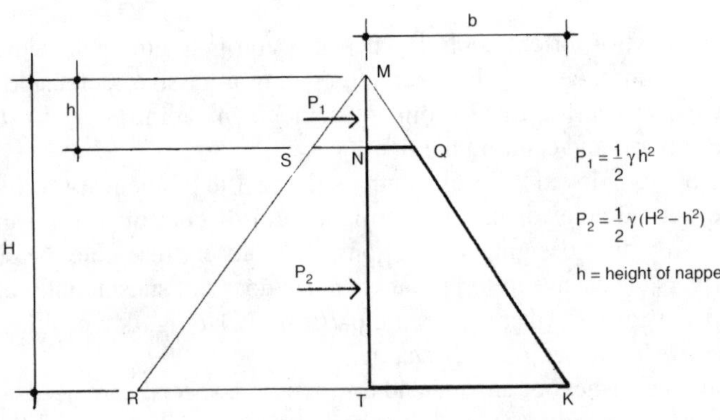

Figure 41. Quick method for calculating weir stability

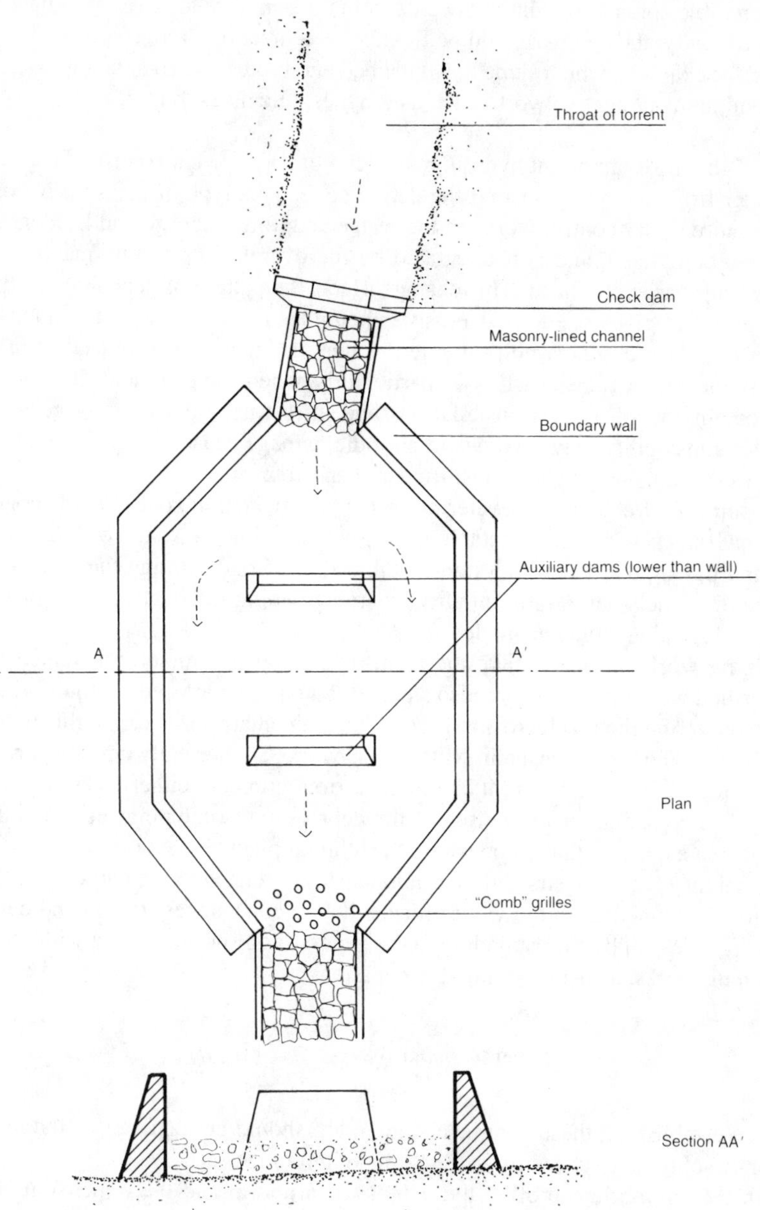

Figure 42. Diagram of a settling basin

- Non-erodible aprons extending outwards from the dam face to cover the adjacent bed area. Ideally, the aprons should be flexible — a layer of large, coarse rocks or gabions, for example, which slope down the bed and protect the foundations.
- Discontinuous protective works such as groynes, pile dikes, piling, etc.

One of the most important hydrological techniques in torrent control is used to stop water from spreading beyond the debris cone. This type of measure is normally required after control works in the watershed, torrent gorge and headwater have been completed, and is necessitated by the overall drop in the quantity of sediment discharge produced. This change affects the pattern of deposition in the torrent area and gives rise to new erosive phenomena in response to the tractive force of the clear, and now non-saturated, waters. In many cases, indeed, it may be advisable to act rather earlier — particularly when the sediment deposition zone contains people, crops, installations and infrastructural works — because the water's instability may give rise to periodic damage caused by sedimentation processes that encourage channel shifting and anastomosis.

The purpose of channelling water in torrent sedimentation zones, debris cones or alluvial fans is to counter unstable flows by restricting the water with training walls and paving the bed with a non-erodible floor. Concentrating the flow also reverses the zone's natural torrentiality by strengthening the tractive force of the waters and keeping them channelled.

Training works normally take the form of a stepped channel punctuated by small grilled weirs; the weirs are also stepped to help give the bed an equilibrium profile, rendering the reach erosion-proof. The main characteristics are illustrated in Figure 43. The type of reach in which these works are normally employed runs from the toe of the dam, where it closes the torrent gorge, to either its confluence with the main channel or to the foot of the debris cone at the point in which the cone ends in a channel that empties into the alluvial plain.

The height H of the weirs and their number N are related to the length L of the reach to be channelled, to the values for the debris cone slopes ($\tan \alpha$) and equilibrium profile ($\tan \beta$) corresponding to the generating flow, and to the width b of the training works, as per the following equations:

$$H = \ell(\tan \alpha - \tan \beta) \qquad \ell = L/N$$

tan

When establishing these parameters, attention should be focussed on the most economic solution — normally in the 1-4 m height range.

Both the equilibrium profile, the depths (of h and z) and the dimensions for obtaining stable grilled weirs are calculated according to the method described earlier for check dams.

The design tested by Lombardi and Marquenet (1950) may be adopted for the apron at the base of the weir. The design involves giving the apron a slight (5-8 percent) counterslope and a length $\ell_1 = 1.521\, z^{4/9}\ H^{1/1.8} + 0.3z$ in which $z = h + V_0^2/2g$, the hydraulic head of the design flow above the overflow.

To calculate the depth h_2 in a grilled reach, any of the equations for uniform flow in open channels may be used; for example, applying the Manning formula in this case gives (assuming a roughness coefficient of $n = 0.04$)

$$Q = 25\, bh_2 \left(\frac{bh_2}{b + 2h_2} \right)^{2/3} (\tan \beta)^{1/2}$$

in which Q (m^3/s) is the maximum volumetric rate of flow computed for the protected channel.

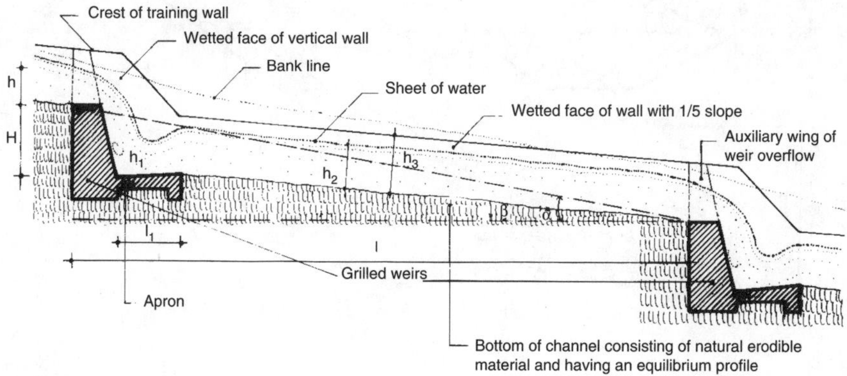

Figure 43. Diagram of a stepped reach in a debris cone

For safety reasons, the height h of the lateral walls should exceed h_2 by at least 0.30 m, depending on the discharge.

The weir profile should be trapezoidal (as in the figure) or hydrodynamic. The latter type is usually employed when the h/H ratio is greater than 0.5, since with trapezoidal profiles there is a risk of inadequate aeration in the lower part of the free-falling nappe. Since the water's mass is relatively large compared to the inertia of the weir, its impact on the face of the structure potentially threatens its stability. Even where the h/H ratio is low and a trapezoidal profile is adopted as the most economic solution, steps should be taken to facilitate aeration of the nappe. The width of the overflow should be slightly narrower than that of the channel, achieved by having two auxiliary wings that extend a minimum of 0.50 m from the lateral walls.

In some torrential debris cone channels where the streams are not big enough or wide enough for channelization, a better alternative may be to have a rapid channel with a continuous non-erodible apron. The lining should consist of crude stone bound together with concrete or cement mortar, the latter being more suitable for hard stone as it has a lower coefficient of abrasion than ordinary concrete (concrete is vulnerable to sediment erosion). In this type of channel, where the discharge regime is usually hypothetical because of the steep slope required, rectangular flow sections are advisable, since sharp bends and abrupt changes in

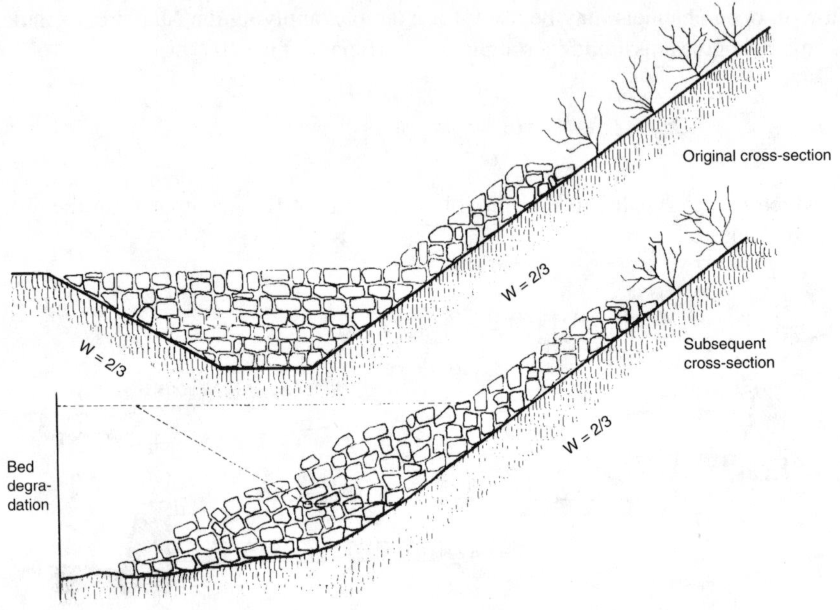

Figure 44. Rock revetment

section and slope in the channelled reach can result in vertical turbulence or sediment deposition that can modify the discharge regime.

Bank revetment is another kind of longitudinal protection work in common use in torrential channels. It is usually employed in areas of high sediment transport and localized lateral erosion. Rigid concrete or masonry structures, similar to those used in rivers, can also be used for torrent control, provided that they are capable of withstanding the severe stresses involved and that measures (such as those referred to above) are taken to protect the foundations from undercutting.

Flexible structures, rock-filled gabions, stone revetments, fascine mattresses, etc., are also suitable, providing the sediment load does not consist of anything larger than gravel. The impact of boulders and large rocks, however, can be so great that a revetment consisting of massive stonework — carefully placed or simply dumped — will be necessary. The type of revetment best suited to preventing downcutting of torrential origin is illustrated in Figure 44.

Another important factor in view of the high tractive force of torrential waters is the determination of the diameter of materials to be used in protective works. It can be calculated on the basis that

$$\tau_L = (\tau_0)^L$$

in which τ_L is the tractive force acting on the banks. This force varies according to the height of the nappe supported, although an approximate estimate may be obtained as follows:

$$\text{for } h \geq \frac{2}{3} H \qquad \tau_L = K_L \, \gamma \, H \, i$$

$$\text{for } h \leq \frac{2}{3} H \qquad \tau_L = \frac{3}{2} K_L \, \gamma \, h \, i$$

where

h (m) = height of water above point where material is placed

H (m) = maximum height of water in the section

γ (t/m^3) = specific gravity of water

i = bed slope

K_L = Lane's distribution coefficient, a function of the shape of the channel and the ratio b/H, where b is the mean width of channel with design discharge (obtain b from the table below)

Type of channel	*b/H*				
	0	1	2	3	4
Rectangular	0.00	0.50	0.70	0.72	0.73
Trapezoidal with 1/1 sides	0.56	0.70	0.73	0.74	0.75
Trapezoidal with 2/1 sides*	0.63	0.73	0.76	0.77	0.78

* Horizontal/vertical ratio.

The critical tractive force on bank materials is given by the formula

$$(\tau_0)^L_\omega = (\tau_0)_\omega \left(\cos\theta \sqrt{1 - \frac{\tan^2\theta}{\tan^2\varphi}} \right)$$

where $(\tau_0)_\omega$ (t/m^2) $= K(\gamma_s - \gamma)\,d$, the critical tractive force on bed materials, similar to that used in the earlier calculations for transverse structures

θ = angle of bank slope above the horizontal

φ = angle of internal friction of revetment material.

This formula allows us to determine the diameter d (m) characterizing the material to be used in the revetment. One factor to remember here is that loose dumping of coarse, highly resistant materials leaves up to 50-percent gaps (needing to be filled in with finer materials); even in paving the proportion can be as high as 30 percent.

Rock size should be as uniform as possible and should conform to the following requirements:

$$\frac{d_{max}}{d_{50}} \leq 2 \qquad\qquad \frac{d_{50}}{d_{50}} \geq 2$$

A gravel filter at least 0.20 m deep should be laid between the natural slope and the protective revetment, with the following approximate specifications (in relation to the average size of slope materials):

$$\frac{d_{50}\ \text{(filter)}}{d_{50}\ \text{(slope)}} < 40$$

$$5 < \frac{d_{15}\ \text{(filter)}}{d_{15}\ \text{(base)}} < 40 \qquad \text{(permeability condition)}$$

$$\frac{d_{15}\ \text{(filter)}}{d_{85}\ \text{(base)}} < 5 \qquad \text{(stability condition)}$$

2.7 Energy dissipation

Effect of water at the dam toe

The nappe in Figure 45 has velocity V_1 which is very much higher than V_2. Velocity is a function of discharge velocity at the overflow and the height H.

According to Veronese, the extent of scouring can be calculated as follows:

$$h_s = 1.9 \cdot H_t^{0.225} \cdot q^{0.54}$$

where

h_s (m) = maximum depth of scouring

H_t (m) = head between the levels of water in the basin and the level of the discharge

q (m^2/s) = Q/b

in which

Q (m^3/s) = discharge

b (m) = width of overflow.

Schocklitsch formula:

$$h_s + h_2 = 4.75 \frac{y^{0.2} \cdot q^{0.57}}{d_{90}^{0.32}} y = h_0 + z$$

There are two possible solutions: energy dissipators and aprons.

2.7.1 Energy dissipators

The phenomenon considered here is the hydraulic jump, which occurs when water velocity suddenly passes from rapid to slow and its energy is absorbed as a result of the impact. The relationship between the two depths h_1 (rapid flow) and h_2 (slow flow) can be expressed by:

$$h_2 = -\frac{h_1}{2} + \sqrt{\frac{h_1^2}{4} + \frac{2q^2}{gh_1}} \quad \text{(Bélanger formula)}$$

where
h_1 (m) = depth of water at toe of check dam
h_2 (m) = depth derived from h_1
q (m^2/sec) = rate of discharge per unit width.

Merriman's simplified expression may be used:

$$h_2 = 0.45 \frac{q}{\sqrt{h_1}}$$

The error factor is only around 3 percent when $h_2/h_1 = 10$ but as much as 20 percent when $h_2/h_1 = 2$.

Energy dissipators are of two types: water cushions or stilling basins enclosed by a subsidiary weir.

Bureau of Reclamation guidelines, based on the Froude number:

$$F_1 = V_1 \sqrt{\frac{1}{gh_1}}$$

$F_1 < 1.7$ Energy dissipator unnecessary; an apron of length $4h_2$ provides sufficient protection.

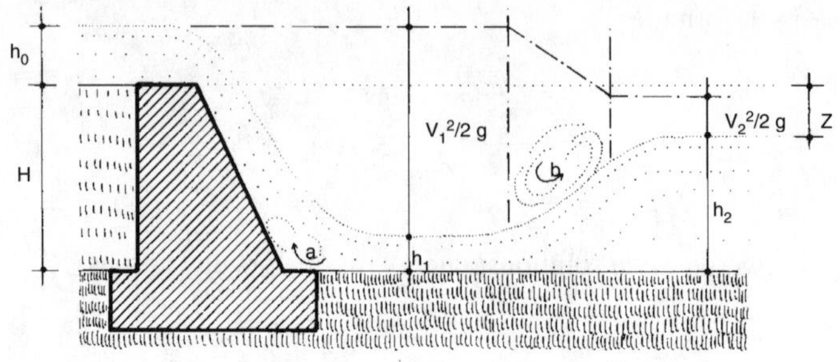

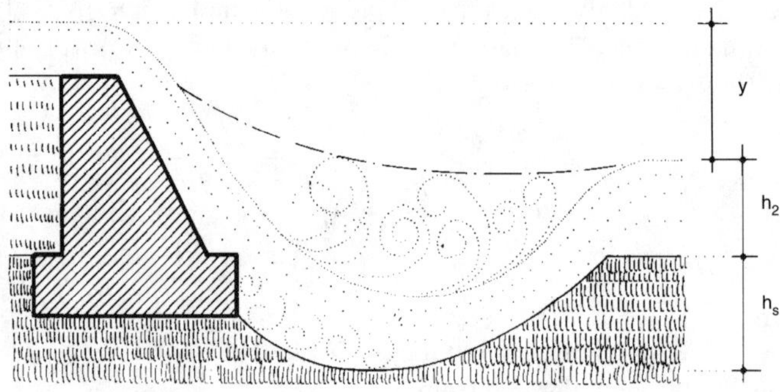

Figure 45. Effects of water at toe of check dam

$1.7 < F_1 < 2.5$	Energy dissipator may be used, but not absolutely necessary.
$2.5 < F_1 < 4.5$	A difficult "in between" area. Neither stilling basins nor aprons are really suitable since the hydraulic jump is not stable, and waves can extend past the basin. However, the dimensions of the overflow can be modified to prevent the discharge regime coming into this range.
$F_1 > 4.5$	Ideal conditions for energy dissipators.

The assumption of clear water in the calculations provides a safety margin, since suspended sediment and bedload reduce the erosive force of the stream.

Calculation of submerged stilling basins

Hydrodynamic overflow (Figure 46)

- Design flow: the same value for Q is used for torrential streams and for defining the overflow.

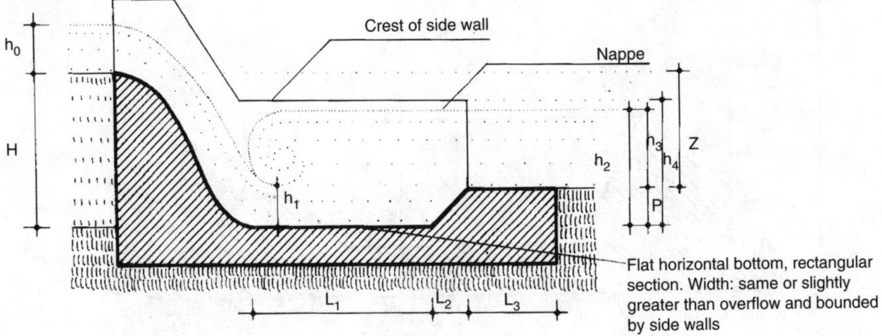

Figure 46. Hydrodynamic profile of submerged stilling basin

- Calculation of h_3: since Q is fixed and h_3 is the depth in the free reach, all that is needed is to make a topographic survey of the section and calculate h_3 by applying one or other of the conventional formulae for uniform flow in open channels (Bazin, Manning, etc.).
- Calculation of h_1: applying the law of the conservation of energy gives

$$h_1^{\,3} - \left(H + h_0 + \frac{V_0^{\,2}}{2g}\right) h_1^2 + \frac{q^2}{2g \cdot \varphi^2} = 0$$

φ being the energy loss between the overflow sill and the dam toe. In masonry dams, $\varphi^2 = 0.85$

- Calculation of h_2:

$$h_2 = \frac{h_1}{2} + \sqrt{\frac{h_1^2}{4} + \frac{2q}{gh_1}}$$ (Bélanger formula or Merriman's approximate formula)

$$h_2 = 0.45 \frac{q}{\sqrt{h_1}}$$ (especially where $\frac{h_2}{h_1} = 10$)

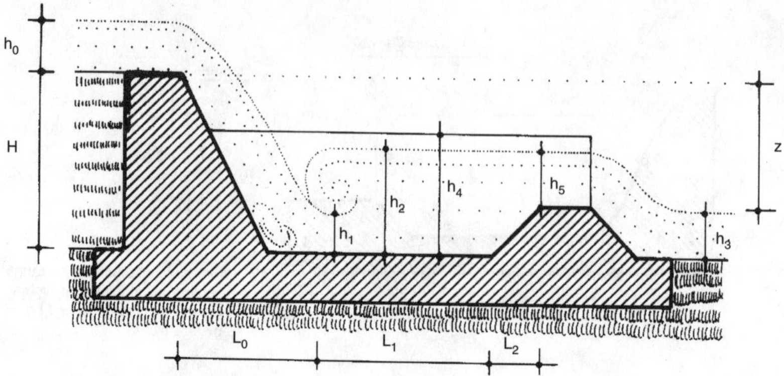

Figure 47. Stilling basin and auxiliary weir at toe of free overflow dam

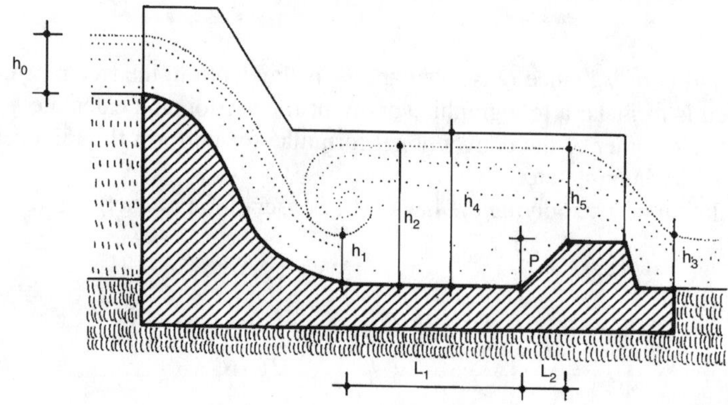

Figure 48. Stilling basin with auxiliary weir at toe of hydrodynamic overflow dam

- Depth of basin: $p = 1.15 / h_2 - h_3$
- Height of lateral walls: $h_4 = h_2 + 0.1\ (h_1 - h_2)$
- Length of basin bottom: $L_1 = 5\ (h_2 - h_1)$ (Lindquist formula)
- Calculation of $L_2 : 2p \leq L_2 \leq 4p$
- Calculation of $L_3 : 2.5h_3 \leq L_3 \leq 3.5h_3$

Calculation of stilling basins at toe of free overflow dams (see Figure 47)

- Calculation of h_1: as before, except $\varphi^2 = 0.65$
- Calculation of $L_0 : L_0 = \sqrt{2H\ h_0\ +\ h_0^2}$

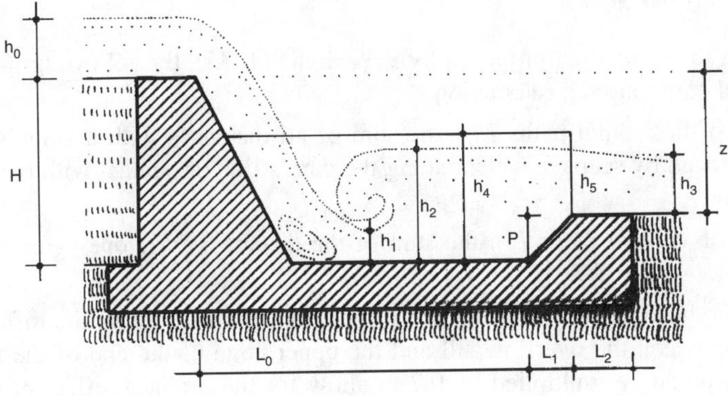

Figure 49. Submerged stilling basin with free overflow

The other design calculations are as for hydrodynamic overflows.

Stilling basin and auxiliary weir at toe of hydrodynamic overflow dams

For h_1, h_2, L_1 and h_4, use the formulae already described (Figure 48). For computing h_5, use the height that corresponds to the discharge Q over the overflow. Having defined h_5, $p = h_2 - h_5$ (in this case, $h_5 \simeq h_0$ is clearly acceptable).

L_2 is calculated as before, but with a free overflow (Figure 49).

Piping: aprons

Piping is the name given to the type of erosion that occurs in permeable foundations when seepage velocity below the structure exceeds the critical scouring velocity of the finest bed materials. The detachment of these small particles leaves a pipe-like space in the earth that can cause the dam to burst; however, such damage requires prolonged action by seepage waters exposed to continuous hydraulic pressure. Consequently, dams with permeable foundations are only affected: (1) if they have already silted up; (2) if the absence of weep-holes gives rise to prolonged liquid storage; (3) if there is sustained surface flow movement in the silt; or (4) if movement beneath the streambed keeps the piezometer level close to that of the siltbed.

The danger may be averted by forcing seepage water to travel a greater distance through the earth by constructing aprons downstream. They can also protect the dam toe, providing there are cutoffs in the upstream foundations and at the bottom of the apron. Drains consisting of permeable pipes surrounded by a well-graduated filter can also be laid below the base of the dam foundations.

Piping: safety margins

According to the method proposed by E.W. Lane (1935), the following parameters should enter into the calculation:

- Length of horizontal paths L_H : the sum of all distances with a slope of less than 45° traced by seepage waters along the dam's line of contact with the foundation floor.

- Length of vertical paths L_v : the sum of the distances for slopes greater than 45°.

- Hydraulic head above the structure H: measured in this case by the difference in height between the overflow sill and the upper edge of the end of the apron. The head should be multiplied by 0.7 to allow for the drainage effect of weepholes.

- Compensated length of path L_c : $L_c = L_v + L_H/3$
- Compensated head ratio R_c : $R_c = L_c/0.7\,H$
- Compensated failure ratio R_f : an empirical dimensionless parameter that depends on the characteristics of the foundation floor. However, the maximum values given by Lane for this parameter are too high for design purposes. Suitable average values are provided by Mollet and Pacquant:

Fine sands	4.0
Medium sands	3.5
Coarse sands	3.0
Gravel and stones	2.5
Clays	2.0

- Calculation of the piping safety margin requires the satisfaction of the following condition: $R_c / R_f \geq 1$.

2.7.2 Aprons

Aprons protect the streambed from erosion by overflow waters. Water is prevented from coming into contact with movable bed materials while its velocity is higher (because of the acceleration caused by the step effect of the dam structure) than it is in the free reach downstream. The transition flow section between the dam toe and the free channel is covered with an apron of erosion-proof materials — either by using blocks large enough to resist scouring in the reach caused by water velocity or by building a non-erodible structure made of masonry or concrete.

There are two types of apron: horizontal or sloping (i.e. following the downstream channel slope, see Figure 50). The calculations are based on the equations for variable flow in open channels.

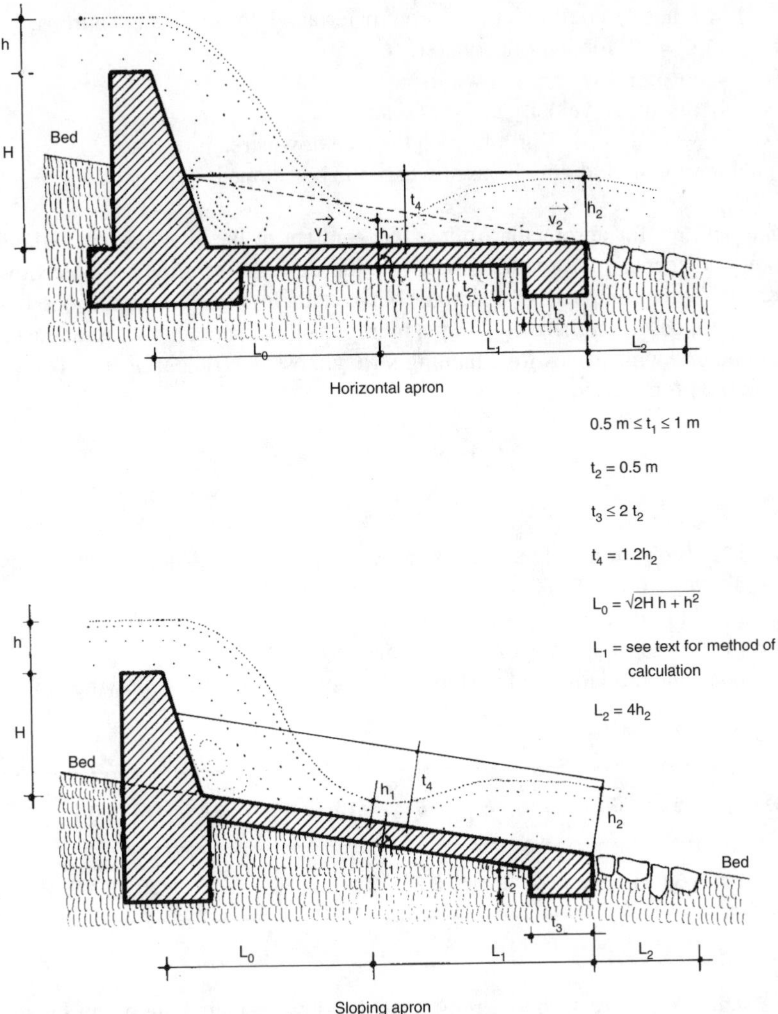

Figure 50. Horizontal and sloping aprons

- Horizontal aprons: the length of the structure is given by:

$$L_1 = \frac{c^2 q}{g}\left(\frac{1}{V_2} - \frac{1}{V_1}\right) - \frac{c^2 q^2}{4}\left(\frac{1}{V_2^4} - \frac{1}{V_1^4}\right)$$

where:

L_1 (m) = length of apron (in the case of a vertical drop structure, length is reckoned from the point at which the nappe hits the toe of the dam)

C (m$^{1/2}$/s) = Chezy's coefficient for apron materials. For fairly rough aprons, $C = 20$; for smooth concrete, $C = 50$
q (m^2/s) = design flow per unit width
V_1 (m/s) = discharge velocity at toe of dam
V_2 (m/s) = velocity of uniform flow in the free downstream reach.
Horizontal aprons should only be used where the bed slope is very gentle.

• Sloping aprons: for aprons that follow the gradient of the channel (best where the ground is steeper), the mathematical relation derived from the variable flow equations is rather complex, so a simpler but nonetheless fairly accurate one has been obtained, based on these equations, by regression. It covers the usual check dam parameters, with values for Manning's roughness coefficient of 0.05 for the apron and 0.04 for the bed.

$$L_1 = \varphi \cdot H^{0.5} \cdot h_0$$

where:
L_1 (m) = length of apron (the same observation applies as for horizontal aprons above)
H (m) = height of dam
h_0 (m) = depth of design flow at the overflow
φ = coefficient relating to the slope of the apron, as per the following table.

Slope (%)	5	6	7	8	9	10	11	12	13	14	15
φ	4.61	4.16	3.80	3.51	3.27	3.07	2.89	2.72	2.56	2.41	2.27

These structures have to be extremely secure before their length can be reduced. Masonry, consisting of coarse material from the channel itself or from a quarry, bound with concrete or cement mortar, is far more resistant than mass concrete alone.

In normal circumstances, the thickness of the apron will vary between 0.50 m and 1.00 m, depending on the height of the dam and the volume of the discharge. A cutoff made of the same material and penetrating at least 0.50 m into the ground is usually placed below the end of the apron; it should be twice as wide as it is deep.

The water's transition from apron to channel can be made smoother by adding coarse material without any binder to the end of the apron over a distance four times the depth of the design discharge in uniform flow conditions. Should downcutting occur, this ramp will prevent gradient shift.

Unless made of rock, banks along the apron will normally need to be protected with lateral walls. These walls should be of the same material as the dam, rectangular in section, and 1.2 times as high as the discharge in the downstream free channel.

2.8 Natural vegetation in torrent bank management

Although correct use of the jetties, groynes and other works discussed in Chapter 3 provides effective torrent bank protection, the construction and maintenance costs of many such structures are high. However, if they are not properly looked after, they will gradually deteriorate or possibly give way altogether. Furthermore, to be fully effective they need to be adapted to their particular environment; otherwise, they will not only prevent the bank vegetation on which wildlife depends from establishing itself (biotopes containing only a few species tend to be less stable), but will be eyesores as well. On the other hand, the complete or partial substitution of normal building materials by vegetation has certain advantages. Although plants provide little initial protection, their effectiveness increases as they grow and develop. Provided they do not obstruct the flow, they can be useful as streambank protection, enhancing the site and improving the quality of the water.

2.8.1 Ecological factors

Streams differ in size and ecology. Studies should cover both longitudinal and cross-sections as well as ecological factors.

Longitudinal section. A channel's longitudinal section consists of three parts: an upper one (Crenon), characterized by steep slopes in narrow valleys and gravel and shingle deposits; a central one (Rithron), with gentler slopes, broader banks and finer soils; and a lowland one (Potamon), with much flatter, smoothly sloping banks and fine deposits.

This sediment and ecology-based classification is applicable primarily to large rivers running from mountains through tablelands to the sea. For lesser flows emptying into rivers, the lower part may bear a closer resemblance to the central (Rithron) or upper (Crenon) parts. Similarly, a stream that rises in flat terrain may have Potamon characteristics throughout.

Cross-section. The streambank consists of the area between the low water and five-year flood levels. The channel boundary follows the bed on both sides up to the five-year flood mark.

The term, bank vegetation, covers everything growing in this area.

Ecological factors. Bank vegetation is affected not only by soil, topographic and biotic factors, but by hydraulic ones as well: discharge, depth and velocity are crucial elements in determining the type of vegetation that can be used to rectify a torrential channel axis. However, since these hydraulic aspects are dealt with in Chapters 1 and 3, we will not go into them here.

Moreover, although discharge, depth and velocity all affect the location of vegetation and the zoning of plant associations, other properties such as trophic balance, transparency, turbidity and temperature, combined with soil and climatic factors, also play a role in determining which species succeed in competing with other plants and establishing themselves.

2.8.2 Zoning of vegetation

There are four zones of vegetation: aquatic, cane-brake, riparian and brush.

Aquatic zone

Plant associations. The aquatic zone is populated by water crowfoot, with pondweed and water-lilies growing in quiet meanders and backwaters. These plants grow in shallow water on the streambed or on gently sloping banks. Their main requirements are a low level of bedload transport and plenty of light; in narrow channels, shade from trees on the bank stunts plant development.

Protective action. Aquatic plants reduce water velocity and blunt its erosive force. They protect the bed from erosion, especially when flattened against it by strong flows. Ideally, therefore, flat banks should be covered with plants, although not too thickly.

Introduction of a living structure. It is not easy to introduce aquatic plants artificially, and until recently it was scarcely even attempted. However, the plants can be established quite easily where there is an existing cane-brake, so the best method would appear to be to plant reeds first.

Cane-brake zone

Plant associations. Depending on the prevailing ecological conditions, different types of *Phragmites* association appear in the cane-brake zone. Reeds and rushes may be found in stagnant waters and in the lower reaches of torrential streams, estuaries and so on. They grow at depths of 0.3-1.5 m in fresh or brackish water; rushes can grow down as far as 2 m in moderately to highly eutrophic soils ranging from silty clay to fine sands.

Of the various plants such as calamus, *Glyceria*, reedmace and sedge, one in particular — *Phalaris* (reedy canary grass) — stands out, especially in small or medium-size channels. It prefers oxygen-rich running water, up to 0.30 m deep, and will take root in silty, sandy or gravel soils and sometimes even in low or high marshy ground.

Protective action. Cane-brakes protect banks and fix soil below the water-line (in some cases, a little way above it as well), while their aerial parts provide as much, if not more, protection. The vegetation acts as a permeable barrier helping to deaden the impact of waves and streamflows on the soil surface. This kind of active bank protection by cane-brakes is only feasible in zones permanently under water, i.e. lying below the mean water level.

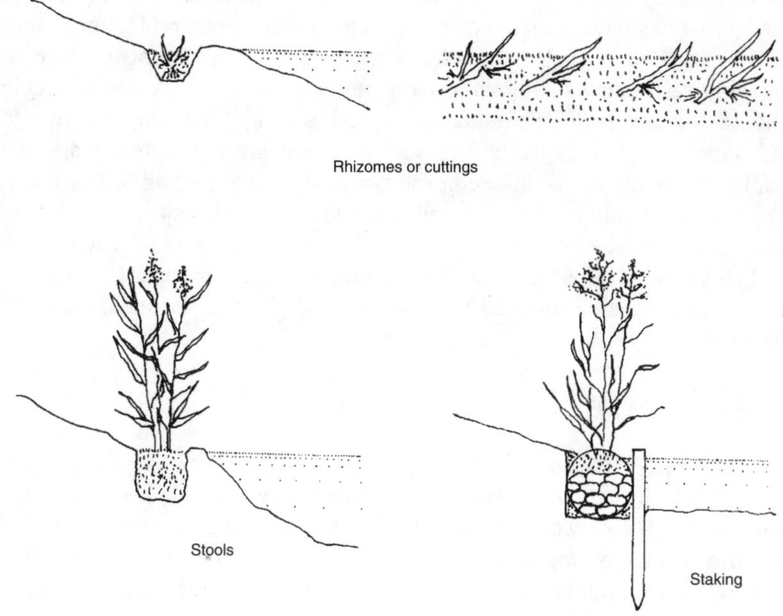

Figure 51. Methods of introducing a living structure in the cane-brake zone to protect torrent banks

The protection afforded by the various types of cane-brake association varies; for example, some protect the zone affected by changes in the water-level. The most important association is the *Phragmites* one; these robust plants have stems which lignify in autumn, enabling them to provide protection during the winter as well, thanks to the dense tangle of plant residues and strongly rooted rhizomes. No other type of reed is so effective at fixing the soil. It has other advantages too: all the aerial and underground stems have node buds, facilitating regeneration, planting and vegetative propagation.

Introduction of a living structure. There are various methods of establishing cane-brakes and rush beds (Figure 51). The oldest method, applicable to all plants, is stool planting. The aerial parts are severed and the cube-shaped stools placed in previously dug holes, ensuring that they are at least two-thirds covered.

Many species can be successfully planted from rhizomes or cuttings, thus necessitating fewer plants. They are placed in holes or narrow trenches along the mean summer water-line, so that only the aerial shoots can be seen above the soil.

Phragmites cuttings can be planted alongside stagnant or slow-flowing water. Generally, three cuttings are placed in each 30-50 cm deep hole. In compact or stony soil, the holes are best made with a dibble. *Phalaris* and *Glyceria* can also be planted in very damp bank soils, provided they are not flooded in the ensuing six months.

Since banks are often not sufficiently consolidated immediately after planting, combined structures have been developed in which initial bank protection is provided by inert materials such as bundles of canes; these have been shown to be effective along both slow- and fast-moving stretches of water. A trench 40 cm wide and 40 cm deep is dug behind a row of stakes and wire netting laid in it to cover the sides as well; filling materials such as coarse gravel are then heaped on top; finally, the stools are positioned. The two ends of the netting are then fastened together with galvanized wire, ensuring the bundles do not rise more than 5 cm above the water-level. The final stage is to cover everything over with earth and stool residues. A cane-brake can be combined with paving or riprapping by inserting rhizomes or cuttings between joints and gaps at the mean summer water-level.

Riparian zone

Plant associations. This zone consists of clumps of trees and shrubs, mainly willow and alder. There are associations of riparian willow, marsh alder, and other riverside species. *Salix alba*, *Salix fragilis*, *Salix rubens* and *Populus nigra* will grow on gravel soils. *Salicetum albae* prefers cool, moist soils, which are alkaline to slightly acid, on high or low ground. *Salicetum fragilis* is normally found in neutral to acid soils and also does well in mountainous areas. Coppices composed of these species are a highly effective form of bank protection.

However, true riparian associations, composed mainly of *Alnus glutinosa*, are *Stellario-Alnetum*, *Carici remotae-Fraxinetum* and *Pruno-Fraxinetum*. These grow on cool moist banks on medium to high ground where the soil is acid to slightly alkaline. The main genera are *Fraxinus*, *Prunus* and *Ulmus*, together with shrubby species such as *Viburnum*, *Corylus*, *Evonymus*, *Rhamnus*, *Crataegus*, *Cornus* and *Sambucus*.

In these formations, ash, sycamore and all the above shrubs play an important role, particularly in maturing the soil; nearer the bank, willows can be very useful.

Protective action. In every tree association, the roots help prevent soil erosion; in particular, they protect banks from the effects of water and torrential flows. A tree association is the deepest type of bank soil protection, reaching down even to zones permanently under water. Banks criss-crossed by roots rarely break up unless undercurrents have already made inroads into the unconsolidated soil beneath the root system; even then, however, the shrub is not always uprooted. The root system of alders is capable of fixing banks that are almost vertical.

The upper parts of the plant help reduce the velocity of flow and thus the erosive capacity of the water, although only during peak flows. Indeed, the role of shrubs in this zone is analogous to that of plants in the cane-brake zone.

Branches act as an elastic check on water flow, thus helping prevent bank erosion. No inert material could provide such active protection. Flood damage to riparian formations is quickly repaired by vigorous new plant growth.

Introduction of a living structure. The considerable regenerative capacity of riparian coppices means that they have long been used in bank protection. All the different species produce suckers. The trunks and cut branches of willows are capable of developing secondary roots; the trees also have large numbers of dormant buds. Cuttings, branches or stems can be planted and fixed in a variety of ways to provide immediate protection. They may be interwoven (wattling) or fastened with wire (fascines or fascine mattresses).

Wattling may take the form of fencing or matting. If the wattling is to root and send out shoots, it needs to be buried at least as far down as 20 cm. Fascines (Figure 52) and fascine bundles are cylindrical in shape, 4-20 m long and 10-40 cm in diameter; they contain scarcely branched stems tightly fastened with wire and are placed in the bank so that the parts that are meant to take root stay out of the water and in contact with the soil. Covering over with earth prevents desiccation. Coarse gravel or shingle is used to fill the fascine mattresses.

The degree of protection can be increased by employing anchor hurdles, or rock-brush fascines. Anchors are made with 2-3 year-old willow stems (1.5-2.0 m long) laid out in parallel rows 1-5 cm apart and perpendicular to the direction of flow. The bottoms of the stems are placed in a 15-cm deep ditch and covered over. Willow branches are fastened firmly together with wire, fascines or willow plaiting, using stakes 0.6-1.0 m long for wiring; anchoring the plaiting involves first driving stems into the ground until they protrude 10-20 cm above it. Once the branches are in position, the stakes are joined together with galvanized wire; they are then driven in again until the bed of stems is tightly pegged to the ground.

When willow fascines are used for consolidation, leave a 1.0-1.2 m gap between them and cover thinly with earth so that the branches are flattened but not completely hidden. Hurdling is composed of layers 10-20 cm wide for brushwood fixed by fascines 60-80 cm apart and laid parallel to the direction of flow or at an angle of 30° to it. The ends of the bottom layer cover the base of the layer above; the base of the bottom row is positioned in a trench dug previously at the foot of the slope. Everything is then covered over with earth or fine gravel to a depth of 15-25 cm.

Rock-brush fascines basically consist of 20-30 cm thick compressed layers of brushwood, which are covered with fascines of green branches and secured by stakes and (if possible) forked branches. The spaces between the fascines are filled with gravel, stones and earth, and another 20-30 cm thick brushwood layer is laid on top (Figure 52). Rock-brush fascines are particularly useful for restoring badly scoured banks along deep streams.

In banks where the root system has not had time to develop properly, additional temporary protection may be provided by inert materials such as riprapping or paving. Sites unsuitable for replanting may be grassed over with species such as *Angelica archangelica, Chaerophyllum bulbosum, Agropyron repens* and *Festuca arundinacea*; these plants help consolidate banks without the need for maintenance. All are tufted species, with stolons and quickly spreading root systems.

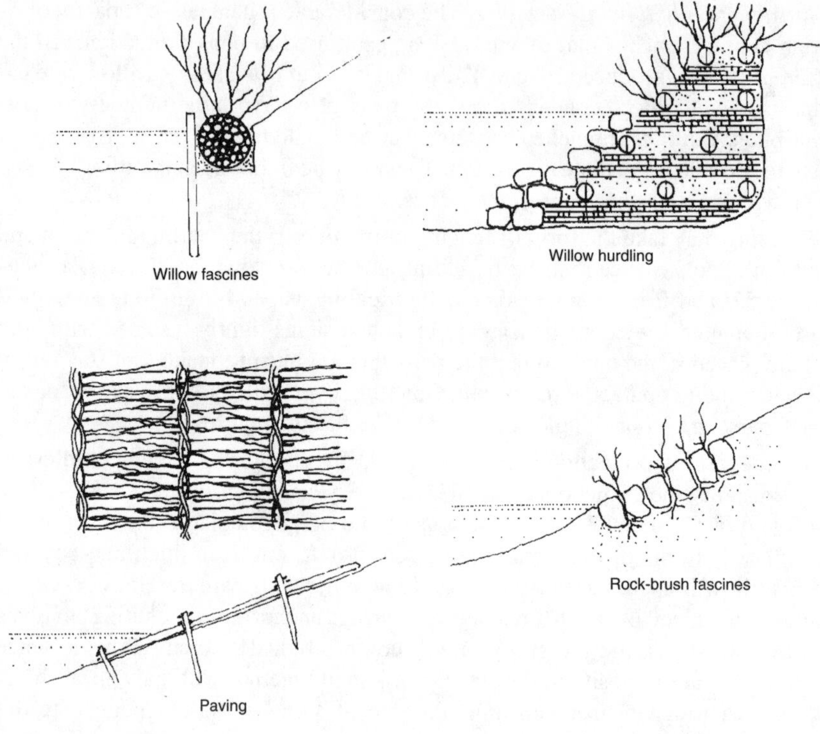

Figure 52. Introduction of riparian vegetation to protect torrent banks

Brush zone

Plant associations. These consist of *Fraxino-Ulmetum*, *Pruno-Fraxinetum* and *Stellario-Carpinetum*. On fertile sites managed for pasture, ash tends to be the dominant species in the association; in moist zones, *Alnus glutinosa*; and in dry zones, *Quercus robur* and *Acer pseudoplatanus*. In *Fraxino-Ulmetum* associations with moderately alkaline soil, ash will predominate. Other important species are: *Ulmus campestris*, *Populus alba* and *P. canescens*, *Tilia cordata* and *Acer campestris*.

The shrub layer is particularly rich in species. In addition to those mentioned above, the genera *Viburnum*, *Ligustrum*, *Prunus* and *Rubus* may also be added. The latter is particularly effective at fixing the soil in hydrophilous forests and can easily be planted between gaps in the paving or riprapping. In older associations, *Carpinus betulus* is often found.

Protective action. This zone has a smaller role in bank protection since it is less subject to flooding and water erosion. However, the zone's vegetation has a definite influence on that of other zones, particularly as far as shade is concerned, since most associations in the other zones require plenty of light.

Introduction of a living structure. Formations in the woody zone proper are created by planting different rooting species of shrubs and trees (Figure 53). Maintenance cuts should be used to create as natural a formation as possible. Trees should be densely planted to ensure compact formations.

2.8.3 Arrangement and combination of vegetation zones adapted to stream morphology

Asymmetrical cross-section

As waters tend to follow a winding course, the characteristic depth and width of the channel cross-section will be constantly changing: in particular, there will be asymmetry (Figure 54). While on the inside the slide bank is fairly flat, the angle and shape of the slope at various points above the water-level has a considerable influence on the zoning of vegetation. The gentler the slope in a particular zone, the more vegetation will be encouraged. In banks sloping steeply into the water, for example, the forest zone may extend almost to the water-line, leaving no room for a cane-brake (for which there would not be enough light anyway). On the other hand, a fairly flat bank, particularly in the zone around the mean flow level, facilitates the establishment of a broad belt of reeds.

Advantages of cross-sectional asymmetry

In farming areas, streams and bank vegetation are expected to take up as little room as possible, with gently sloping banks only being permitted if they consist of exploitable grassland. Since woody formations on gentle slopes take up much of the cross-section, the slope needs to be kept vertical on the outside of the bend, although on the inside it can be much flatter and protected by grass and reeds.

Banks exposed to the full force of the waters should have woody formations to provide active protection during peak flows. Slide banks require less protection and can be farmed right up to the cane-brake zone. It is here that deposition occurs.

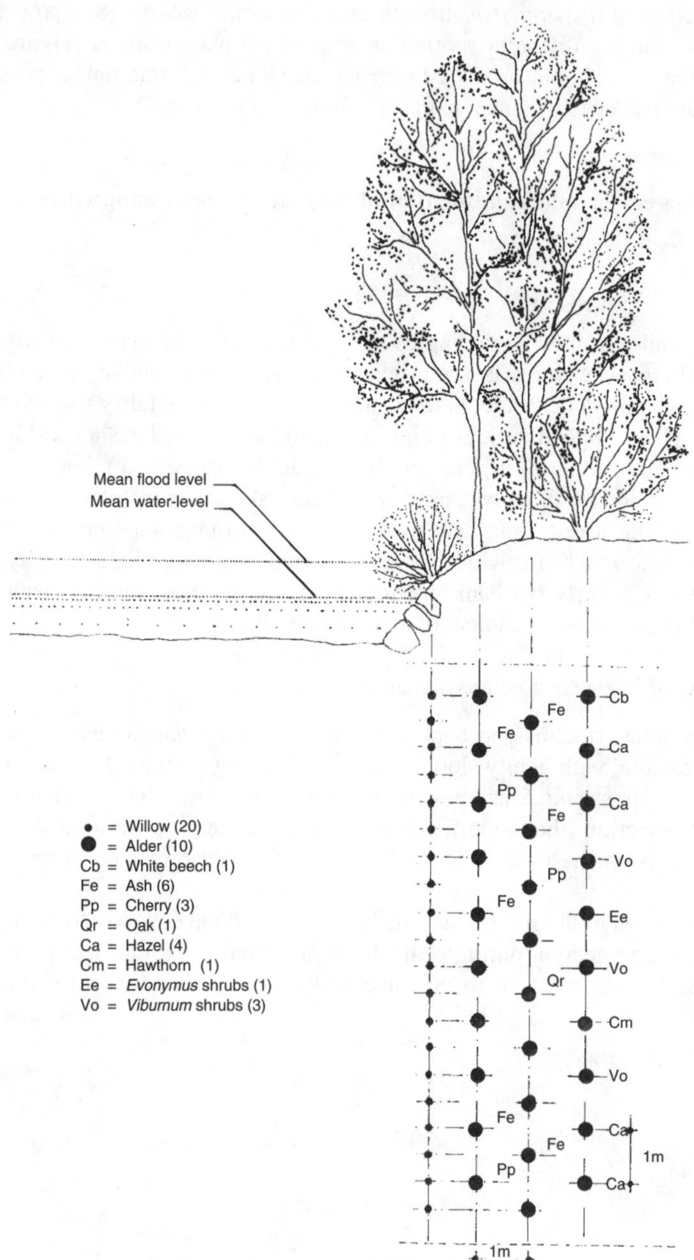

Figure 53. Brush zone design for torrential streambanks

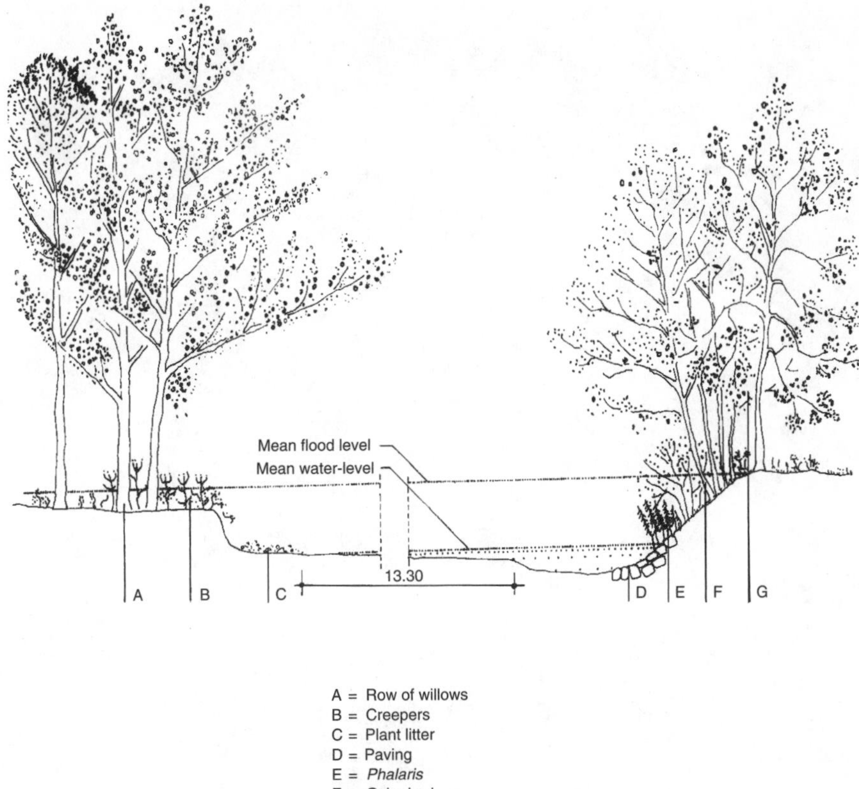

A = Row of willows
B = Creepers
C = Plant litter
D = Paving
E = *Phalaris*
F = Osier bed
G = Alders and ashes

Figure 54. Cross-section of a natural streambed showing vegetation zones

3. Protection of primary channels

3.1 General

For the most part, training walls are built along reaches affected by sediment deposition and characterized by zones of discontinuous lateral erosion (usually along just one bank). These structures may be classified according to whether they protect primary channels from lateral erosion or from flooding. Groynes are probably the most common method of countering lateral erosion. Training walls also protect banks directly from lateral erosion and help stabilize the channel section by tightening the outside bend and smoothing the inside one. They are made of strong materials such as concrete and masonry, although gabions may be used where the ground is not firm, because their construction enables them to absorb differential settlement at their base without breaking up.

Another way of protecting torrential streams from water erosion is bank correction and revetment. This step involves covering the bank with loose materials (riprapping) and is a simple and economic method, providing the channel contains materials large enough to enable the revetment to resist the tractive force of peak flows. The loose rock is dumped on the slope, and all gaps are filled in with finer materials to allow the planting and development of shrubby riparian species, thereby increasing the strength and effectiveness of the protection.

Another kind of non-erodible bank revetment is wire mesh of the type used in gabions. The mesh is either simply placed over the slope materials to keep them from being detached by the water or made into "bags", which are then filled with stones. Since the stones do not have to be particularly large, this technique is useful where the only available materials are too small for riprapping, even if hand-placed rather than dumped.

Although strictly biological, there is another form of streambank revetment that protects against lateral erosion: the establishment of shrubby or sub-shrubby plant cover, preferably after some initial slope correction work.

In channels whose upper banks are nearly always above water, fast-growing, quick-rooting riparian species can be used. In the slope area beyond the bank crest, however, growth should be checked before the tree stage is reached.

Bank flood protection works usually take the form of non-submergible jetties that stabilize and strengthen streambanks and ensure a cross-section capable of dealing with even the largest floods. A similar role can be played by submergible jetties. The resulting floodway is able to handle ordinary, frequently recurring floodflows. Jetties also help control the circulation of water and protect the riverside from the erosive effects of heavy flooding.

From the viewpoint of clear water hydraulics, the wide channels along which waters in these reaches normally flow facilitate the design of training works; this step involves keeping the streambed flat and constructing two jetties to produce a cross-section wide enough to virtually rule out the possibility of overtopping. However, since the characteristics of sediment transport in the reach remain the same, the bed level will continue to rise, entailing a systematic reduction in discharge capacity and nullifying the effectiveness of the training works.

By narrowing the channel section, the water's tractive force could be sufficiently increased to virtually eliminate mass deposition. This would obviously so reduce discharge capacity that there would be little point in constructing the training works in the first place. Flood protection works along torrent banks cannot be effective in the long term unless a global approach is taken to control torrentiality in catchments and their headwaters, so that waterflow and sediment transport during peak discharges is kept to a minimum.

3.2 Bend protection

Undercutting or scouring on bends increases water depth and velocity along the extrados, resulting in lateral displacement of the channel. This is a particularly dangerous form of scouring and can cause serious damage. The outer bend is therefore usually protected with groynes and bank revetments; both methods aim to divert high-velocity streamlines away from bank materials and prevent their detachment.

Groynes are structures jutting into the stream but keyed into or supported by the bank. They not only divert streamlines away from the bank, but encourage sediment deposition in the gaps between them. They are simple and cheap to build, with maintenance costs actually shrinking as time goes by. If the groyne head becomes worn, the remainder of the structure is still effective, while the destruction of one groyne does not pose any special threat to the others. Repairs, moreover, are quite straightforward.

Streambank revetments and protection works rest directly against the bank slope and the channel bottom and are made of materials that cannot be detached by the flow. A filter is normally placed between gaps in the revetment. The main advantage of streambank revetments is that they permanently fix the shape of the bank, preventing subsequent displacement. However, they are more difficult to build than groynes and therefore cost more. They also need careful maintenance, as even a small fault can damage the whole structure.

3.3 Groyne design

The main points to be borne in mind when designing groynes are:

- location in plan: radius of bends, length of tangents, width of stream (stable);
- length of groynes;
- spacing of groynes;
- height and slope of crest;
- angle of orientation to the bank;
- groyne permeability; construction materials;

- undercutting of bend and local scouring at groyne head.

The first five points are discussed below. The other two will be commented on only briefly.

Location in plan

Protective works may be designed to follow the existing bank or a corrected one, but in either case the channel axis should be drawn in plan, together with a line running parallel to it along the bank (which the groynes will meet). The length of each groyne is given by the distance of the actual bank from this line. The width *B* between the new banks will depend on the outcome of the flow stability study.

When correcting sandy or silty channels, the radii of the curves (measured up to the channel axis) should as far as possible be of length *R* as follows: with a uniform curve (correction), all the groynes are the same length, the same distance apart and at the same angle. If the above radii are respected, groynes will provide effective protection. The shorter the radii, the smaller the gap between the groynes, making it more economical to protect the bank directly. Longer radii cause the stream to curve in within the bend itself, and groyne action will not be uniform.

If the aim is simply to protect existing stream banks, and correction works are not feasible, then the line joining the groyne heads should be as uniform as possible, without necessarily keeping the same radius throughout. Because this type of work is comparatively inexpensive, it is most commonly carried out during the initial phase of a region's development (Figure 55). With irregular stream banks, the length and the distance between groynes should vary; indeed, the bank itself will differ at each anchoring point.

Whether it is a single bend or an entire reach that is being protected, the first three upstream groynes should always be of different lengths. The first groyne should be as short as possible (equal to water depth), with the length of the second and third groynes increasing uniformly until the design length is reached with the fourth groyne. All groynes should have the same crest slope.

Length of groynes

A groyne's total length is made up of the anchor length and the working length, the anchor being that part which is initially embedded in the bank, and so not in the stream itself.

Recommendations

Working length. This is measured along the crest and is chosen independently. It should ideally fall within the following range:

$$h \le L_t \le B/4$$

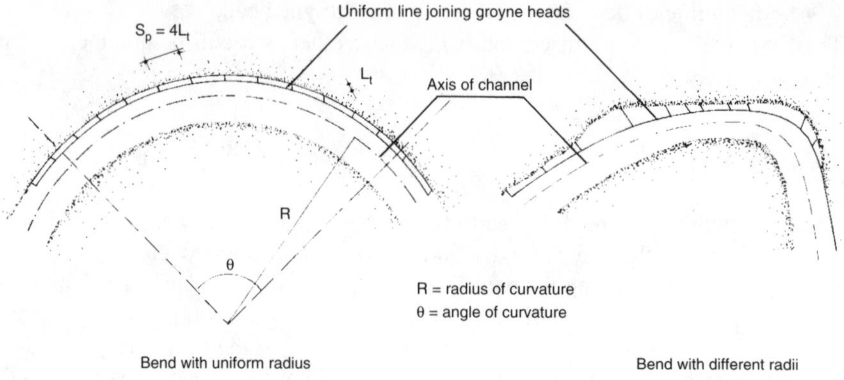

Figure 55. Groyne design: various types of location in plan

in which B is the average width of the channel and h the average depth, both of these under dominant discharge conditions.

Anchor length. Anchors are not essential, i.e. groynes do not necessarily have to be keyed into the bank.

Remarks

Although it was stated above that working length is decided independently, all the groyne heads should still meet the same design line. If the groynes are to be of predetermined length, this line will move nearer to or further away from the main bank, but will always be parallel to it.

For reasons of economy, the anchoring should be as short as possible. The ends of the groynes should be set directly against the bank, keying in only about 4 percent of them. It is much cheaper to repair any eventual damage to a few groynes than to anchor all of them. Repairs are carried out at the next low water by lengthening the groyne until it rejoins the eroded bank. If groynes break up at all, it is usually during the first flood. Once repaired, however, they continue their action without much further maintenance. If it is necessary to avoid damage to groynes in a particular reach, then the spacing between them should be reduced, or they should be keyed in (to a maximum distance of $L_t/4$).

Spacing of groynes

The spacing is measured at the bank between two groyne bases and depends mainly on the length of the upstream groyne. The angle that the groyne makes with the downstream bank and the theoretical widening of the flow (by 9°-11°) as it passes the groyne head should also be taken into account (Figure 56).

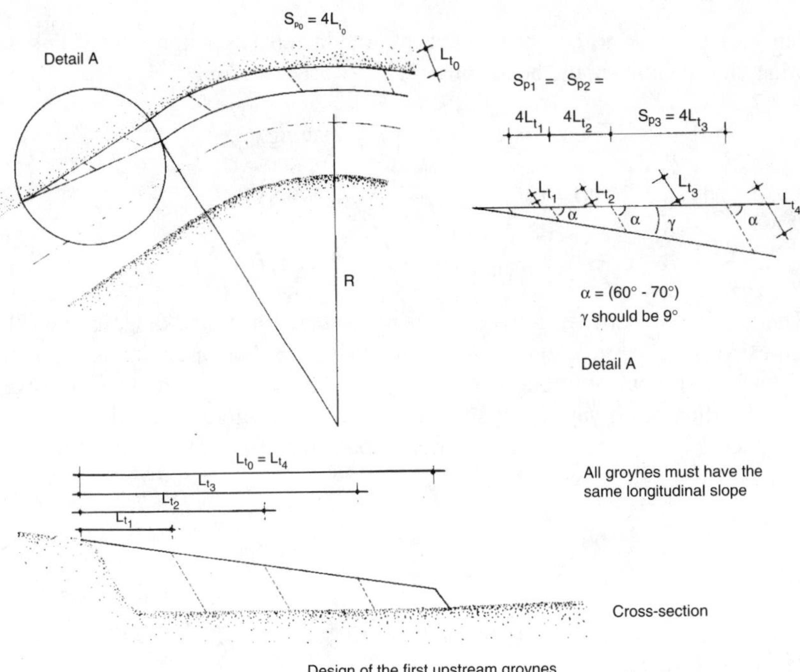

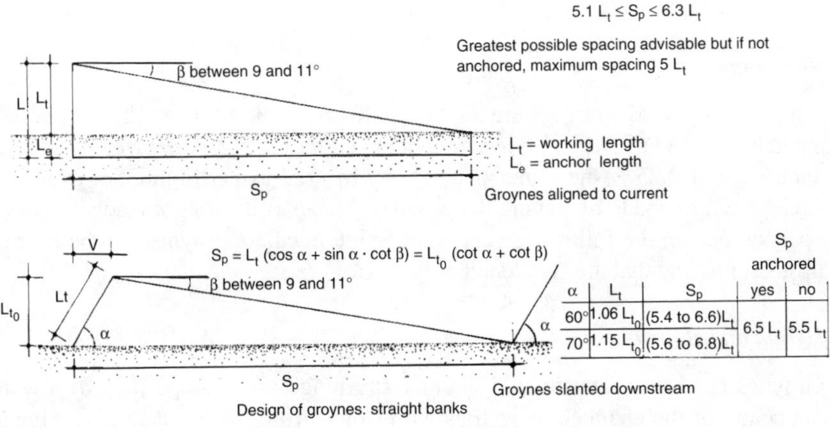

α	L_t	S_p	S_p anchored yes	no
60°	1.06 L_{t_0}	(5.4 to 6.6)L_t	6.5 L_t	5.5 L_t
70°	1.15 L_{t_0}	(5.6 to 6.8)L_t		

Figure 56. Detail of groyne design

Recommendations

When groynes have to be constructed in straight reaches without any bank anchoring, the spacing should be as follows:

α	Spacing, S_p
90°-70°	(4.5-5.5) L_t
60°	(5-6) L_t

The spacing S_p between groynes on bends is best illustrated diagrammatically (Figures 55 and 57). In a regular bend with a single radius of curvature, good results have been obtained with S_p = (2.5-4) L_t. If the curve is irregular, however, or if the radius of curvature is particularly small, a diagram is needed to determine spacing (Figure 57); angles of orientation can be fixed at the same time.

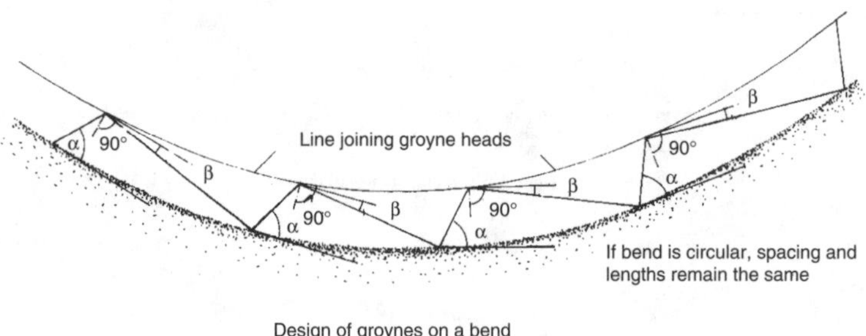

Figure 57. Spacing of groynes (in plan)

Remarks

The recommended spacings are slightly narrower than the theoretical ones indicated in Figure 56 as the groynes are not keyed into the bank. However, given an anchorage of 0.25 L_t the same spacing may be used as per Figure 56. If desired, savings can be made by having the groynes 8 L_t apart in straight reaches and 6 L_t apart on bends; the following year, shorter intermediate groynes can be inserted upstream of any that are weakened or broken.

Height and slope of crest

Groynes have been constructed without any longitudinal slope (S = 0) towards the centre of the channel, as well as with slopes from 0.02 to 0.25. Experiments with groynes having a horizontal crest and slopes of 0.1-0.5 and 1 have also been made.

Recommendations

Groynes should be constructed so that they slope toward the centre of the channel; they should start either at the top of the bank or at the free surface level corresponding to the dominant discharge. The head should be no more than 30 cm above the channel bottom. This placement produces slopes of between 0.05 and 0.25, with satisfactory results (Figure 58).

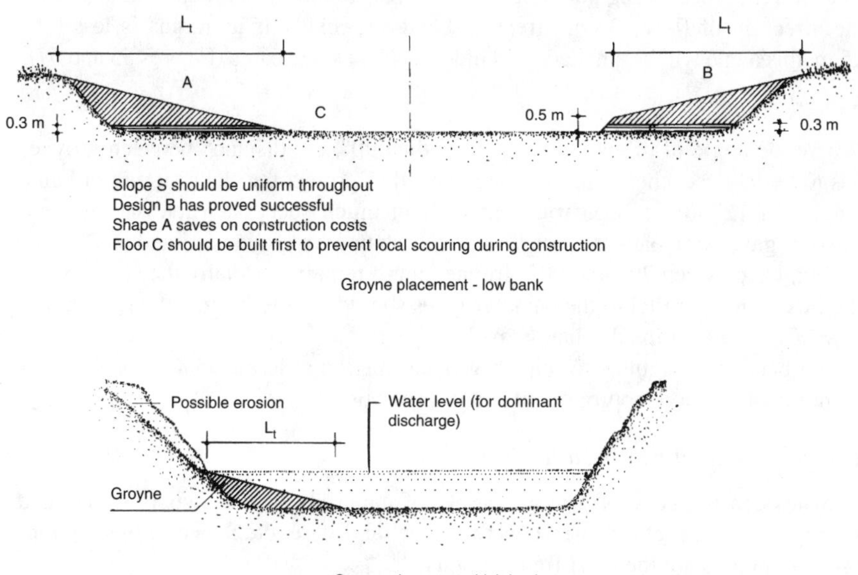

Figure 58. Height and slope of a groyne crest

Remarks

The advantages of having groynes that descend so steeply into the channel are as follows: (1) virtually no scouring occurs at the groyne head; (2) if the groyne has vertical sides with sheet piling there will only be some slight erosion at the upstream face; (3) if, on the other hand, its sides are not vertical but have a slope of 1.5/1 with riprapping, sediment deposition will occur immediately behind the downstream face, providing valuable protection; (4) each groyne requires only 40-70 percent of the material needed to construct a horizontal crest groyne (the greatest savings are made using riprapping or gabions); (5) deposition of sandy materials between groynes is faster than with a horizontal slope; groynes having these slopes and separated by a gap of 4 L_t are unlikely to break up. They have, however, only been tested on bends.

Angle of orientation to the bank

Groynes may be angled upstream or downstream or placed normal to the flow. Groyne orientation is measured by taking the angle formed by the groyne's longitudinal axis and the downstream tangent to the bank at the point of anchorage (Figures 55 and 57).

Recommendations

In a straight reach or regular bend, the groynes should form an angle of 70° with the direction of flow. On an irregular bend, especially if its radius is less than 25 m, this angle will be smaller — as little as 30° in some cases (Figures 55 and 57).

Remarks

Where the angle of orientation is greater than 90°, the distance between groynes has to be reduced; therefore more are needed to protect the same stretch of bank. Angles of 120° have been tried but without much success; when one of these groynes gave way, bank erosion was greater than with groynes angled at 70°-60°. For angles between 70° and 90°, groyne length remains virtually the same. Since the flow is not parallel to the bank, groynes should ideally be angled at 70° rather than 90°, whatever the discharge level.

If a bend is so tight as to require groynes angled at less than 40°, bank revetment may be a more appropriate form of protection.

Groyne permeability. Construction materials

Groynes can be made of a large variety of materials such as wood, trunks and branches, stone, prefabricated concrete, steel and wire, etc.; sheet piling, riprapping or gabions are the most frequently used.

Groynes intended to be left permanently in the main channel should be impermeable, which makes them more effective at diverting the flow away from the bank. On the other hand, if groynes are used to reduce the velocity of flow in a zone so that it can be filled in with bedload transported by the stream (for bank formation), they should be permeable; in this way, they let the water through while slowing it down sufficiently to induce sediment deposition (Figure 59).

Groynes should be constructed of materials strong enough to withstand not only flow pressures but also the impact of any trunks, trees and other floating bodies transported by the river. In fact, groynes that are themselves made of tree trunks and branches are usually destroyed.

Undercutting of groynes

Local scouring at the groyne head is a major problem during construction if loose materials (bags, stones, gabions, etc.) are being used. If the velocity of flow exceeds 50 cm/s, the bottom on which the groyne is to rest should be covered with a layer 30 cm thick of stone prior to building (from the bank outwards). Without such a floor, more materials will be needed. Local scouring at the groyne head is much less of a problem if the groyne itself is given a steep longitudinal slope.

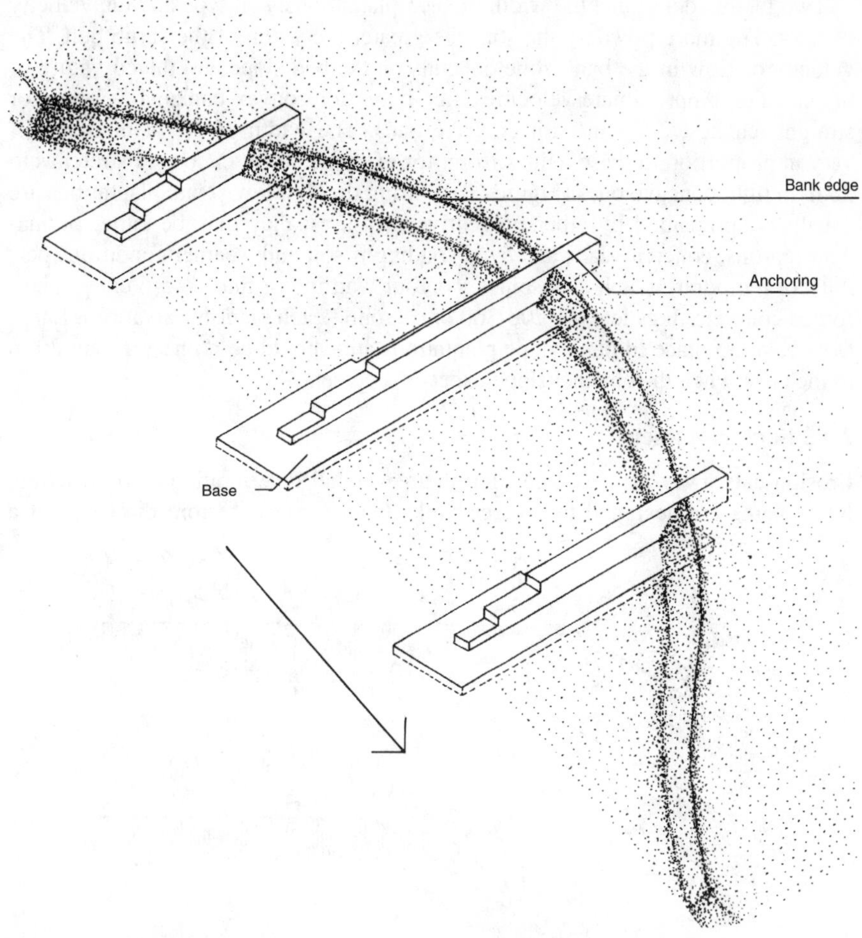

Figure 59. Series of gabion groynes on a gabion base along an eroded bank

3.4 Revetments

3.4.1 Systematic use of shrubs for bank slope fixing and stabilization

The soil characteristics of bank slopes (for example, soil that is too powdery) and climatic factors (such as long summer droughts and lack of capillary moistening of the soil) limit the opportunities for establishing grassy vegetation; however, dense shrubby bush (max. height 5 m) may be used instead to fix and stabilize slopes. Small-scale trials have confirmed that this planting system can protect soil from erosion, reduce water velocity in the bank zone and control the velocity of floodwaters in riverside areas.

Two factors determine the width of such plantations: soil type and the velocity of flow. The more powdery the soil, the greater the width of the shrub belt. The velocity of flow in the bank zone depends on the bed slope and the curvature of the channel. Approximate velocities are: 1 m/s for convex banks; 1.5-2 m/s for straight reaches; 2-2.5 m/s for concave ones. The width of the plantation will vary in proportion to these values from, for example, 10 m in convex stretches to 25 m in tight concave ones (Figure 60). During the first few years, plantations are usually accompanied by other preventive measures; they may be either permanent (aprons, concrete slabs and even sodding if soil and weather conditions permit), or temporary (such as fascines, contour wattling or thin — 5-6 cm — reinforced concrete flags leaving 200-300 cm^2 around each plant for aeration). Large trees have no place in bank slope plantations and should be no nearer than 20 m to the crest when the channel slope exceeds 5 percent.

3.4.2 Bank revetment

Erosion eats away at banks, causing their eventual deterioration or destruction. Revetments are designed to protect banks from erosion, restore the slope of a

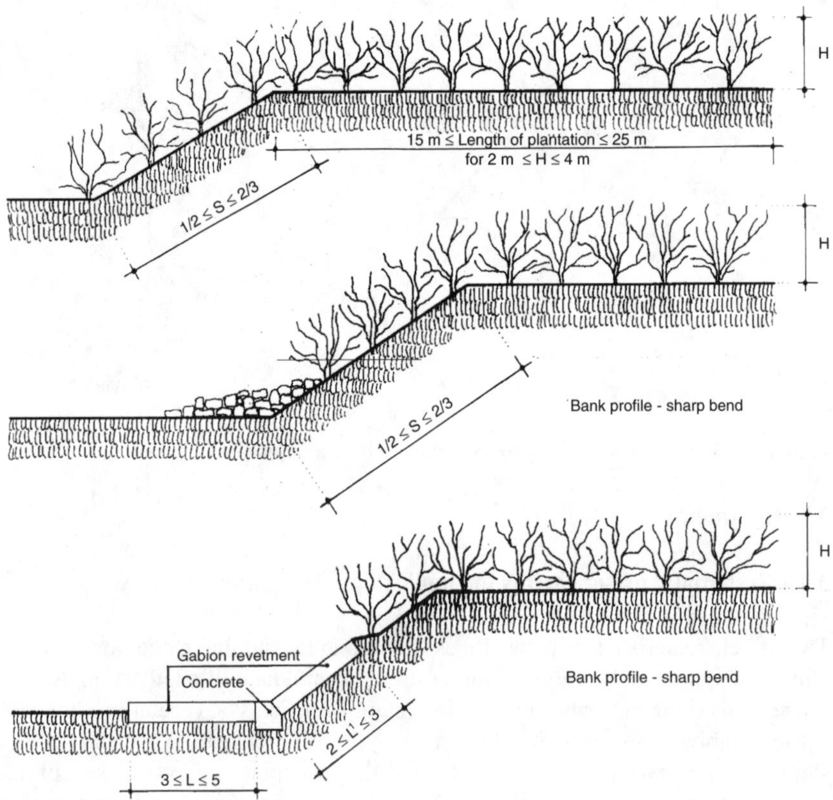

Figure 60. Types of cross-section in bank revetments with a mixed system including vegetation

deeply eroded bank and repair damage to bank protection works in certain reaches. In choosing the type of revetment, one should bear in mind that the bank slope consists of three zones:

- the permanently submerged zone below the low water level;
- the zone lying above the 5-year flood level (this being the period needed for shrubby plantations to become fully effective) and which is only temporarily submerged;
- the intermediate zone between the previous two.

Calculating the different stages in a given section of the channel over a 20-year period will help establish the boundaries between the three zones.

Measures to be taken in the first zone are: large boulders or artificial slabs resting on rockfill and put in place when water velocity has dropped below 0.8 m/s. Bank slopes should all be less than 1/1. Sandy slopes may require the use of sheet piling or cribbing, etc. (Figures 61-63).

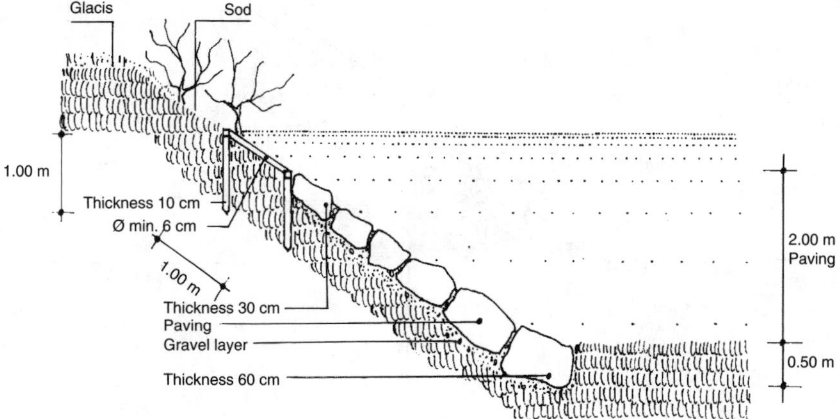

Figure 61. Bank revetment (various types)

In the second zone, grassing is recommended where soil and climatic conditions permit; if not, shrubs can be planted instead.

In the final zone, there are three possible types of revetment:

- Revetments composed of loose elements laid side by side: these structures depend on their own weight and the placement of their elements for their stability. Examples of materials are riprapping, drystone masonry, thin concrete flags and concrete slabs weighing up to 75-80 kg. Figure 64 shows what to do when the foot of the bank slope has been eroded by water. The revetment should rest on a layer of stones and have a trapezoidal section 1-1.5 m high and 2 m wide, with 2/3 slopes.
- Gabion revetment: several designs for this form of bank protection are given in Chapter 4 on gabions (Figure 65).
- Monolithic revetments: these structures are made of such materials as 0.3-0.6 m concrete slabs with contraction joints, reinforced concrete slabs, etc. (Figure 66).

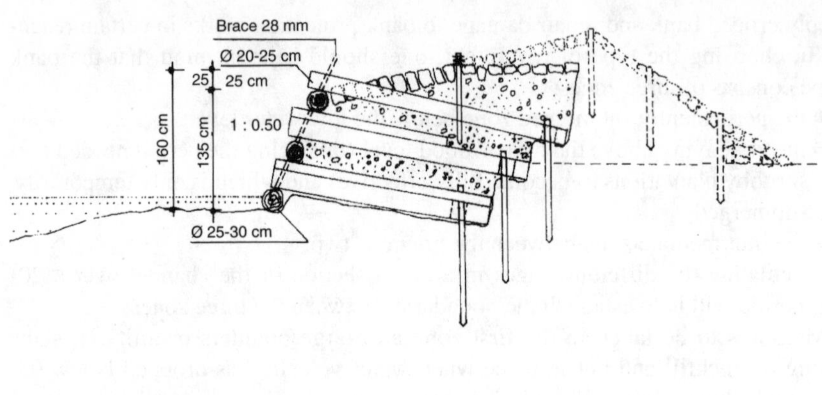

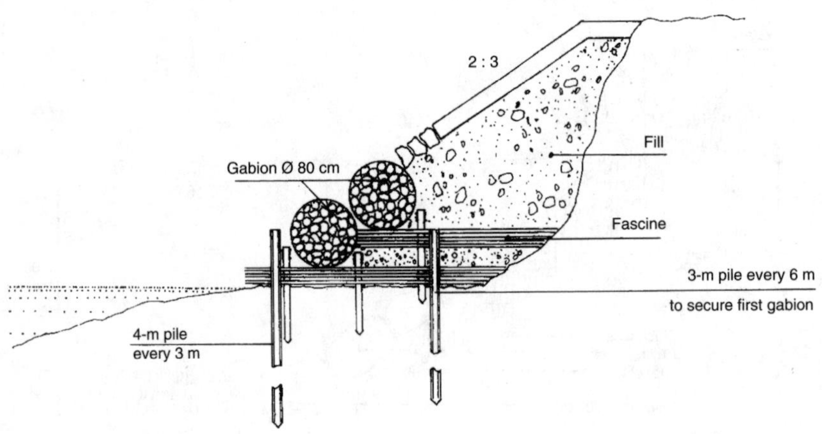

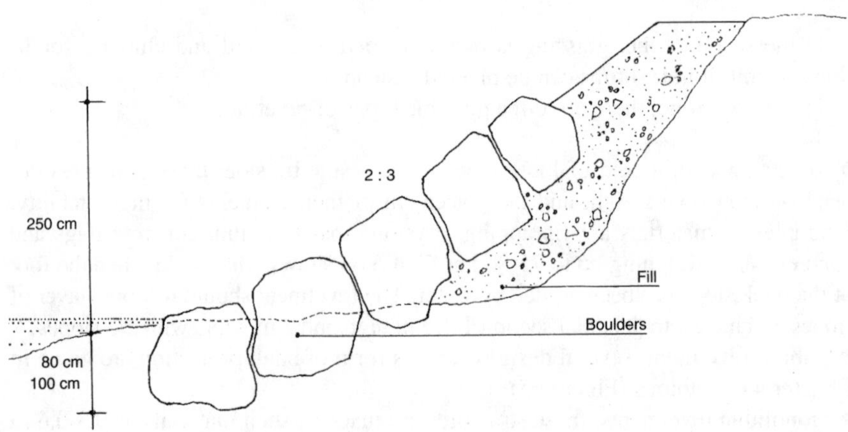

Figure 62. Bank revetment (various types)

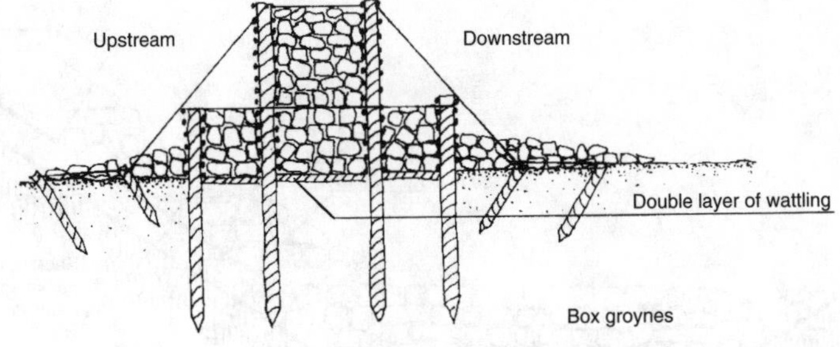

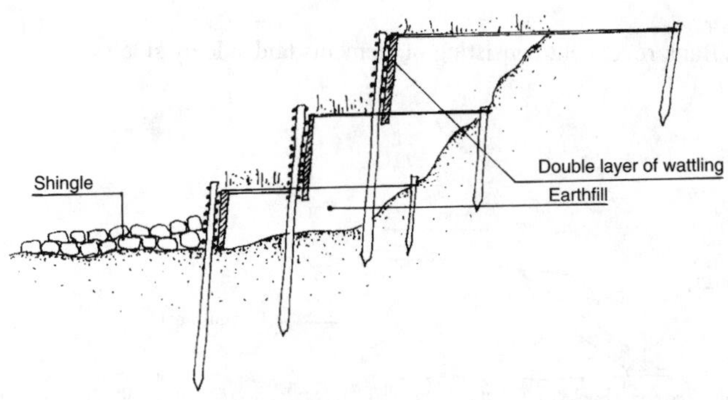

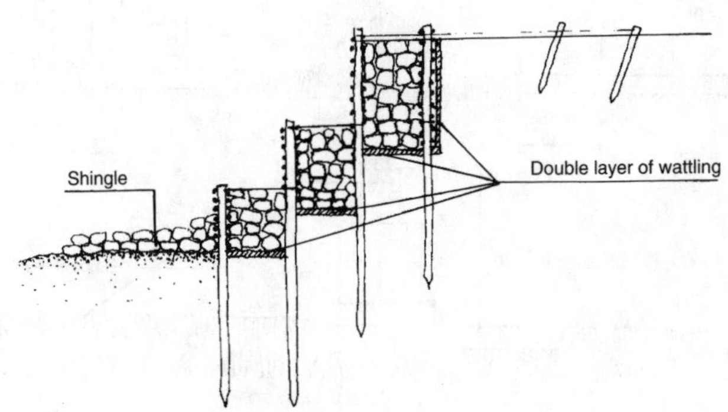

Figure 63. Bank revetment (various types)

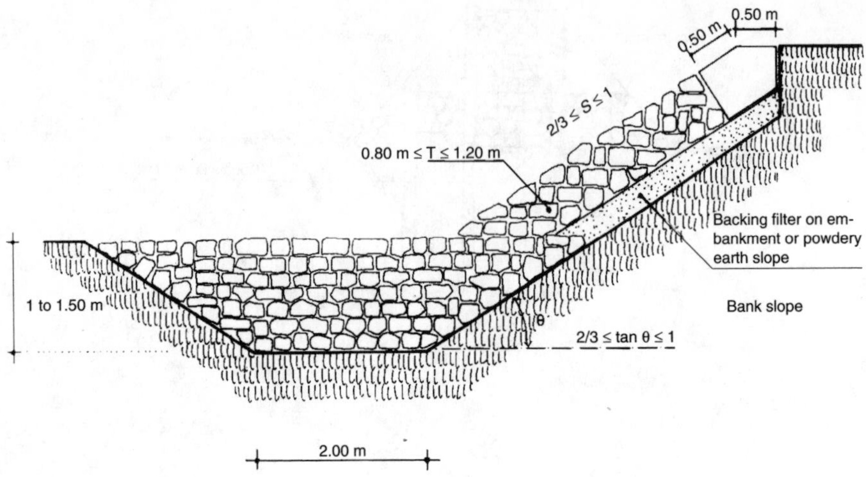

Figure 64. Bank revetment consisting of elements laid side by side

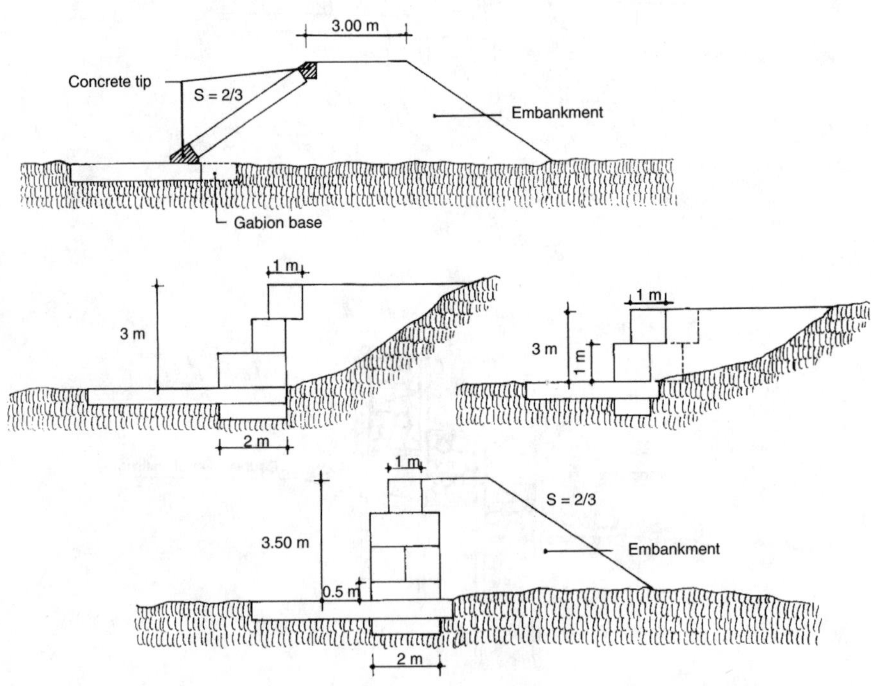

Figure 65. Cross-sections of different types of gabion revetment (shallow foundations)

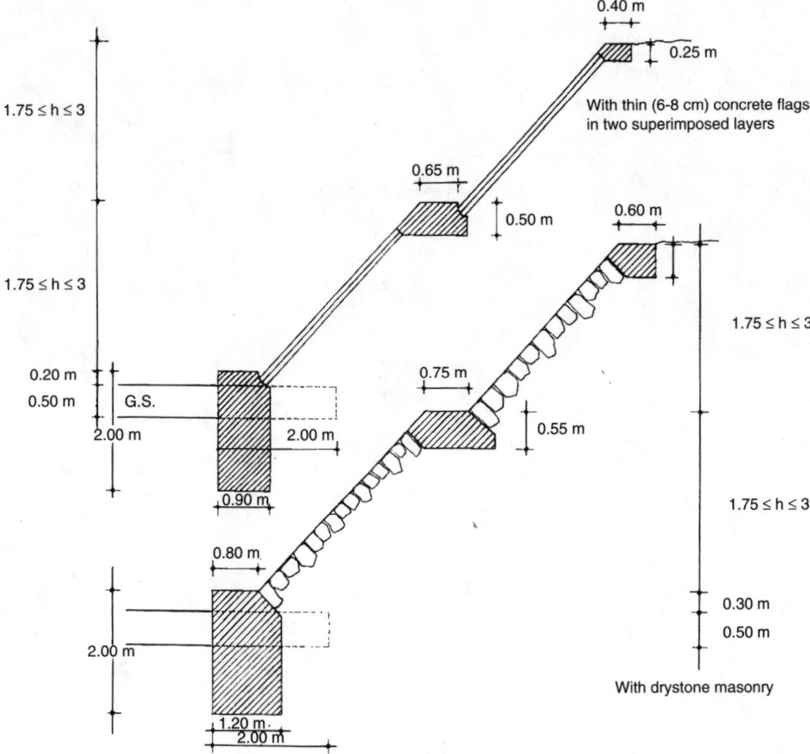

Figure 66. Cross-sections of bank revetments (monolithic type)

4. Gabion structures

Gabions are crates or boxes made of wire mesh and filled with stones; they may be prismatic or cylindrical in shape.

4.1 Characteristics and types of gabion

The prismatic gabions used in dams, walls, groynes, etc. are rectangular parallelepipeds made of wire mesh that has been galvanized or plasticized to protect the wire from nitrates in the water. Gabion dams may be classed as loose material dams on account of their origin, action, filling materials, flexibility and filtering capacity as well as their role at the interface between structure and foundation floor. From a static point of view, their outer metal covering permits the use of a transverse profile and a method of determining dimension similar to that for gravity dams.

Gabions are used where:

- suitable filling materials are available;
- any other material would pose transport problems (empty gabions are light and easy to handle);
- enough manpower is available.

The disadvantage of gabions is that the wire can become oxidized or snap under pressure from the materials transported by the water. This can be solved by galvanizing and plasticizing the wire, or covering the mesh with concrete.

Prismatic gabions are described by the following characteristics:

- the length in metres of the three edges converging at a corner, expressed as the length, width and height;
- the mesh width in centimetres;
- the thickness of the galvanized wire.

Characteristics of galvanized wire gabions (5 x 7 cm mesh)

Dimensions				Weight (kg)
Length (m)	Width (m)	Height (m)	Volume (m^3)	Without diaphragms 2.4 mm ø wire
2	1	0.5	1	13.6
3	1	0.5	1.5	19.5
1.5	1	1	1.5	15.6
2	1	1	2	19.0
3	1	1	3	26.0

Characteristics of galvanized wire gabions (6 x 8 cm mesh)

Dimensions				Weight (kg)
Length	Width	Height	Volume	Without diaphragms
(m)	(m)	(m)	(m^3)	2.4 mm ø wire
2	1	0.5	1	11.0
3	1	0.5	1.5	15.0
1.5	1	1	1.5	12.0
2	1	1	2	15.0
3	1	1	3	20.0

The characteristics of galvanized cylindrical gabions and galvanized plasticized gabions used in apron support or streambank revetment are:

Characteristics of galvanized cylindrical gabions (8 x 10 cm mesh)

Dimensions			Weight (kg)
Length (m)	Diameter (m)	Volume (m^3)	3.0 mm ø wire
2	0.65	0.65	9.6
3	0.65	1.00	13.5
2	0.95	1.40	15.7
3	0.95	2.15	21.0

Characteristics of galvanized plasticized gabions (8 x 10 cm mesh)

Dimensions			Weight (kg)
Length (m)	Diameter (m)	Volume (m^3)	2.7 mm ø wire
2	0.65	0.65	9.4
3	0.65	1.00	13.0
2	0.95	1.40	15.2
3	0.95	2.15	21.2

For the 8×10 mm mesh, SAE 1010 wire is used; it has a low carbon content and a resistance of 45 kg/mm^2. SAE 1040, which has a high carbon content, is used for the 5×7 mesh and has a resistance of 83 kg/mm^2. Binding wire is flexible, 2.4 mm thick and triple galvanized. After galvanization (250 g/m^2 of zinc), wire should be able to resist abrasion, twisting, blows and oxidization; the zinc will need to be blended with steel to improve adhesion. In particularly corrosive conditions, the galvanized wire should be given a coating of polyvinyl chloride as well.

4.2 Instructions for use of gabions

A prismatic gabion has three parts: the body and two end-pieces (Figure 67). Rectangle I forms the lid of the gabion, rectangle III the base, and rectangles II and IV the sides. The structure is closed by two end-pieces (*T*), fixed like hinges at either end.

The wire used for the edges is usually one size up from that used for the meshing. For ease of transport, prismatic gabions are folded. Assembly is in three stages: (1) unfold the gabion and lay it flat on the ground; (2) raise rectangles II and IV and the two end-pieces (*T*) until their edges coincide, thus forming an open-top crate; and (3) tie edges *AI*, *BJ*, *EH* and *FG* firmly together with galvanized wire.

Use 2.4-mm diameter wire to sew the gabion together. The quantity of wire needed for the operation amounts to about 5 percent of the gabion's total weight. Above a certain height, the gabion will need to be braced by joining opposite faces horizontally with wire the same thickness as the mesh. This reinforcement keeps the gabion from being pushed out of shape by the weight of the fill material. The horizontal spacing between braces should be 70-80 cm, with a 33-cm vertical gap between two horizontal rows. The braces in one row should alternate with those in the row immediately below.

In all gabions, and especially those at the ends of rows, adjacent faces are usually braced as well. Gabions used in foundations also have vertical braces linking the base to the lid. Before filling, the gabion's longest sides should be squared with planks supported by iron struts to prevent buckling (Figure 67).

The filling should be as dense as possible. To stop stones escaping, only the largest ones should be in contact with the mesh, while the smaller stones should be kept for the inside. After filling the gabion, the lid is closed and secured. Similarly, the edges of each gabion should be tied to those of its neighbours so that the whole structure is bound tightly together. Gabions are suitable for building dams up to 10 m high. Their flexibility enables them to adapt to the differential settlement of tiers and foundations.

Since monolithic masonry and concrete structures call for firm foundations, the cost of the extra volume required if the terrain is not suitable can be prohibitive. In such circumstances, gabions provide the best solution.

Characteristics of galvanized wire gabions (8x10 cm mesh)

Dimensions			Volume (m^3)	Weight (kg)						Diaphragm No.
				Without diaphragms			With diaphragms			
Length (m)	Width (m)	Height (m)		2.4 mm Ø wire	2.7 mm Ø wire	3.0 mm Ø wire	2.4 mm Ø wire	2.7 mm Ø wire	3.0 mm Ø wire	
2	1	0.5	1	9.3	11.5	14.0	10.0	12.5	15.0	1
3	1	0.5	1.5	12.6	15.7	19.4	14.5	17.5	21.5	2
4	1	0.5	2	15.9	20.2	24.6	18.8	23.0	28.0	3
1.5	1	1	1.5	10.2	12.8	16.0	–	–	–	–
2	1	1	2	12.5	15.7	19.2	13.7	17.0	21.0	1
3	1	1	3	17.0	21.3	26.0	20.0	24.5	30.0	2
4	1	1	4	22.0	27.0	32.4	26.3	31.5	38.5	3

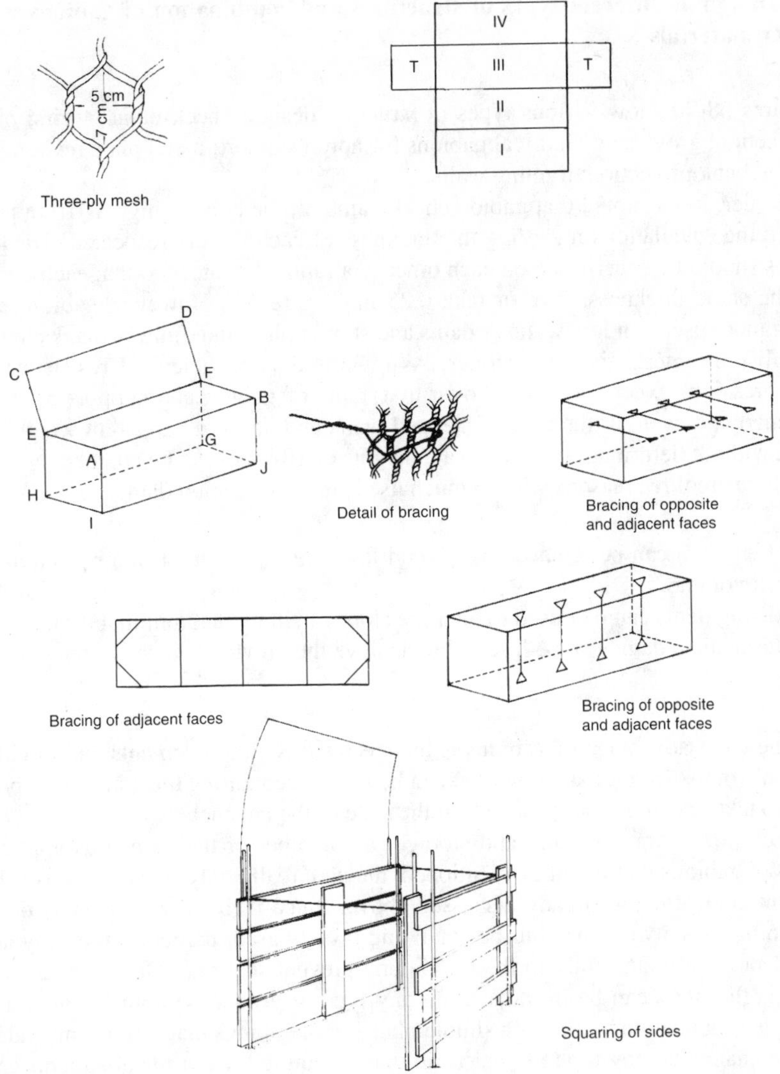

Figure 67. Instructions for use of gabions

Another advantage compared to masonry or concrete is that the latter requires lime or cement, sand and water to prepare the mortar. Transporting these ingredients, particularly to a site high up in the mountains, adds considerably to the cost of the operation. Gabions, on the other hand, are factory-folded and delivered unfilled.

4.3 Design of different types of structures and combination of gabions with other materials

Figures 68-70 show various types of structure design: check dams; weirs; pipe protection; groynes; cylindrical gabions for apron support; metal plate revetment; mixed bank protection; training walls.

Earlier, it was noted that gabion check dams can be built as high as 10 m provided the calculations regarding the thickness of each tier are respected. The gabions should be superposed on each other in a rational manner so that each tier is of the same thickness, give or take 0.25 m (Figure 67). However, gabions are even more useful in low walls or dams and stay in place indefinitely thanks to the stability the mesh gives the stones. As regards the coefficient of resistance to compression, experience has shown that 1 m^2 of gabion can support 5 t (0.5 kg/cm^2) and even, in the case of stepped walls and dams, an apparent weight of 20 t, without deformation; in this way, heights of 10-12 m can be attained.

There are three reasons why so much use is made of gabion dams:

- A high dam can be replaced by several lower ones, resulting in a reduction in overall volume.
- Existing dams can be raised to alter the slope of siltation at minimal cost.
- Intermediate dams can be inserted to achieve the previous objective on a larger scale.

The chief advantage of gabions is their versatility; improvements and modifications (in the form of small works) can be introduced during the course of a project to take account of any changes in the state of the channel.

Weirs (both for diversion and storage) are another of the numerous applications of gabions that might be mentioned; they are really only special cases of the torrent control dams already discussed above. Since their main characteristic is flexibility, such weirs need to be small and broad-based, particularly if they are to adapt quickly and fully to the terrain and prevent scouring. One great advantage is that they can be introduced on any type of ground without the need for complex foundation works — a simple platform of gabions that can be embedded in the channel at any time of year is all that is required. Even the abutments can be made of gabions (Figure 68).

At first sight, gabions do not appear to give much assurance of impermeability. However, all the gaps between the stones will have filled up with sediment after two or three basic-stage floods; gabion structures are therefore just as effective and long-lasting as those built of other kinds of material.

In a gabion dam it is particularly important to have as long a stilling pool apron as possible with a cutoff wall at the end deep enough to prevent undercutting. Upstream, a cutoff is also required below the bottom step, perhaps in combination with a short apron of similar width to the step.

It is also necessary to prevent the nappe from damaging the abutments, i.e. the

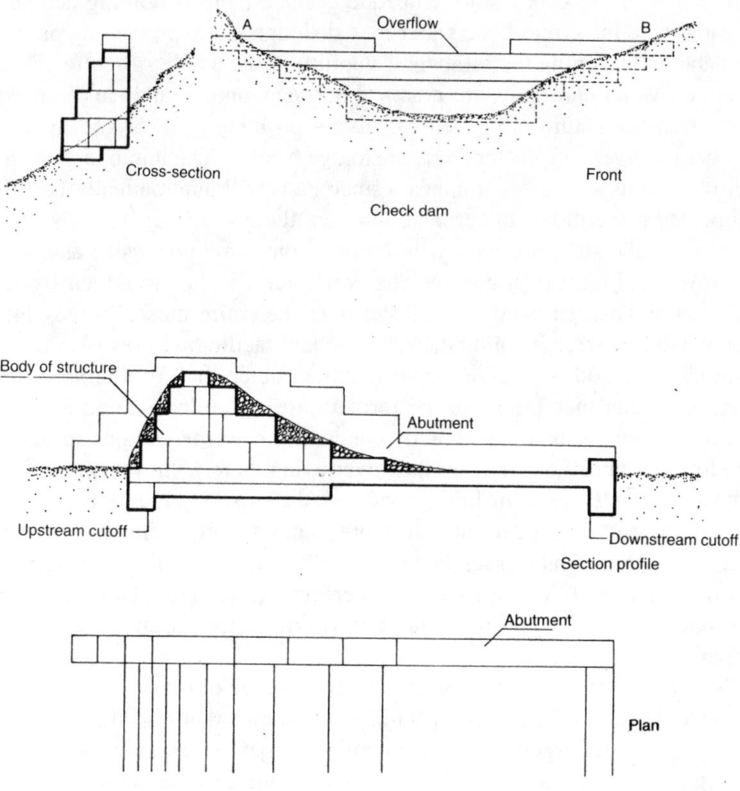

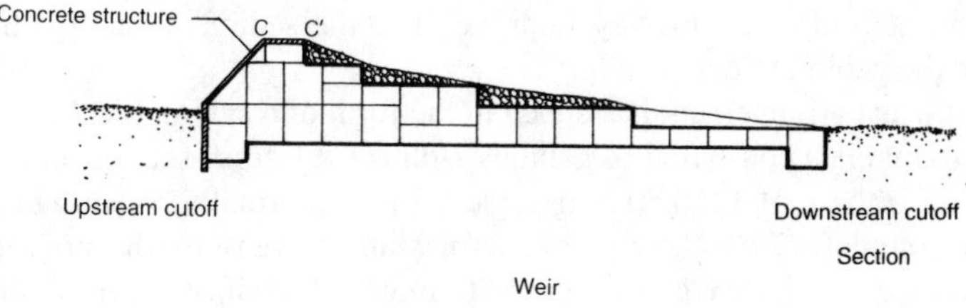

Figure 68. Bank protection using gabion structures in combination with other materials

point at which the gabions are embedded. Since there is nothing actually fixing the gabions to the ground, the water may dislodge them, preventing proper settlement and undermining the safety and stability of the whole structure.

Gabion weirs and dams are practical and economical and can be used whenever a small structure is needed to solve a problem quickly and inexpensively (e.g. stream diversion, coffer dams or storage basins). The initial lack of impermeability is not as serious as it appears since gaps will automatically be filled with sediment. Furthermore, impermeability can always be increased by enveloping the body of the structure with wire mesh of the same mesh size as the gabions. As shown in Figures 68 and 69, the weir face can be smoothed by filling in with stones. The next step is to plaster over the entire mesh, thereby improving impermeability, strengthening the structure and facilitating flow over it.

Another method is to give the structure an outer shell or alternatively an impermeable inner membrane. In the former case, a similar method is used to that described above. It involves directly concreting over the gabions so that the face is no longer stepped but flat and then overlaying them with wire mesh. This technique is normally used in low, broad-based dams. Structures between 10 and 12 m high that have been built to store water for domestic use in towns and places with inadequate groundwater resources are examples of when the latter method is adopted. These structures perform quite satisfactorily, since heavy rains once or twice a year are enough to fill the reservoir and ensure supplies in dry periods.

The most common solution in the case of storage or diversion weirs up to 6 m high is to use an extremely compact clay membrane that runs through the middle of the gabions. In larger works, the membrane may be tarpaulin or even concrete although the latter has a tendency to crack owing to the settlement that takes place in any elastic structure. The membrane consists of a 40-cm thick layer of clay packed between two layers of tarpaulin running the entire breadth and height of the structure (Figure 69).

Groynes made of gabions can be stepped, especially at the ends, to help restore the bank's natural slope. The average slope of the stepped cross-section should facilitate flow and promote deposition. Normally, the groynes are designed so that the slope ($S = 1/2$) is the same on both sides, making a stability test unnecessary. Stability will anyway improve once the sediment has had time to consolidate the gabion structure.

The most usual arrangement is stepped in the form of a symmetrical trapezium (generally triangular) consisting of gabions with a 1×1 cross-section and resting on a platform or base of 1×0.50 transverse gabions (normally 3-4 m wider than the groyne foundation itself). However, for stability reasons the groyne axis should not coincide with the platform axis; to improve stability, a gap is normally left on each side, the downstream one being twice as wide as the upstream one (Figure 68). The proportions of the gaps can vary — indeed they may sometimes be equal — depending on a detailed analysis of flow variations in the spaces between groynes. As a general rule, the drop-down curve should always hit the platform.

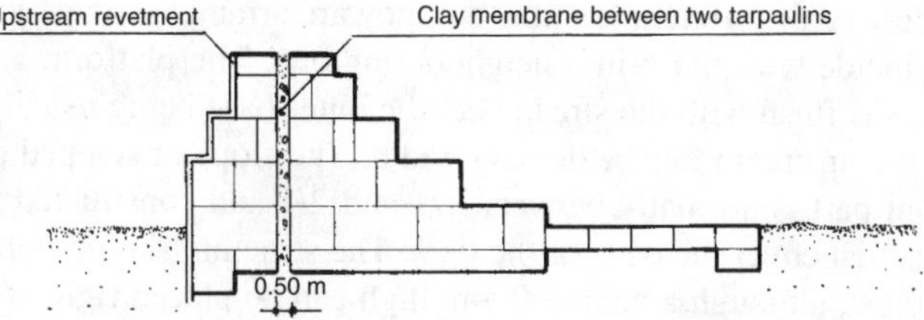

Weir with upstream revetment and impermeable central membrane for storage and diversion

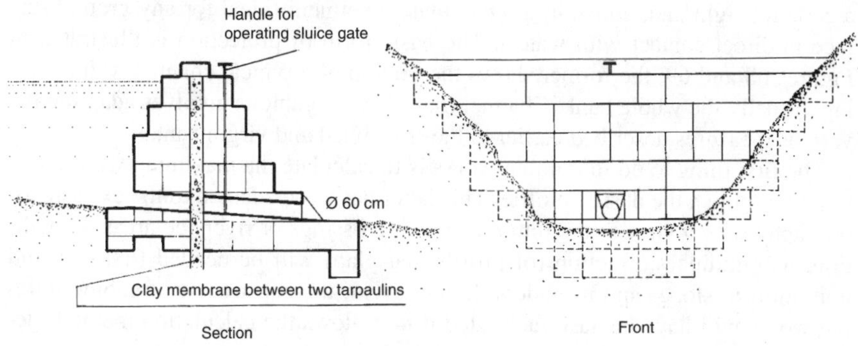

Gabion storage weir with impermeable central membrane

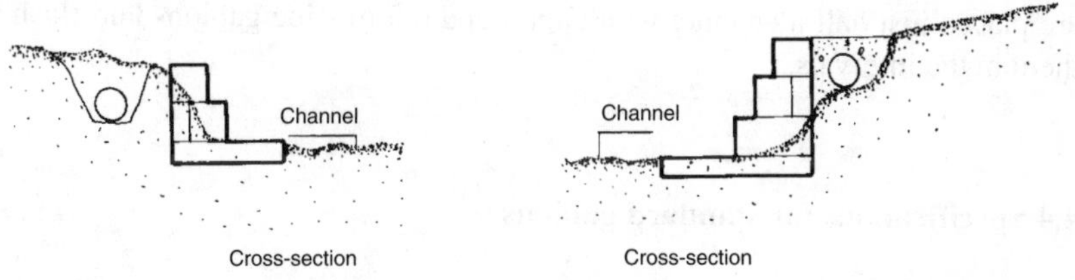

Bank pipe protection

Figure 69. Methods for improving the impermeability of gabion structures

Gabions may be of different lengths, but they are arranged so that joints in one tier never coincide with those in a neighbouring one. The platform is buried, so that its surface is flush with the streambed, the outer base being usually two-and-a-half times the upstream free settlement width. The slope or stepped profile given to the front part is normally between 1/1 and 2/1 and constructed with transverse gabions that cover the ends of the tiers. The structure should normally have a 2-m wide crest, although a gabion 0.5 m high can be placed right at the top instead. Where floods are not particularly violent, the crests of small groynes can be designed on the basis of a gabion 1 × 1 m without threatening its stability; the section is thereby reduced to a right-angled isosceles triangle.

When the platform is not thick enough to compensate for the slope of the bed and its irregularities, or when the depth of the waters prevents proper grading of the excavated site bottom, then cylindrical gabions may be used as a subfoundation to facilitate horizontal settling of the platform (Figures 69 and 70).

A more effective mixed form of bank protection is to have a gabion wall up to a certain height and, above it, a metal plate revetment (ideal for any ground surface in direct contact with water). The basic form of protection is illustrated in Figures 68 and 69; the former shows the section of a typical channel wall covering virtually the whole bank. Channel training with gabions involves adapting the various measures described earlier to the streambed and virgin banks.

The first thing to do in training works is to calculate the maximum wetted section to establish the design profile. This latter has to be adapted to the existing topography with a view to the future levels of crossings or riverside areas. In addition, longitudinal correction (of profile and plan) will be needed first to avoid non-uniform slopes and meanders. In any event, the constructor of gabion training works will have his task facilitated if he follows the calculation methods described earlier.

Composite training works for channel correction and fixing are supported by bottom sills that extend across the streambed from the lateral wall platform. These consist simply of a row of 1 × 1 gabions positioned to protrude 25 cm above the ground (Figure 71). The commonest and most straightforward system is to fix the distance between such supports at one-and-a-half times the width of the channel. This spacing may be narrowed, especially if the stream is subject to frequent heavy flooding. If bed paving or revetment is envisaged, the supports are placed just half a channel width apart and 0.5 m wide gabions laid flush with them in the intervals.

4.4 Specifications for standard gabions

1. Standard gabions (of the types and dimensions referred to below) should be strongly galvanized and have reinforced edges with mesh size and type as specified in the following paragraphs. They may be divided by cellular membranes no more than one-and-a-half times as long as the gabion is wide.

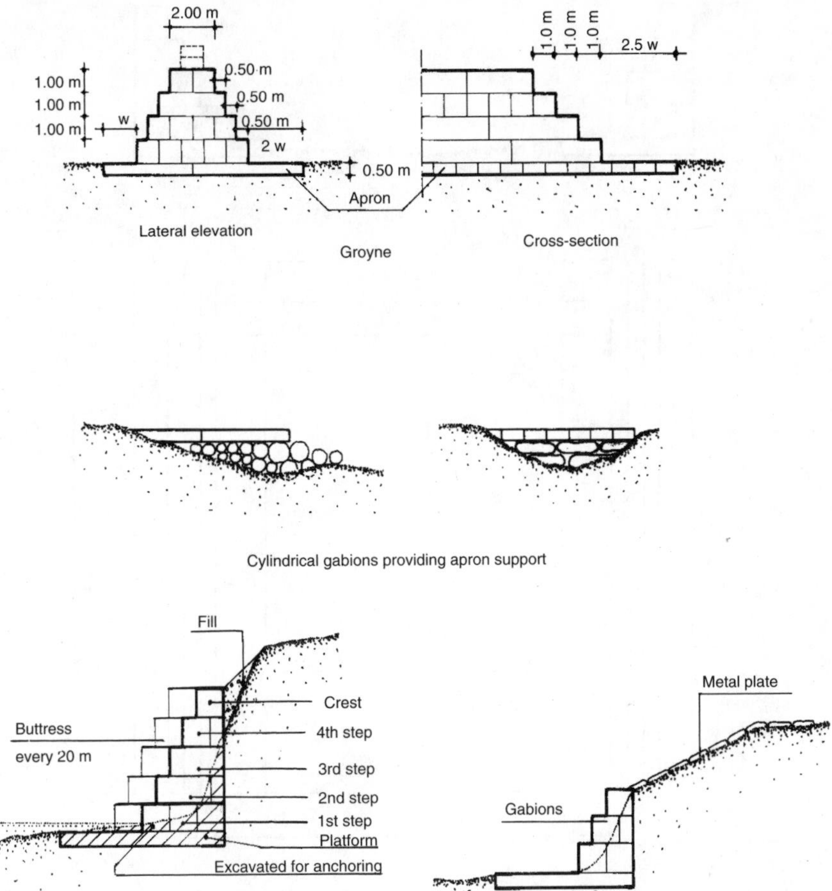

Figure 70. Bank protection with subfoundations

2. The meshes used should be hexagonal and two-ply (i.e. with two wires interlaced for three half turns, and hence sometimes described as three-ply). Mesh size should conform to the manufacturer's specifications: 10 × 12 is standard.

3. Both gabion wire and binding wire should conform to BSS 1052/1942 *mild steel wire*; alternatively, the wire should have a mean breaking load of 38-50 kg/mm^2 (prior to netting manufacture). The diameter should be 2.7 or 3.0 mm, depending on requirements.

4. A sample of the wire 30 cm long should be tested prior to making the netting. It should be capable of being stretched at least 12 percent.

5. Wire used for manufacturing or binding gabions should be galvanized in

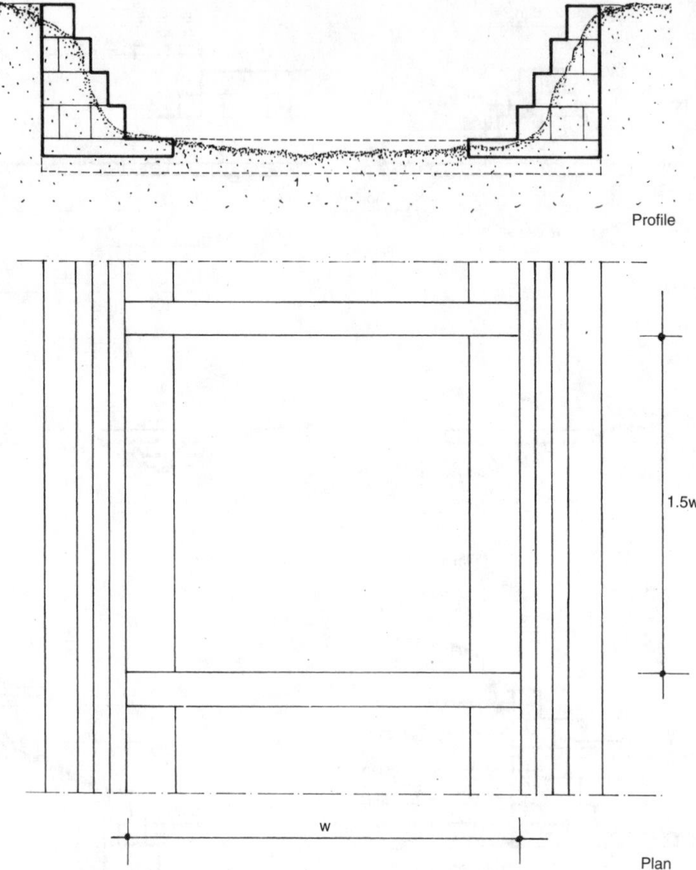

Figure 71. Channel correction with bottom sills

accordance with BSS 443/1969 *galvanized coating on wire*, i.e. the zinc quantity should not fall below the levels indicated in the table below.

Nominal diameter of wire (mm)	*Minimum weight of coating* (g/m²)
2.2	240
2.4	260
2.7	260
3.0	275
3.4	275
3.9	290

The zinc's adherence should be such that the wire can be wound six times around a cylinder four times its diameter without the coating flaking or cracking to the point that it can be scratched off.

6. All gabion edges, including lateral panels and diaphragms, should be mechanically reinforced to give them the same strength as the mesh and to prevent the netting coming apart. The diameter of the wire used to strengthen the edges should be larger than that of the netting wire itself:

- ⩾ 3.9 mm, for a 10 × 12 mesh with 3.0-mm diameter wire;
- ⩾ 3.4 mm, for a 10 × 12 mesh with 2.7-mm diameter wire.

7. Standard gabion dimensions are:

- width: 1.00 m;
- length: 2.00 m, 3.00 m or 4.00 m;
- height: 0.5 m or 1.00 m.

8. A quantity of wire will be needed at the same time as the gabions, so that all binding operations can be carried out while the structure is being built. The wire should total about 5 percent of the weight of the gabions supplied. Its diameter should be:

- 2.4 mm for gabions made of 3.0-mm diameter wire;
- 2.2 mm for gabions made of 2.7-mm diameter wire.

Binding wire with a polyvinyl chloride (PVC) coating will amount to about 8 percent of the weight of the gabions supplied. Its diameter should be 2.2 mm.

9. With PVC-coated wire, at least 0.4 mm of grey PVC is applied after galvanizing; the wire should be able to withstand natural corrosion and immersion in salt water without any alteration to its initial characteristics. These characteristics are:

- breaking load: no less than 230 kg/cm^2, in accordance with ASTM D412;
- stretching: no less than 190 percent, in accordance with ASTM D412;
- cold bend temperature: no greater than –35°C, in accordance with BSS 2782/1965, method 104 A;
- corrosion penetration: the maximum depth to which corrosion should penetrate from the end of a completely severed wire is 25 mm.

10. A margin of 2.5 percent is allowed with respect to the diameter of the wires mentioned above (BSS 1052/42); consequently, the weight of the gabion can vary by up to 5 percent. For gabions, width and height margins are 5 percent and the length margin 3 percent.

5. Small storage dams and reservoirs

Using small dams and reservoirs to store rainwater can help the recovery of areas depressed by advanced desertification. The technology was developed in zones where a sharp decline in agricultural and livestock resources had led to severe desertification. Protective action was focused on water control, the channelling of excess storm water infiltration through terraces and outlets and storage behind earth dams.

The water thus obtained has many uses: supplying rural people and their livestock; irrigating forage crops for livestock feeding during the dry season; providing relief irrigation to meadows adjacent to the basin; practising aquaculture (for both recreational and commercial purposes); and controlling runoff and sediment deposition.

The amount of water stored depends on the area's soil and weather profile, existing crops and the safety margin deemed necessary to cover possible shortages. However, there is little point in capacity exceeding the level required in a dry year; for example, for an annual irrigation module of 1 500 m^3 and an irrigated area of 40 ha, useful storage capacity will be somewhere in the region of 16 000 m^3. In calculating this figure, possible evaporation losses, seepage beneath or through the structure, or at the bottom of the storage basin itself must all be estimated; one particularly important factor is the quantity of water that is unusable either because it is inaccessible or because of sedimentation.

5.1 Siting criteria

Prior to taking any decision about a site, functional, topographical, hydrological, geological and geotechnical factors all have to be considered. The dam should be located either in the valley it is wished to irrigate or just upstream of it. When good arable land and suitable conditions for irrigation exist downstream, the choice of a site will be determined by whether there is a spring or permanent stream nearby, of whatever size, to cut the cost of irrigation channels.

Since the most expensive part of the operation is the construction of the earth dam itself, the site chosen has to maximize the upstream retention capacity. The project is reckoned to be economically feasible when the ratio of storage volume to dam volume is greater than 8. Thus a dam 8 m high and 200 m long should be able to impound more than 100 000 m^3 of water; however, this figure is counterbalanced by the higher distribution cost of large concentrations of stored water. Both aspects will therefore have to be taken into account when ascertaining the structure's optimum volume. When selecting a site, 1 : 10 000 or 1 : 20 000 maps are usually sufficient, although smaller scales (e.g. 1 : 1 000) will be needed for calculating dam and reservoir volume.

The hydrological study is based primarily on an estimate of likely water input into the basin; this is a function of runoff from rainfall and can be calculated approximately from the formula

$$V\,(\mathrm{m}^3) = 1\,000 \cdot H \cdot A \cdot R$$

in which H is the mean annual rainfall in mm, A the area of the catchment basin in km^2 and R the mean runoff coefficient (whose value varies between 0.3 and 0.5).

Another point to analyse is the effect of rises on the reservoir. After heavy rain, large quantities of material are washed down into the basin which, in extreme cases, may be filled completely. This circumstance is particularly serious for earth dams as they can be destroyed by overtopping. The dam will therefore need some form of gate at the bottom to evacuate some of the flow downstream and avoid damage to the structure. Detailed prior hydrological study will help in estimating peak floodflows as well as the discharges needed for dimensioning auxiliary works.

The geological and geotechnical study involves analysing the materials that will be active or passive components of the structure. The study of slopes and banks helps determine their stability in relation to the wing walls and streamflow. The materials lining the bottom of the reservoir should be impermeable — clays or silts are best — since seepage through materials such as sand or gravel can threaten the economic feasibility of the project. Materials for building the dam should be locally available. They are analysed in a laboratory to determine their compaction and usage characteristics; the most satisfactory tend to be clay silts or sandy clays, provided the moisture content is not too high. Generally speaking, all silts and clays are acceptable, while loose and peaty soils are not.

The earth dam's appurtenant works consist of intakes and conveyance structures leading to irrigation points; the intake is generally a metal pipe running through the dam. The undersluice takes the form of a conduit that runs through the structure at bed level and is closed by a gate located either downstream or, preferably, upstream. The spillway is made of concrete or masonry, or lined with plastic, and is built to coincide with the reservoir's normal level. The spillway requires as well an outlet channel and an energy dissipator in the form of a stilling basin, which acts as a brake on water coming from the canal at periods of high flow.

5.2 Earth structures

Dam volume is determined by knowledge of the area in conjunction with the construction provisions already referred to in Chapter 2. A summary of these provisions is provided below. The following characteristics of the structure have to be determined:

- Crest width (3-5 m).

- Crest elevation.
- Face slope (downstream 1/2, upstream 1/2.5).
- Crest treatment with 20 cm of gravel to keep the dam from drying out and bursting.
- Face protection: sodding is recommended for the upstream face, but for the downstream face it is only appropriate if little erosion has occurred; otherwise, a layer of rocks is laid on a filter bed of sand and gravel or, sometimes, textile material.
- Drainage of dam body to keep the upstream face from becoming saturated and destabilizing the structure: sand or gravel should be used as they prevent downstream seepage.
- The terrain for the foundations needs to be completely clean and excavated deeply enough to ensure firm anchorage, even for small structures 3-4 m high.
- A complete geotechnical study is not required for structures below 8 m in height.

As for compaction of the dam body, 80 percent on the standard Proctor test is quite sufficient, which yields a substantial energy saving and gives the structure the necessary flexibility. Compaction is done by pneumatic scrapers on layers no more than 0.20 m thick.

Spillways should be designed to cope with maximum floods; whenever possible, provision should be made so that when the reservoir is at capacity, water is channelled into a lateral streambed or at any rate kept at least 100 m from the toe of the dam.

If no suitable site for the dam is available but the other conditions mentioned above are present, a form of sunken reservoir may be constructed instead. In a wide, centrally drained valley a circular basin is excavated with 1/2 slopes (i.e. not too steep for tractors). The water entry area is protected by plastic skirting so that the outlet does not become blocked. The disadvantage of this type of basin is that it costs more and holds less than a dam.

Maintenance work should begin once construction is completed to prevent cracking caused by desiccation when the dam is empty as well as the seepage, compaction and sliding that occur as soon as the reservoir starts filling up. Quick action is needed or the whole structure will be threatened.

5.3 Techniques for use of dams and construction of multipurpose reservoirs

5.3.1 Land preparation

The first step is to find a suitable site. It should be free of rocks (unless they can be broken up) down to an acceptable level and have a slope not exceeding 25 percent (the exception being where the present or future qualities of the soil are such that plots can all be put to the same use).

Eliminating natural non-shrubby vegetation may, if it is particularly thick, require the use of a brush-beater or, where the ground is very uneven or there are largish trunks, a mechanical digger. If there is no surface rock formation (or if it is extremely weathered), this vegetation can be taken out by ploughing. For the latter operation, a heavy harrow with twelve 32-inch discs is used; it is highly efficient at slashing stems and roots and thus preventing subsequent regrowth.

If the rock has to be broken up prior to ploughing, a subsoiler is used to a depth of 40 cm, and caterpillar tractors of at least 100 hp are required. The work will have to be carried out again a year later to ensure that all plant residues and regrowth have been eliminated. Frequently, however, a cereal crop is sown straight away, following a few passes with a light harrow and application of a phosphate fertilizer. Whatever method is used, terraces still have to be built, during or after ploughing, wherever the slope requires it; this step stabilizes soil which would otherwise be quickly washed away by rain.

When establishing pasture, the distance given by Saccardy's formula ($H^3 = 2.60\ P$) for spacing between terraces should be increased by 20-50 percent, depending on the zone's maximum expected daily rainfall.

On undulating ground with slopes not exceeding 10-12 percent, erosion may not be the only problem; clay soils, for instance, can become waterlogged. In such cases, terraces should not be constructed horizontally but with a gradient of around 0.2 for channelling away any surplus water.

5.3.2 Water control

Terracing is the first and the most important phase in water control since it keeps runoff from forming rills and gullies, and either increases infiltration (contour terraces) or assists drainage (sloping terraces). Terraces help evacuate surplus water following heavy rainfall by collecting it in specially constructed channels. Without a complete drainage network, the operation cannot be a success.

In flat terraces, water flows from end to end. As in horizontal channels, the water-level rises at the end opposite to the point of entry; to prevent damage from overtopping, the distance between outlets should therefore not exceed 400 m. Since water tends to concentrate in the channels, action may be necessary to prevent gullying unless, of course, the flow runs over bedrock. Protection takes the form of a stepped series of small drystone dams to absorb water energy and encourage deposition of the coarser elements as the first stage in sorting.

From the point of view of conservation, it is better and more economical for water to be used near the place in which it falls. Consequently, water which cannot be taken up by plants and which is channelled away by terraces and drainage outlets should be put to use in the farm itself, particularly if there is a likelihood of severe water shortage for much of the year.

The size of the reservoir catchment can be increased by having the terraces capture water and channel it into the reservoir, thus making the most of storage capacity and helping establish grazing areas.

5.3.3 Establishment and exploitation of pasture

After first sowing a cereal, a dressing of P_2O_5 is applied and worked in with a light harrow, articulated so that it follows the land. Grass seed is then broadcast and covered over with a smoothing harrow. The only action needed in subsequent years is to apply fertilizer — usually granulated lime superphosphate — to ensure even distribution. If the annual rate is less than 200 kg/ha it is better to cut down on costs and apply a double dose every other year.

In the third year, some scrub regrowth may be noted. If it is densely concentrated in particular zones, it may be best to resow. More scattered regrowth, however, is best dealt with by manual pulling; this job should not require the work of more than one person per day per hectare, and considerably less the following year if it has to be repeated.

Grass is usually left for grazing. When there is a surplus, it may occasionally be harvested for hay or silage.

Since growth can be checked by spring droughts, fresh grass should be sown each year to ensure a supply of early forage. It should be sown in places where reseeding has not already taken place, where scrub regrowth has occurred or where the quality of the grass is poor.

Grazing should not be allowed until the ground is dry enough for vegetation to withstand trampling. In wet weather, the animals should be confined to an area near the farm buildings, which is supplied with hay and water and large enough for them to move about freely (40-50 ha for every one thousand).

Paths and fencing are important for the smooth operation of the farm, and special care should be taken in laying them out. Ideally, all plots should be linked, without being interrupted by paths; however, this would involve fencing the paths on both sides — a costly operation in terms of manpower.

If it is too expensive to build the whole fencing network at once, it is better to plan to spread the work over several years. A main path, which can be extended later, should be laid out in such a way that it links as many plots as possible to the grazing area and the farm installations.

Grazing areas vary in size from 25 ha for the best land, to 80-100 ha for poorer land or unimproved land with little exploitable value.

5.3.4 Use of stored water

Stored water has a variety of uses: direct consumption by livestock or humans or indirect consumption for irrigation and aquaculture.

Direct use of water. One of the constraints facing people who keep livestock is water shortage and rural supply difficulties. Reservoirs solve this problem since their storage potential far exceeds requirements. They should be fenced to keep out livestock. Water can be extracted in several ways, the most usual one being for the dam to have a 2-inch pipe running through it about 50 cm from the base; the part of the tube inside the reservoir is elbowed and blocked at the end so that the water can only penetrate through small holes or grooves made in the end section. The end section is threaded so that unperforated extension pieces may be fitted as the basin silts up. At the outlet, a coupling connects to a 1-inch pipe leading to the watering troughs, whose level is controlled by a ball-cock. The end of the pipe has a stop that can be removed during cleaning to let the pressurized water expel any sediment. Reclosing the pipe is easier with a stop-valve.

When the water is for human consumption or for supplying watering troughs some distance away from the basin, the pipe is connected to a pump operated by the power take-off of a tractor. The water is pumped along 2-inch polyethylene pipes, often for a kilometre or more. If the water is for human use, the pipes terminate at a reservoir; if for livestock, at a raised location from which it is fed by gravity to the watering troughs.

Irrigation. The advantage of having suitable land downstream for irrigation has already been mentioned above. An annual forage supply equilibrium can only be achieved in zones where harvesting provides enough silage or hay to tide livestock over dry periods. Experience shows that 12-15 percent of total farm area, consisting of the best land, needs to be given over to this end. However, if irrigation is at all possible, even where soil quality is not so high, 8-10 percent of the area may be enough to cover normal deficits. With exceptional deficits, it is cheaper to purchase the fodder than to overburden installations that would not normally be exploited to the full.

Sprinkling is the most common system, carried out by using power pumps coupled to a tractor and fully mobile piping that can sometimes be used for more than one basin. Equipment should be suitable not only for normal irrigation of the area concerned but also elsewhere (for example, supplementary irrigation to ensure successful sowing, or winter irrigation to improve cereal harvests). In short, the aim should be maximum flexibility to be able to effectuate whatever action required in those years when monthly rainfall falls below the norm.

Water for irrigation is usually drawn directly from the basin to take full advantage of the head. During dry periods, the area within 500 m of the basin may still be irrigated, although with some difficulty, using a hand-held pipe.

Aquaculture. This complementary activity ideally requires a relatively constant water level in the reservoir and is perfectly compatible with other uses.

The species chosen need to be able to adapt to the low oxygen level in the water, to variations in temperature (depending on atmospheric conditions at various altitudes) and to the periodic disturbances caused by storms. Usually, they are phytophagous or omnivorous and can be farmed either intensively or extensively.

Cyprinids, Cyclids and Tetraquids are the families most commonly used for exploitation either on a recreational or a commercial basis. In the latter case, substantial yields of both adults and fry may be obtained. Recreational fishing calls for a certain amount of landscaping, involving reforestation of the area immediately bordering the reservoir.

5.3.5 Sealing of sunken basins

In the section on earth structures, reference was made to sunken basins used in irrigation and water supply. As they are usually of limited capacity, more control has to be exercised over seepage losses than in larger dam reservoirs. However, since sealing can double or even triple the cost of small storage basins, the economic aspect needs to be carefully studied.

Sealing generally involves coating the surface, bottom and slopes with butyl rubber, polyvinylchloride (PVC), polyethylene or, less commonly, propyethylene rubber (PER). If clay is plentiful locally, a clay revetment can be used instead, but it usually requires more hours of labour and greater care. Butyl rubber is more expensive than PVC or polyethylene, but it does not need to be covered with soil to protect it from the elements. Although these revetments are all chemically inert and the water can safely be used for irrigation or human consumption, they can be damaged by petrochemicals.

The soil should be sterilized to keep plant growth from damaging the revetment and giving rise to seepage losses. The revetment consists of sheets that are positioned in such a way as to keep the number of joins to a minimum — particularly horizontal joins at water-level. The outer edge of the revetment is anchored inside a 30 × 30 cm trench dug along the crest of the embankment.

Butyl rubber revetment. The sheets used come in three thicknesses: 0.75 mm, 1 mm and 1.5 mm (0.75 mm being the most common). Width varies between 1.40 and 1.75 m according to thickness. Size is limited by considerations of weight and manoevrability — a 30 × 30 m sheet weighs 1 000 kg. The sheets are joined either with adhesive or by using portable vulcanizing equipment. Rocky soils are usually covered with sand prior to laying the sheets. The soil should also be sterilized to prevent plant growth.

PVC revetment. PVC is a hard thermoplastic polymer given greater flexibility during manufacture. It is an effective revetment although prolonged exposure can cause the plasticizer to deteriorate, so that after ten years it may be fragile and liable to break. Its life can be extended by covering the slope with a 30 cm layer of soil and ensuring the bottom is always covered by at least 30 cm of water.

To preserve the stability of the earth layer, slopes should not be much steeper than 1/3. The earth layer may sometimes be reinforced by covering it with synthetic fibre or pebbles. PVC sheets are normally 0.35 mm thick and joined together by heat-welding or with solvent adhesive. In the factory, radio frequency thermic welding is used to produce 1 000 kg prefabricated sheets. The use of PVC is, however, limited by the fact that it becomes harder and less flexible when the temperature drops to freezing point.

Polyethylene revetment. Polyethylene is a flexible thermoplastic polymer which, for revetment purposes, is manufactured in black sheets 7.5 m wide, 20 m long and 0.38 mm thick. Although it deteriorates more slowly under the effects of exposure than PVC, on slopes it too is usually covered over with earth. On stony ground, a layer of sand or synthetic fibre is applied first. Sheets are joined on the spot by means of beading between the overlapping edges and a pressure-sensitive adhesive strip.

Propyethylene rubber (PER). This substance was introduced fairly recently and is still not widely used. It has similar physical properties to butyl rubber, but is better suited to tropical climates and more resistant to exposure. Although it now costs more than butyl rubber, the price would probably fall if it were used on a large scale.

6. Concluding remarks

Over the ages, people's attitude to natural resources has changed. In the past, the emphasis was on satisfying immediate subsistence requirements and involved comparatively little interference with the environment. Today the pattern is quite different: the environment is under intense pressure, and resources are shrinking and poorly controlled. Resources, therefore, should be rationally utilized for optimal exploitation and protected from irreversible damage through indiscriminate use.

Implicitly or explicitly, resource management has been a theme of a number of international conferences over the last decade. Among the resolutions of the Stockholm Conference's "Plan of Action for the Human Environment" (1972) was one pertaining to the management of agriculture in relation to the water regime. Mountain watershed management was advocated by the Council of Europe first in its resolution on alpine areas (1975) and then in its Ecological Charter (1976). The United Nations Water Conference (Mar del Plata, 1977) included among its recommendations the need to "give attention to problems of soil and water conservation through good management of watershed areas, which includes rational crop distribution, pasture improvement, reforestation, torrent and avalanche control as well as the introduction of appropriate agricultural soil conservation practices, taking into account the economic and social conditions existing in the respective watershed areas".

Finally, the United Nations Conference on Desertification (Nairobi, 1977) declared that watersheds should be viewed "as working units for the purpose of soil conservation and water exploitation, these being factors in the integrated development of these units; comprehensive measures should be adopted to promote the conservation, improvement and rational use of soils with a view to preventing and controlling desertification".

There is, therefore, at least theoretically, a clear perception of the need for rational use of natural resources — water, soil and vegetation — within the physical framework defined by watersheds. In short, natural resources are now seen as a complex, interdisciplinary system that depends on the hydrological cycle and is territorially defined by the watershed and affected by any changes in it.

Today, the relationship between people and this complex natural resource system has worldwide relevance, and environmental studies of water, soil and vegetation now take into account the impact of human intervention. The importance of this relationship is even greater in countries with fragile ecosystems, damage to them being less easy to repair.

The torrential phenomena that occur in favourable climatic conditions and cause water erosion, sedimentation and flooding can have catastrophic consequences. Unfortunately, when constructing engineering works, dams and training walls it is often overlooked that the root of the problem lies chiefly in deforestation and the lack of rational crop management in the watershed.

Since the objectives of management are soil conservation, flood control and water supply, the influence of natural ecosystems on the economy and quality of soils and waters assumes particular importance. Wooded areas, for example, are of great strategic value in watersheds, as they are situated in the upper and middle reaches where rain and snow are heavier and the terrain more rugged. Here, the role of the most developed of such systems — forests — needs to be stressed.

Studies show that forests create a microclimate of their own, modifying sunlight and radiation, air and soil temperatures, wind speeds and atmospheric moisture. This aspect has beneficial consequences for the hydrologic cycle and gives forests a crucial place in the water economy. The role of forests in the water cycle basically arises from their ability to control surface runoff, as soils in forest ecosystems have a much greater capacity for water infiltration, retention and storage. Furthermore, the water balance differs from that in open or shrubby areas owing to the substantial extra inputs into the system from increased condensation (dew, frost and hidden precipitation) and moisture from mist and fog (Suering's horizontal precipitation).

In addition, forest cover eliminates soil erosion so that most surface runoff ends up as percolation water, resulting in the virtual disappearance of sediment from channels draining forested areas. This action prolongs the useful life of the reservoirs in which all this clean water is impounded. Forest ecosystems also have the advantage of introducing fewer nutrients, such as nitrogen and phosphorus, into the waters they drain. This greatly improves water quality, not only preventing eutrophication of reservoirs, but also averting the risks associated with excess nitrates in drinking water — always a problem for water treatment plants.

These factors all serve to explain the importance of hydroforestry restoration works in agrohydrological watershed management, especially in highly torrential basins.

As a sectoral response to the challenge of torrentiality, hydroforestry covers biological activities, such as afforestation and the introduction or improvement of other forms of plant cover, as well as engineering works for torrent or avalanche control and bank protection. Although these two aspects, the biological and the engineering, should complement each other, afforestation takes pride of place.

Afforestation of torrential watersheds is a way of assisting nature by reversing degradation and speeding up the development of a true forest ecosystem, the stage at which vegetation is most capable of controlling these phenomena. However, total effectiveness depends on maximizing biological potential at all levels — from water retentive mosses to tall trees whose crowns intercept the rain and whose roots reach deep into the soil, fixing it and facilitating infiltration. This range can be achieved by introducing into the shrub layer indigenous species corresponding to the actual site clan, at least at the subclimatic level, and by attempting to promote the establishment of climax species with a view to encouraging growth at the higher plant levels. Mixed or irregular formations that contain both shrub and grass layers gradually developing toward the climax constitute the ultimate aim of afforestation works in torrential basins.

As for hydraulic engineering works, the whole purpose of channel correction in torrential reaches is to reduce, eliminate or control sediment transport and bed/bank erosion, and to prevent sediment, whatever its source, from entering the channel; torrentiality and its effects are closely linked to the volume of bedload discharge.

Reaching this goal involves taking appropriate steps to prevent sediment discharge from occurring or, if it has occurred already, to reduce it to a minimum if not eliminate it.

Transverse dikes are the most effective and economical way of achieving these objectives as well as of stabilizing banks and protecting them from erosion. Longitudinal structures are another way of controlling torrential damage to channels, their purpose being the elimination of sediment transport. They complement transverse structures in the sense that while the latter are designed to control bed erosion, the role of the former is restricted to preventing bank erosion and flooding. The action of longitudinal structures is passive and protective; transverse structures, on the other hand, act directly on the torrential process.

This is not to say that longitudinal works do nothing to reduce torrentiality; after all, by helping to consolidate or strengthen unstable banks or the foot of erodible slopes, they undoubtedly remove one source of sediment from the stream. However, they are best kept for solving specific localized problems caused by or contributing to torrentiality. They are quite unsuitable for use as a primary torrent control technique.

Moreover, the capacity of these protective works to protect the bank zone and its infrastructure from flooding for any length of time is totally dependent on the existence of watershed and upstream torrential control works designed to drastically reduce high flows and sediment discharge.

Bibliography

Aguilo Bonin. 1977. Agua y agricultura de secano. In *Proc. United Nations Water Conference*, Mar del Plata, Argentina, 14-25 March.

Associazione Italiana di Idronomia; Instituto Italo-Latinoamericano. 1983. *Manual para el diseño de diques de corrección de torrentes.* Rome, IILA.

Bureau of Reclamation. 1973. *Design of small dams.* United States Department of the Interior, Washington DC, United States Government Printing Office.

Calabri, G. 1970. *Note on the prototype dam made of prefabricated metallic elements experimented by the State Forest Administration in Italy.* In *Report of 9th session of the Working Party on Torrent Control, Protection from Avalanches and Watershed Management, FAO European Forestry Commission,* Munich, 1-3 June. Rome, FAO.

FAO. 1981. *Torrent control terminology.* FAO Conservation Guide, No. 6, Rome.

Fattorelli, S. 1972. *Criteri per il calcolo di progetto delle briglie in conglomerato cementizio.* In *Opere per la correzione dei torrenti. Moderne tecniche costruttive e nuovi procedimenti di calcolo.* Ministero dell'Agricoltura e delle Foreste, Direzione Generale per l'Economia Montana e per le Foreste, Collana verde, No. 29, Rome.

García Nájera, J.M. 1962. *Principios de hidráulica torrencial. Su aplicación e la corrección de torrentes.* Ministerio de Agricultura, Dirección General de Montes, Caza y Pesca Fluvial; Instituto Forestal de Investigaciones y Experiencias, Madrid.

Gilmour, D.A. 1877. Logging and the environment, with particular reference to soil and stream protection in tropical rainforest situations. In *Guidelines for watershed management.* FAO Conservation Guide, No. 1, Rome, FAO.

Giudici, P. 1969. *Briglie per la correzione dei torrenti.* Accademia Italiana di Scienza Forestali, Florence.

Hattinger, H. 1976. Torrent control in the mountains with reference to the tropics. In *Hydrological techniques for upstream conservation.* FAO Conservation Guide, No. 2, Rome, FAO.

Hattinger, H. 1979. Protective constructions for forest roads in endangered areas. In *Mountain forest roads and harvesting. Technical report of 2nd FAO/Austria Training Course on Forest Roads and Harvesting in Mountainous Forests,* Ort and Ossiach, Austria, 2 June to 2 July 1978. FAO Forestry Paper, No. 14, Rome, FAO.

Hattinger, H. 1985. Case studies of wooden and concrete check-dams in connexion with forest roads. In *Logging and transport in steep terrain.* Report of 4th FAO/Austria Training Course on Mountain Forest Roads and Harvesting in Mountainous Forests, Ossiach and Ort, Austria, 30 May to 26 June 1983. FAO Forestry Paper No. 14, Rev. 1, Rome, FAO.

Hofmann, F. 1973. *Mitteilungen der Forstlichen Bundes-Versuchsanstalt Wien,* No. 12. Colloquium on Torrent Dams, Vienna.

Hughes, A.B. 1977. Waterproofing of earth irrigation reservoirs in England and Wales. In *Proc. European Regional Conference, International Commission on Irrigation and Drainage,* Rome, 10-12 May. ICID.

Jedlitschka, M. 1982. Torrent engineering works for the protection of mountain forest roads in the region "Salzkammergut", Austria. In *Logging of mountain forests. Report of 3rd FAO/Austria Training Course on Mountain Forest Roads and Harvesting in Mountainous Forests,* Ossiach and Ort, Austria, 1-28 June 1981. FAO Forestry Paper, No. 8, Rome, FAO.

Keller, H. 1970. Torrent control in the Alps. In *Proc. Joint FAO/USSR International Symposium on Forest Influences and Watershed Management,* Moscow, 17 August to 6 September. Rome, FAO.

Kronfellner-Kraus, G., Swanston, D.N., Stefanovic, P., Rula, B., Midriak, R., Tavsanoglu, F., Moser, M., Hoffmann, L., Lied, K., Gand, H.R. in der, Aulitzky, H., Fiebiger, G. & Laatsch, W. 1978. *Mitteilungen der Forstlichen Bundes-Versuchsanstalt Wien,* No. 125. XVI World Congress of IUFRO, Vienna.

López Cadenas de Llano, F. 1965. *Diques par la corrección de corsos torrenciales y métodos de cálculo.* Ministerio de Agricultura, Dirección General de Montes, Caza y Pesca Fluvial; Instituto Forestal de Investigaciones y Experiencias, Madrid.

Muntean, S.A. 1970. Contributions to the problem of underdimensioned gravity dams. In *Report of 9th session of the Working Party on Torrent Control, Protection from Avalanches and Watershed Management, FAO European Forestry Commission,* Munich, 1-3 June. Rome, FAO.

Quesnel, B. 1963. Traité d'hydraulique fluviale appliquée. Vol. I. *Travaux d'aménagement du lit de pleines rives et du lit majeur.* Paris, ED. Eyrolles.

Riedl, O. & Zachar, D. 1984. *Forest amelioration.* Amsterdam, Elsevier.

Rula. B., Stefanovic, P., Midriak, R. & Gand, H.R. in der. 1976. *Mitteilungen der Forstlichen Bundes-Versuchsanstalt Wien,* No. 115. Research on torrent erosion and avalanches, Vienna.

Weber, A. 1958. Static considerations on dam-building. In *Report of 4th session of the Working Party on Torrent Control, Protection from Avalanches and Watershed Management, FAO European Forestry Commission,* Austria, 9-20 September. Rome, FAO.

WHERE TO PURCHASE FAO PUBLICATIONS LOCALLY
POINTS DE VENTE DES PUBLICATIONS DE LA FAO
PUNTOS DE VENTA DE PUBLICACIONES DE LA FAO

25/1/93

• ***ANGOLA***
Empresa Nacional do Disco e de Publicações, ENDIPU-U.E.E.
Rua Cirilo da Conceição Silva, No. 7
C.P. No. 1314-C
Luanda

• ***ARGENTINA***
Librería Agropecuaria
Pasteur 743
1028 Capital Federal

• ***AUSTRALIA***
Hunter Publications
P.O. Box 404
Abbotsford, Vic. 3067

• ***AUSTRIA***
Gerold Buch & Co.
Weihburggasse 26
1010 Vienna

• ***BAHRAIN***
United Schools International
P.O. Box 726
Manama

• ***BANGLADESH***
Association of Development Agencies in Bangladesh
House No. 1/3, Block F, Lalmatia
Dhaka 1207

• ***BELGIQUE***
M.J. De Lannoy
202, avenue du Roi
1060 Bruxelles
CCP 000-0808993-13

• ***BOLIVIA***
Los Amigos del Libro
Perú 3712, Casilla 450, Cochabamba
Mercado 1315, La Paz

• ***BOTSWANA***
Botsalo Books (Pty) Ltd
P.O. Box 1532
Gaborone

• ***BRAZIL***
Fundação Getúlio Vargas
Praia do Botafogo 190, C.P. 9052
Rio de Janeiro

CANADA (See North America)

• ***CHILE***
Librería - Oficina Regional FAO
Avda. Santa María 6700
Casilla 10095, Santiago
Tel. 218 53 23
Fax 218 25 47

• ***CHINA***
China National Publications Import & Export Corporation
P.O. Box 88
100704 Beijing

• ***COLOMBIA***
Banco Ganadero, Revista Carta Ganadera
Carrera 9ª Nº 72-21, Piso 5
Bogotá D.E.
Tel. 217 0100

• ***CONGO***
Office national des librairies populaires
B.P. 577
Brazzaville

• ***COSTA RICA***
Librería, Imprenta y Litografía Lehmann S.A.
Apartado 10011
San José

• ***CUBA***
Ediciones Cubanas, Empresa de Comercio Exterior de Publicaciones
Obispo 461, Apartado 605
La Habana

• ***CYPRUS***
MAM
P.O. Box 1722
Nicosia

• ***CZECH REPUBLIC***
Artia
Ve Smeckach 30, P.O. Box 790
11127 Prague 1

• ***DENMARK***
Munksgaard, Book and Subscription Service
P.O. Box 2148
DK 1016 Copenhagen K.
Tel. 4533128570
Fax 4533129387

• ***ECUADOR***
Libri Mundi, Librería Internacional
Juan León Mera 851,
Apartado Postal 3029
Quito

• ***ESPAÑA***
Mundi Prensa Libros S.A.
Castelló 37
28001 Madrid
Tel. 431 3399
Fax 575 3998
Librería Agrícola
Fernando VI 2
28004 Madrid
Librería Internacional AEDOS
Consejo de Ciento 391
08009 Barcelona
Tel. 301 8615
Fax 317 0141
Llibreria de la Generalitat de Catalunya
Rambla dels Estudis, 118
(Palau Moja)
08002 Barcelona
Tel. (93)302 6462
Fax 302 1299

• ***FINLAND***
Akateeminen Kirjakauppa
P.O. Box 218
SF-00381 Helsinki

• ***FRANCE***
La Maison Rustique
Flammarion 4
26, rue Jacob
75006 Paris
Librairie de l'UNESCO
7, place de Fontenoy
75700 Paris
Editions A. Pedone
13, rue Soufflot
75005 Paris

• ***GERMANY***
Alexander Horn Internationale Buchhandlung
Kirchgasse 22, Postfach 3340
D-6200 Wiesbaden
Uno Verlag
Poppelsdorfer Allee 55
D-5300 Bonn 1
S. Toeche-Mittler GmbH
Versandbuchhandlung
Hindenburgstrasse 33
D-6100 Darmstadt

• ***GREECE***
G.C. Eleftheroudakis S.A.
4 Nikis Street
10563 Athens
John Mihalopoulos & Son S.A.
75 Hermou Street, P.O. Box 10073
54110 Thessaloniki

• ***GUYANA***
Guyana National Trading Corporation Ltd
45-47 Water Street, P.O. Box 308
Georgetown

• ***HAÏTI***
Librairie "A la Caravelle"
26, rue Bonne Foi, B.P. 111
Port-au-Prince

• ***HONDURAS***
Escuela Agrícola Panamericana, Librería RTAC
Zamorano, Apartado 93
Tegucigalpa
Oficina de la Escuela Agrícola Panamericana en Tegucigalpa
Blvd. Morazán, Apts. Glapson - Apartado 93
Tegucigalpa

• ***HONG KONG***
Swindon Book Co.
13-15 Lock Road
Kowloon

• ***HUNGARY***
Kultura
P.O. Box 149
H-1389 Budapest 62

• ***ICELAND***
Snaebjörn Jónsson and Co. h.f.
Hafnarstraeti 9, P.O. Box 1131
101 Reykjavik

• ***INDIA***
Oxford Book and Stationery Co.
Scindia House, New Delhi 110 001;
17 Park Street, Calcutta 700 016
Oxford Subscription Agency, Institute for Development Education
1 Anasuya Ave., Kilpauk
Madras 600 010

• ***IRELAND***
Publications Section, Stationery Office
4-5 Harcourt Road
Dublin 2

• ***ITALY***
FAO (See last column)
Libreria Scientifica Dott. Lucio de Biasio "Aeiou"
Via Coronelli 6
20146 Milano
Libreria Concessionaria Sansoni S.p.A. "Licosa"
Via Duca di Calabria 1/1
50125 Firenze
Libreria Internazionale Rizzoli
Galleria Colonna, Largo Chigi
00187 Roma

• ***JAPAN***
Maruzen Company Ltd
P.O. Box 5050
Tokyo International 100-31

• ***KENYA***
Text Book Centre Ltd
Kijabe Street, P.O. Box 47540
Nairobi

• ***KOREA, REP. OF***
Eulyoo Publishing Co. Ltd
46-1 Susong-Dong, Jongro-Gu
P.O. Box 362, Kwangwha-Mun
Seoul 110

• ***KUWAIT***
The Kuwait Bookshops Co. Ltd
P.O. Box 2942
Safat

• ***LUXEMBOURG***
M.J. De Lannoy
202, avenue du Roi
1060 Bruxelles (Belgique)

WHERE TO PURCHASE FAO PUBLICATIONS LOCALLY
POINTS DE VENTE DES PUBLICATIONS DE LA FAO
PUNTOS DE VENTA DE PUBLICACIONES DE LA FAO

• ***MAROC***
Librairie "Aux Belles Images"
281, avenue Mohammed V
Rabat

• ***MEXICO***
Librería, Universidad Autónoma de Chapingo
56230 Chapingo
Libros y Editoriales S.A.
Av. Progreso N° 202-1° Piso A
Apdo Postal 18922 Col. Escandón
11800 México D.F.
Only machine readable products:
Grupo Qualita
Kansas N° 38 Colonia Nápoles
03810 México D.F.
Tel. 682-3333

• ***NETHERLANDS***
Roodveldt Import B.V.
Browersgracht 288
1013 HG Amsterdam
SDU Publishers Plantijnstraat
Christoffel Plantijnstraat 2
P.O. Box 20014
2500 EA The Hague

• ***NEW ZEALAND***
Legislation Services
P.O. Box 12418
Thorndon, Wellington

• ***NICARAGUA***
Librería Universitaria, Universidad Centroamericana
Apartado 69
Managua

• ***NIGERIA***
University Bookshop (Nigeria) Ltd
University of Ibadan
Ibadan

• ***NORTH AMERICA***
Publications:
UNIPUB
4611/F, Assembly Drive
Lanham MD 20706-4391, USA
Toll-free 800 233-0504 (Canada)
800 274-4888 (USA)
Fax 301-459-0056
Periodicals:
Ebsco Subscription Services
P.O. Box 1431
Birmingham AL 35201-1431, USA
Tel. (205) 991-6600
Telex 78-2661
Fax (205) 991-1449
The Faxon Company Inc.
15 Southwest Park
Westwood MA 02090, USA
Tel. 6117-329-3350
Telex 95-1980
Cable F W Faxon Wood

• ***NORWAY***
Narvesen Info Center
Bertrand Narvesens vei 2
P.O. Box 6125, Etterstad
0602 Oslo 6

• ***PAKISTAN***
Mirza Book Agency
65 Shahrah-e-Quaid-e-Azam
P.O. Box 729, Lahore 3
Sasi Book Store
Zaibunnisa Street
Karachi

• ***PARAGUAY***
Mayer's Internacional - Publicaciones Técnicas
Gral. Diaz 629 c/15 de Agosto
Casilla de Correo Nº 1416
Asunción - Tel. 448 246

• ***PERU***
Librería Distribuidora "Santa Rosa"
Jirón Apurimac 375, Casilla 4937
Lima 1

• ***PHILIPPINES***
International Book Center (Phils)
Room 1703, Cityland 10
Condominium Cor. Ayala Avenue & H.V. dela Costa Extension
Makati, M.M.

• ***POLAND***
Ars Polona
Krakowskie Przedmiescie 7
00-950 Warsaw

• ***PORTUGAL***
Livraria Portugal, Dias e Andrade Ltda.
Rua do Carmo 70-74, Apartado 2681
1117 Lisboa Codex

• ***ROMANIA***
Ilexim
Calea Grivitei No 64066
Bucharest

• ***SAUDI ARABIA***
The Modern Commercial University Bookshop
P.O. Box 394
Riyadh

• ***SINGAPORE***
Select Books Pte Ltd
03-15 Tanglin Shopping Centre
19 Tanglin Road
Singapore 1024

SLOVENIA
Cankarjeva Zalozba
P.O. Box 201-IV
61001 Ljubljana

• ***SOMALIA***
"Samater's"
P.O. Box 936
Mogadishu

• ***SRI LANKA***
M.D. Gunasena & Co. Ltd
217 Olcott Mawatha, P.O. Box 246
Colombo 11

• ***SUISSE***
Librairie Payot S.A.
107 Freiestrasse, 4000 Basel 10
6, rue Grenus, 1200 Genève
Case Postale 3212, 1002 Lausanne
Buchhandlung und Antiquariat Heinimann & Co.
Kirchgasse 17
8001 Zurich
UN Bookshop
Palais des Nations
CH-1211 Genève 1
Van Diermen Editions Techniques
ADECO
Case Postale 465
CH-1211 Genève 19

• ***SURINAME***
Vaco n.v. in Suriname
Domineestraat 26, P.O. Box 1841
Paramaribo

• ***SWEDEN***
Books and documents:
C.E. Fritzes
P.O. Box 16356
103 27 Stockholm
Subscriptions:
Vennergren-Williams AB
P.O. Box 30004
104 25 Stockholm

• ***THAILAND***
Suksapan Panit
Mansion 9, Rajdamnern Avenue
Bangkok

• ***TOGO***
Librairie du Bon Pasteur
B.P. 1164
Lomé

• ***TUNISIE***
Société tunisienne de diffusion
5, avenue de Carthage
Tunis

• ***TURKEY***
Kultur Yayiniari is - Turk Ltd Sti.
Ataturk Bulvari No. 191, Kat. 21
Ankara
Bookshops in Istambul and Izmir

• ***UNITED KINGDOM***
HMSO Publications Centre
51 Nine Elms Lane
London SW8 5DR
Tel. (071) 873 9090 (orders)
(071) 873 0011 (inquiries)
Fax (071) 873 8463
HMSO Bookshops:
49 High Holborn, London WC1V 6HB
Tel. (071) 873 0011
258 Broad Street
Birmingham B1 2HE
Tel. (021) 643 3740
Southey House, 33 Wine Street
Bristol BS1 2BQ
Tel. (0272) 264306
9-21 Princess Street
Manchester M60 8AS
Tel. (061) 834 7201
80 Chichester Street
Belfast BT1 4JY
Tel. (0232) 238451
71 Lothian Road
Edinburgh EH3 9AZ
Tel. (031) 228 4181
Only machine readable products:
Microinfo Limited
P.O. Box 3, Omega Road, Alton, Hampshire GU342PG
Tel. (0420) 86848
Fax (0420) 89889

• ***URUGUAY***
Librería Agropecuaria S.R.L.
Buenos Aires 335
Casilla 1755
Montevideo C.P. 11000

• ***USA (See North America)***

• ***VENEZUELA***
Tecni-Ciencia Libros S.A.
Torre Phelps-Mezzanina, Plaza Venezuela
Caracas
Tel. 782 8697-781 9945-781 9954
Tamanaco Libros Técnicos S.R.L.
Centro Comercial Ciudad Tamanaco, Nivel C-2
Caracas
Tel. 261 3344-261 3335-959 0016
Tecni-Ciencia Libros, S.A.
Centro Comercial, Shopping Center
Av. Andrés Eloy, Urb. El Prebo
Valencia, Edo. Carabobo
Tel. 222 724
Fudeco, Librería
Avenida Libertador-Este, Ed. Fudeco, Apartado 254
Barquisimeto C.P. 3002, Ed. Lara
Tel. (051) 538 022
Fax (051) 544 394
Télex (051) 513 14 FUDEC VC

• ***YUGOSLAVIA***
Jugoslovenska Knjiga, Trg.
Republike 5/8, P.O. Box 36
11001 Belgrade
Prosveta
Terazije 16/1, Belgrade

Other countries / Autres pays / Otros países
Distribution and Sales Section, FAO
Viale delle Terme di Caracalla
00100 Rome, Italy
Tel. (39-6) 57974608
Telex 625852 / 625853 / 610181 FAO I
Fax (39-6) 57973152 / 5782610 / 5745090